KAUA'I

1ST EDITION

KAUA'I
GREAT DESTINATIONS
HAWAII

Michele Bigley

 The Countryman Press
Woodstock, Vermont

Dedication
For Eddie and Kai, who were with me all the way, so you'll always know where to find me.

ISBN 978-1-58157-084-7

Cover and interior photos by the author unless otherwise specified
Book design by Bodenweber Design
Page composition by PerfecType, Nashville, TN
Maps by Mapping Specialists Ltd., Madison, WI © The Countryman Press

Published by The Countryman Press, P.O. Box 748, Woodstock, Vermont 05091

Distributed by W. W. Norton & Company, Inc., 500 Fifth Avenue, New York, NY 10110

Manufactured in the United States of America

10 9 8 7 6 5 4 3 2 1

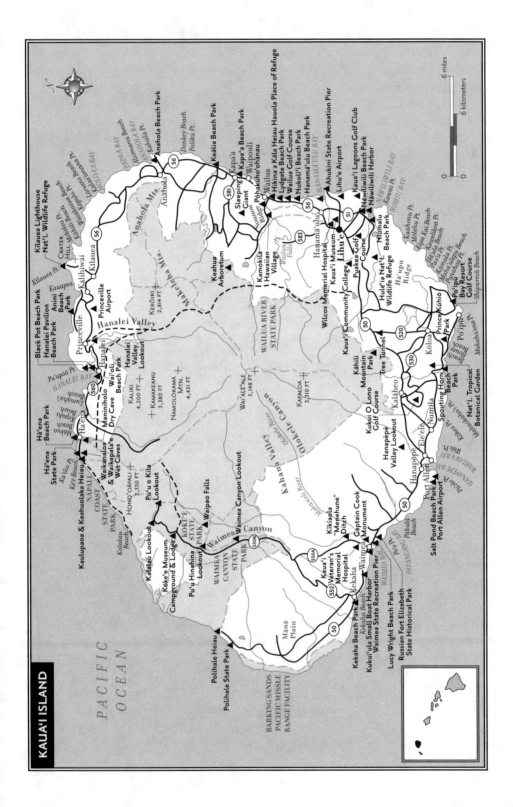

KAUA'I ISLAND

Contents

1

HISTORY
The Kaua'i Kuapapa Legacy
25

2

TRANSPORTATION
Holo Holo
38

3

LODGING
Your Island Hale
47

4

CULTURE
The Origins of Aloha
87

5

SACRED SITES AND NATURAL WONDERS
Na Pana Kaulana o Kaua'i
121

6

RESTAURANTS AND FOOD PURVEYORS
'Ono Kine Grinds
135

Acknowledgments

This book would not be possible without the generous support of my parents, Pat and Bruce Bigley. I would especially like to acknowledge my mom, who not only wrangled beachgoers to tow our car out of the sand for a case of Heineken, but who is also a great travel companion and food taster.

I am indebted to Kim Grant for answering even my silliest questions as if I had just asked about the intricacies of neuroscience. Humble thanks go out to editor extraordinaire, Laura Jorstad, and the whole Countryman Press crew.

Pat Griffin, Rosemary Smith, Sue Kanoho, and Cat Rietow graciously shared their Kaua'i, which helped me to find the heart of this book.

I appreciate all the people, visitors and locals, who offered up their favorite spots for you to enjoy. Most especially: Coralissa and Ivan Delaforce, Ali Nachman, Oliver and Maceo Reyes, Julie and Steve Bierer, and Lorne Bigley and his family.

Eddie, your tireless love, confidence, research, and draft reading continuously makes me feel unworthy.

Mahalo,
Michele Bigley
December 2008

INTRODUCTION

Our first halting place [on Kaua'i] was one of the prettiest places I ever saw . . .
Isabella Bird, Six Months in the Sandwich Islands, *1890*

From a lanai in Haena, I drink Kona coffee and write this during my favorite time of day. The rain, now traveling south, has delivered the smell of plumeria and salty surf pounding onto the white sand beach. As a redheaded honeycreeper sings from the top of the ohi'a lehua tree, it appears. Double arched and stretching from Makana Mountain to the Pacific, I am reminded how every moment on Kaua'i is a *makana*, a gift.

A popular saying here on Kaua'i is: *If you didn't have rain, you wouldn't get the rainbows.* Nor would this isle feel like an outcast sister to the rest of the archipelago. Verdant, yet bursting with shocks of red, pink, yellow, and even blue flowers, this mountainous island represents what all mainlanders imagine when jetting to the Pacific. The remote inland hosts Mount Wai'ale'ale, one of the wettest spots on the planet, inaccessible by car. This lush heart is home to waterfalls that vein in all directions, feeding rivers for the 5 percent of the island that is populated: the mellow coast. Here, no building is higher than a palm tree. Locals, wearing flip-flops and board shorts, talk story over *kalua* pig, leave work early to surf, and are slow to accept change.

Yet change has arrived on the island. The farming industry is hurting; traffic plagues the east shore; the Superferry has created an environmental battle cry; big-box stores threaten mom-and-pop shops; the landfills are nearly full; land is getting too expensive for locals; endangered birds are going extinct at the highest rate in the United States; yet tourism is at an all-time high.

Which is why I had to write this book.

Kaua'i is my favorite place on the planet. I love how the opal-colored Pacific contrasts with the zillion types of green along the north shore coast. I adore the always shocking Na Pali Coast, watching humpbacks migrate past the Kalalau Trail; Mark Twain's "Grand Canyon of the Pacific," the Christmas-colored Waimea Canyon; sneaking up on a sunrise wedding, chatting with the woman who owns the shave ice truck in Poipu, having to get to Country Moon Rising Bakery early enough to get the good sweets, full-moon bonfires, hitting up a local farm stand for fresh lichee, the waterfall you see on the way to the north shore. I love the chickens, the rain, how long it takes to get to Polihale, how everyone from gas station attendants to restaurant workers asks how your day is. I love how the community helps one another out, during storms and for Easter concerts. There's the traveling Children's Museum—a local nonprofit teaching youth the history of local crafts, free hula lessons with Auntie Bev, daily farmer's markets, and the weekly Aloha Center Craft Fair. I try never to miss Friday Night Art Night in Hanapepe, outdoor movie night at the Sheraton, Aloha Fridays lei-making events, and the monthly slack key guitar concerts. Nor can I leave out the simple pleasure of sharing a cocktail at a beach bar while local musicians serenade the sea. Most of all, I love how whenever I return, this Garden Isle feels like home.

Though most visitors to Kaua'i become enamored with the isle as well, lately locals have grown frustrated with tourism. They claim that visitors are disrespectful to the land, their privacy, and, frankly, their intelligence. Since I am sure that you, reader, want to be a

Not many footprints will join yours on the far north shore.

gracious guest in Kaua'i, below I have listed ways you can assure to do your part to understand the impact, both positive and negative, of your footprint on this most fragile and most beautiful environment in the United States.

- As one surfboard, stuck up on the trees on the way to 'Anini Beach, reads, SLOW DOWN. Take off your watch. Turn off your cell phone and just be okay with Hawai'i Time. Things move slower here. Meals take time. Grocery store clerks want to talk story. People (except for some locals, but don't take their lead) drive slower. There is nothing to hurry for. Really.
- *Hemo da slippahs.* Whenever you are invited into a home (or enter your lodging), take off your shoes. The red dirt on Kaua'i stains and is a pain to clean.
- Even though it feels like you have exited the United States, be aware that Kaua'i is a valuable part of the country. So when talking about home, try not to say, "In America . . ." Instead try, "On the mainland . . ."
- I have to take a moment to encourage you to be green. Kaua'i's landfills are filling quickly. Though it might be a small annoyance to drive your paper, bottles, and cans to one of the recycling centers, it is a great gift you can offer the people of Kaua'i. See chapter 10 for specific recycling center information. Even better, try bringing your own reusable water bottle, buying in bulk, unwrapping your toiletries at home, et cetera.
- Respect nature. Okay, I mean that in the hippie way of being green and not picking all the flowers or taking home shells, but I also mean this for your safety. Pay attention to the weather report. If it says rain, you probably shouldn't go on the Kalalau Trail. If the waves or currents are too strong, even if you are an experienced swim-

The majestic Hanalei Bay framed by the famed Bali Hai.

This surfboard tells people how it is.

mer, don't swim. There is a catchphrase in Hawai'i: *When in doubt, don't go out.* Follow this phrase like your life depends on it. Locals do.

· I am a traveler who wants to find every unexplored spot. Except here. Lately, there has been a lot of controversy about guidebooks telling people how to get to locally favored "secret" spots. Unfortunately, tourists visiting these places have created some issues. First off, many people have died or been seriously injured by visiting some of these "secret" adventure spots. This happens in a variety of ways. Visitors not used to the particular mood of a waterfall will rope-swing into the water, not knowing that the water level is unusually low; or they will take a wrong turn on an unkempt trail. If you talk to locals, chances are they will tell you about (and sometimes even take you to) their favorite spots. But when you just arrive, locals feel territorial. Now, those of us who live in big cities may not understand this type of mentality. But the Kaua'i people see land as sacred, something to respect, and something that belongs to them. If you can respect that you are visiting another culture, your visit will be as rich as the soil.

· Wear sunscreen and mosquito repellent. We can always spot the tourists. Aside from being armed with a map and a camera, they always have this lobster hue to their shoulders. The Kaua'i sun is dangerous, even when it's cloudy. Always wear sunscreen of more than SPF 15. And as you might guess, with rain come mosquitoes, a lot of the nasty buggers. Wear repellent, especially in gardens and around Koke'e.

· Leave the pidgin dialect to the locals. It is okay (and even appreciated) to practice pronouncing Hawaiian words, but when *haoles* start chatting away in pidgin, it is like traveling to Britain and taking on a cockney accent.

The Hawaiian Language

With only 12 letters and two punctuation marks, the Hawaiian language is relatively simple to speak and understand. Though English is the primary language spoken on Kaua'i, Hawaiian is experiencing a renaissance, as a way to save it from obscurity. To immerse yourself in the culture, you might consider adding a few useful Hawaiian words to your vocabulary.

Local Hawaiians, however, speak a combination of English, Hawaiian, and slang. Pidgin—as it is called—is difficult to understand. You won't hear it at resorts or even when being served at local restaurants. But hang on the beach next to some surfers or pay attention to locals talking story at Tip Top and you'll soon be scratching your head, trying to make sense of the one rapid thing on the island—this language. If you want to toy with understanding pidgin, check out www.extreme-hawaii .com/pidgin.

Here are a few basic pronunciation rules to make your travels easier.

CONSONANTS

h, l, n, m pronounced the same as English

k, p   pronounced with less breath

w   usually pronounced like a soft *v*, though at the beginning of the word or after an a it can be pronounced like a *v* or *w*.

VOWELS (UNSTRESSED)

a   a as in *above*

e   e as in *bet*

i   *y* as in *pity*

o   o as in *hole*

u   u as in *full*

VOWELS (STRESSED)

When two vowels appear next to each other, stress the first vowel a little less than you would in English.

a   a as in *bar*

e   *ay* as in *play*

i   *ee* as in *see*

o   o as in *mole* (but slightly longer)

u   *oo* as in *soon*

THE USE OF THE *OKINA*, OR GLOTTAL STOP

Though I don't speak fluent Hawaiian, I promised a friend I would attempt to honor the written language as much as possible. In this book, you will notice the use of the *okina* or glottal stop ('). This punctuation mark indicates a pause in the pronunciation of a word. For example, *haoles* pronounce Hawai'i as *Ha-wai*, while locals say *Ha-wai-ee*. I have tried to stay true to this mark even when street signs and company names don't include it. The other Hawaiian punctuation mark (which I do not use in this book) is the *kahako*, which is like a hat over a vowel. When the *kahako* is used, hold the vowel sound slightly longer than other vowels.

Common Words

The best Hawaiian electronic dictionary can be found at http://wehewehe.org. The *New Pocket Hawaiian Dictionary* by Mary Kawena Pukui and Samuel Elbert, published by the University of Hawai'i Press, is a wonderful resource as well.

Below is a list of commonly used Hawaiian and pidgin words.

'ae	to say yes or offer consent
ahupua'a	a triangular division of land reaching from the mountains to the ocean—with the largest piece being oceanfront
'aina	land or earth
akua	god, goddess, or spirit
ali'i	Hawai'ian chief, royal, or person of high rank
aloha	welcome, hello, good-bye, love, or friendship
a'ole	no, never, not
brah	pidgin for "friend"
da kine	pidgin for "thingamajig" or "whatchamacallit"
e komo mai	welcome
halau	a hula group or school
hale	house or building
haole	Caucasian, mainlander, or foreigner
hapu'u	tree fern
heiau	ancient temple or place of worship
hemo da slippahs	pidgin for "take off your shoes"
ho'ike	information
holoholo	cruising
hui	group or club
hula	a form of dance and music
kahuna	priest or priestess; a person well versed in any field
kai	sea
kama'aina	resident of Hawai'i
kane	man
kapa	cloth made from bark
kapu	sacred or forbidden
kapuna	older person
keiki	young child
kiawe	mesquite
koa	rare hardwood tree
kona	leeward
kuapapa	ancient
kukui	candlenut tree
lanai	balcony or patio
lau	leaf
lei	wreath of flowers or shells worn around the neck
mahalo	thank you
makai	toward the sea (used as a directional signifier)

makana	gift
malihini	stranger or newcomer
mana	a kind of spiritual power
mauka	toward the mountain (used as a directional signifier)
mea ho'onanea	relax
mele	ancient chant
Menehune	legendary, dwarf-like ancient Hawaiian people
mu'umu'u	loose-fitting gown or dress
Na pana kaulana	the famous places
nui	significant or important
'ohana	family
pali	cliff-like mountain
paniolo	cowboy
pau	finished or done
pili	a kind of grass
puka	hole or door
tutu	grandparent
wahine	woman
wai	water
wikiwiki	fast

FOOD TERMS

'ahi	yellowfin tuna
aku	bonito (tuna)
'awapuhi	ginger
azuki beans	Japanese sweet red beans used in desserts like mochi and shave ice
bento	a Japanese-style box lunch with meat or fish, rice, and vegetables
crack seed	Chinese sweet-and-sour preserved fruit snack
haupia	sweet coconut pudding
'imu	pit-style oven
kalua pork	preparation for pork cooked in 'imu pit for an extended period of time
kapahaki	cooked Hawaiian food
kaukau	Hawaiian food
ko'ala	broiled food
laulau	pork, chicken, or fish wrapped in taro or ti leaves then steamed
liliko'i	passion fruit
limu	seaweed
loco moco	two scoops of white rice, a hamburger patty with a fried egg, topped with sausage gravy
lomi lomi	raw salmon salted and minced, then mixed with green onions and tomatoes

lu'au	traditional Hawaiian meal
mahimahi	white fish called dolphin, though it really isn't one
mai tai	alcoholic beverage made with rum, grenadine, lemon (or orange), and pineapple juice
malasadas	Portuguese doughnuts
mochi	Japanese sticky rice dumpling, often served sweet or filled with ice cream
nori	dried seaweed
ono	wahoo fish
'ono	delicious
'opae	shrimp
'opakapaka	blue snapper
pao dolce	Portuguese sweet bread
plate lunch	two scoops of rice, meat or fish, and macaroni salad
poke	raw fish (usually 'ahi) with shoyu, sesame oil, salt, onions, and "special" ingredients
poi	a basic Hawaiian food made from pounded taro root
poke	raw fish preparation
pua'a	pig
pupu	snack or appetizer
saimin	the Hawaiian version of noodle soup with pork, scallions, and nori
shave ice	traditional Hawaiian dessert consisting of finely shaved ice smothered in sweet sugary syrup on top of either ice cream or sweet azuki beans
shoyu	soy sauce
star fruit	yellowish green fruit shaped like a star (with five points)
taro (or kalo)	hearty starchy vegetable similar to potatoes or corn
'uala	sweet potato
'ulu	breadfruit

Armed with the first edition of *The Kaua'i Book*, you can have all the tools you need to be a responsible tourist. I thoroughly researched all the information listed in this guide, highlighting locally owned businesses. All the restaurants included have been taste-tested by me, as well as by friends and family. I have chosen to primarily note reasons why you should stay or eat at a particular place instead of bad-mouthing people's businesses. In these pages, you'll find hikes that are well kept, since it is my intention that you have a safe journey, even when you're being adventurous. Culturally, I have done my best to include factual information that bridges the divide between the two Kaua'is: one part American, the other pure Hawaiian.

It is my hope that this book can be a trusted old friend who urges you to run free in this wild region, while respecting the power of nature, history, and a culture that needs listening to. With this information, I am sure you will grow to love Kaua'i as much as I do.

—Michele Bigley

THE WAY THIS BOOK WORKS

This book is divided into 10 chapters. In all cases, entries are listed alphabetically. However, when entries are divided by location, the towns are then listed alphabetically, while the areas are listed in a clockwise fashion, starting with the east shore. The four different location headings are "East Shore" (Anahola, Kapa'a, Lihu'e, Wailua), "South Shore" (Kalaheo, Koloa, Lawa'i, Poipu), "West Shore" ('Ele'ele, Hanapepe, Kekaha, Koke'e, Waimea), and "North Shore" (Haena, Hanalei, Kilauea, Na Pali Coast, Princeville).

Many entries, namely in the Lodging and Restaurant chapters, are listed with a block header. In this heading, I have included useful information like web sites, phone numbers, addresses, and wheelchair-accessibility information. In regard to the handicapped-access information, note that since many hotels and restaurants have grandfather clauses exempting them from being wheelchair accessible, you may want to speak with management in advance to see if they will arrange a ramp. Also, many lodging options have a limited number of rooms that are handicapped accessible. In all cases, I have noted when there is even partial access (which basically means that a wheelchair can enter the facility, but there aren't necessarily grab bars), so always call in advance. I have also put stars (✪) next to particular listings to indicate my favorite places. If you are short on time, I have included a little cheat sheet of my favorite do not miss spots in the Information chapter.

I have fact-checked this information as close to the publication date as possible. Unfortunately, information changes faster than anything else in Kaua'i. Because of this, I have chosen not to list exact times that businesses open and close. So make sure to call ahead before visiting. And don't be put off when the proprietor says they open at 10-*ish*, or if a place says it is open for dinner and you show up at 9 PM to find it closed. In general, you can assume that business hours for shops are 10 AM–6 PM. For food establishments, breakfast generally starts between 6 and 7 AM; lunch runs 11 AM–2 PM; and dinner hours are usually 5 PM–9 PM.

Price Codes

	Lodging	*Dining*
Inexpensive	Up to $150	Up to $10
Moderate	$150–250	$10–19
Expensive	Over $250	$20–29
Very Expensive	Over $375	$30 and over

Credit cards are abbreviated as follows:
AE—American Express
D—Discover Card
DC—Diner's Club
JCB—Japan Credit Bureau
MC—Master Card
V—Visa

Given the rapid rate at which prices change, the publishers and I have decided not to list specific cost information and instead indicate a range. The price range below includes the cost of lodging based on a per-room, per-night, double-occupancy charge during high season (Dec.–Apr. and June–Aug.). Note that off-season rates can be significantly lower, while winter holiday rates can often double or triple. Prices do not include 11.4 percent tax, resort fees, condo cleaning fees, et cetera.

For year-round tourist information, the **Kaua'i Visitors Bureau** (808-245-3971; 4334 Rice St., Suite 101, Lihu'e; www.kauaidiscovery.com) and **Chamber of Commerce** (808-245-7363; 2970 Kele, Suite 112, Lihu'e; www.kauaichamber.org) are wonderful resources to help plan your trip.

Towns in Kaua'i

Though Kaua'i is one island, the towns dotted around the coast can have vastly varying vibes. When you're deciding where to stay, it might help to understand the layout of the land.

The most populated area of Kaua'i, the east shore, is where to find the pulse of the island. The merging towns of **Kapa'a** and **Wailua** stretch up the coast and sit in the shadow of Nounou Mountain. These funky communities house a large number of locals and tourists, looking to be near a variety of food, shopping, beaches, and nightlife. Just south is the county seat of **Lihu'e**. Here you will find government buildings, museums, a mall, most big-box stores, the airport, and a wealth of plate lunch spots. Though not much caters to tourists around here, Lihu'e is rich with history and an unmistakable local flavor. However, once the work crowd leaves, the area slows dramatically.

Travelers wanting a sunny vacation head south to the **Poipu/Koloa** resort area. So the south shore mostly caters to tourists. Here you'll find those postcard-perfect beaches, expensive seafood restaurants, jewelry boutiques, and world-renowned resorts. Still, the old town strip of Koloa retains some of the past plantation-days feel, with mom-and-pop take-out stands and surf shops to offset the lure of the galleries and clothing boutiques. One thing to bear in mind is that at press time there were eight new developments popping up in the Poipu/Koloa area. If you choose to stay here, you might want some earplugs. Drive farther south to the adjoining towns of **Lawa'i** and **Kalaheo** and you'll find where local people actually live. Unless you are staying in these towns, Kalaheo basically offers only a much-needed gas/coffee stop for folks on the way to Koke'e.

We continue clockwise to the west shore, the least populated area on the island. You'll pass the small town of **'Ele'ele**, then arrive in **Hanapepe**, "Kaua'i's Biggest Little Town." Most visitors merely explore the galleries here, since there aren't any places to stay in the direct vicinity. Farther west sits **Waimea**: the historic old town that transports you to another time and acts as the commercial center for this region. And finally, at the end of the road is **Kekaha**, where the dry desert-like conditions and high surf attract locals and some tourists wanting to get away from the crowds, or those of us who like to spend a ton of time exploring Koke'e.

Made legend in photographs and films, the verdant north shore attracts the majority of visitors. This area is traditionally known as *Halelea* (the House of Rainbows), and for good reason—it rains. A lot. Beginning at the farthest north, you'll find the hamlet of **Haena**, popular with hikers and surfers, looking to escape the resort crowd. Drive south to find the heart of this area: the hippie/surfer town of **Hanalei**. This burg, hugged by waterfall-dotted mountains and the picturesque bay, acts as the commercial center for the north shore. Heading south, the decadent **Princeville** appears: a 12,000-acre resort area, created in 1860s by Robert Crichton Wyllie, the foreign minister of the Hawaiian Kingdom, to honor Kamehameha IV and Queen Emma's son, who died when he was four. Condos and resorts sitting atop jagged cliffs suspended over the Pacific make any traveler feel regal. **Kilauea** marks the gateway into this lush northern region. Here grasses and mountains grow taller, restaurants get healthier, and birds congregate on the cliffs just above the migrating humpbacks.

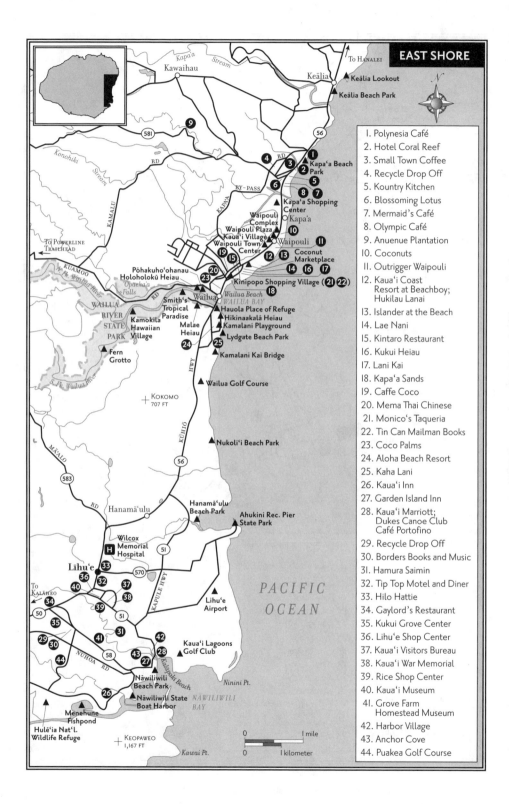

Kawaihau

Kapaʻa Stream

To Hanalei

Keālia

Keālia Lookout

Keālia Beach Park

581

56

Konohiki Stream

RD

BY-PASS

Kapaʻa Beach Park

Kapaʻa Shopping Center

Waipouli Complex

Waipouli Plaza

Kauaʻi Village

Waipouli Town Center

Kapaʻa

Waipouli

Coconut Marketplace

To Powerline Trailhead

KUAMOO

Pōhakuhoʻohanau

Holoholokū Heiau

Kinipopo Shopping Village (21)(22)

ʻOpaekaʻa Falls

Wailua

Wailua Beach

WAILUA BAY

Smith's Tropical Paradise

Hauola Place of Refuge

Hikinaakalā Heiau

Kamalani Playground

WAILUA RIVER STATE PARK

Kamokila Hawaiian Village

Malae Heiau

Lydgate Beach Park

Fern Grotto

S. Fk. Wailua River

Kamalani Kai Bridge

KŪHIŌ

KOKOMO 707 FT

Wailua Golf Course

583

Nukoliʻi Beach Park

56

RD

MAʻALO

Hanamāʻulu

Hanamāʻulu Beach Park

Ahukini Rec. Pier State Park

PACIFIC OCEAN

Wilcox Memorial Hospital

51

Lihuʻe

570

KAPULE HWY

Lihuʻe Airport

To Kalāheo

50

51

Kauaʻi Lagoons Golf Club

NUHOA RD

58

Nāwiliwili Beach Park

Nāwiliwili State Boat Harbor

Kalapakī Beach

Ninini Pt.

NĀWILIWILI BAY

Menehune Fishpond

Huléʻia Natʻl. Wildlife Refuge

KEOPAWEO 1,167 FT

Kawai Pt.

0   1 mile

0   1 kilometer

1. Polynesia Café
2. Hotel Coral Reef
3. Small Town Coffee
4. Recycle Drop Off
5. Kountry Kitchen
6. Blossoming Lotus
7. Mermaid's Café
8. Olympic Café
9. Anuenue Plantation
10. Coconuts
11. Outrigger Waipouli
12. Kauaʻi Coast Resort at Beachboy; Hukilau Lanai
13. Islander at the Beach
14. Lae Nani
15. Kintaro Restaurant
16. Kukui Heiau
17. Lani Kai
18. Kapaʻa Sands
19. Caffe Coco
20. Mema Thai Chinese
21. Monico's Taqueria
22. Tin Can Mailman Books
23. Coco Palms
24. Aloha Beach Resort
25. Kaha Lani
26. Kauaʻi Inn
27. Garden Island Inn
28. Kauaʻi Marriott; Dukes Canoe Club Café Portofino
29. Recycle Drop Off
30. Borders Books and Music
31. Hamura Saimin
32. Tip Top Motel and Diner
33. Hilo Hattie
34. Gaylord's Restaurant
35. Kukui Grove Center
36. Lihuʻe Shop Center
37. Kauaʻi Visitors Bureau
38. Kauaʻi War Memorial
39. Rice Shop Center
40. Kauaʻi Museum
41. Grove Farm Homestead Museum
42. Harbor Village
43. Anchor Cove
44. Puakea Golf Course

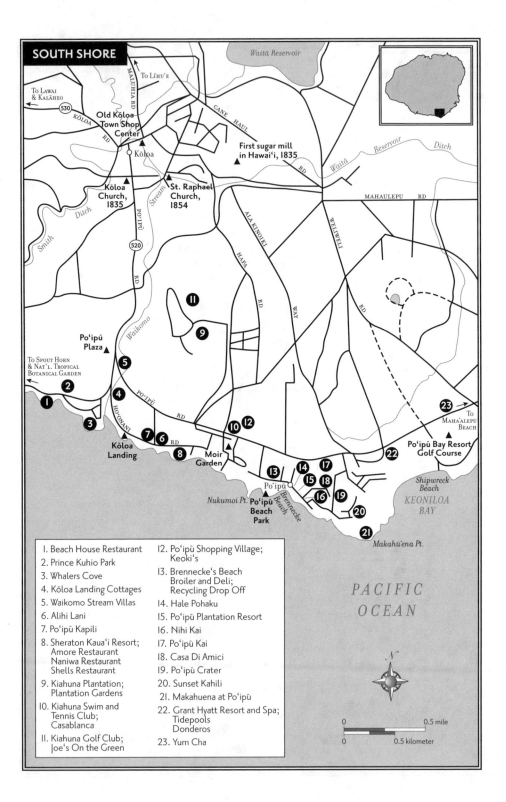

Waita Reservoir

To Līhuʻe

To Lawai
& Kalāheo

530

KŌLOA

MALUHIA RD

CANE HAUL

Old Kōloa
Town Shop
Center

KŌLOA

RD

Kōloa

First sugar mill
in Hawaiʻi, 1835

Reservoir

Ditch

Waitā

RD

MAHAULEPU   RD

Kōloa
Church,
1835

St. Raphael
Church,
1854

Stream

POʻIPŪ

520

ALA KINOIKI

HAPA

RD

WELIWELI   RD

Ditch

Smith

Waikomo

⓫

⑨

Poʻipū
Plaza

WAY

To Spout Horn
& Natʻl. Tropical
Botanical Garden

⑤

POʻIPŪ

④

HOʻONANI

RD

①

③

⑤

②

⑦ ⑥

RD

⑧

Kōloa
Landing

Moir
Garden

⑩ ⑫

⓭

Poʻipū

⑭ ⑰

⑮ ⑱

⑯

㉒

㉓

To
Mahaʻalepu
Beach

Poʻipū Bay Resort
Golf Course

Shipwreck
Beach

KEONILOA
BAY

Nukumoi Pt. Poʻipū
Beach
Park

Brennecke Beach

⑲

⑳

㉑

Makahūena Pt.

PACIFIC
OCEAN

N

1. Beach House Restaurant
2. Prince Kuhio Park
3. Whalers Cove
4. Kōloa Landing Cottages
5. Waikomo Stream Villas
6. Alihi Lani
7. Poʻipū Kapili
8. Sheraton Kauaʻi Resort;
   Amore Restaurant
   Naniwa Restaurant
   Shells Restaurant
9. Kiahuna Plantation;
   Plantation Gardens
10. Kiahuna Swim and
    Tennis Club;
    Casablanca
11. Kiahuna Golf Club;
    Joe's On the Green

12. Poʻipū Shopping Village;
    Keoki's
13. Brennecke's Beach
    Broiler and Deli;
    Recycling Drop Off
14. Hale Pohaku
15. Poʻipū Plantation Resort
16. Nihi Kai
17. Poʻipū Kai
18. Casa Di Amici
19. Poʻipū Crater
20. Sunset Kahili
21. Makahuena at Poʻipū
22. Grant Hyatt Resort and Spa;
    Tidepools
    Donderos
23. Yum Cha

0   0.5 mile

0   0.5 kilometer

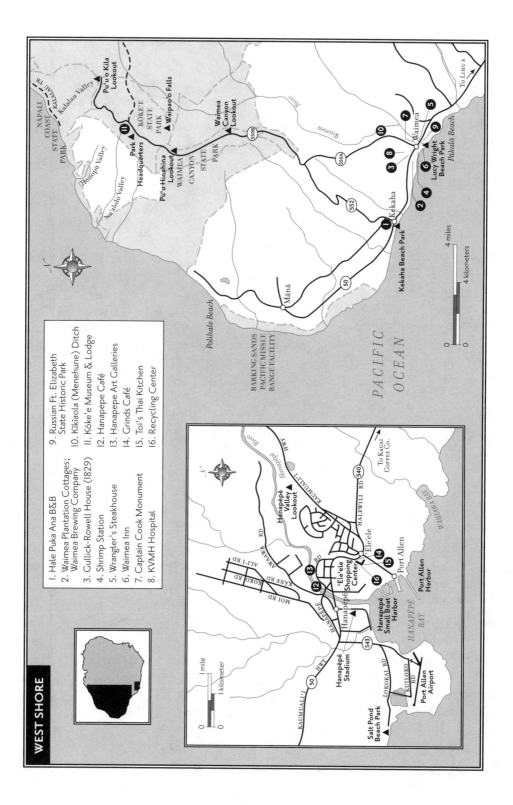

WEST SHORE

1. Hale Puka Ana B&B
2. Waimea Plantation Cottages;
   Waimea Brewing Company
3. Gullick-Rowell House (1829)
4. Shrimp Station
5. Wrangler's Steakhouse
6. Waimea Inn
7. Captain Cook Monument
8. KVMH Hospital
9. Russian Ft. Elizabeth
   State Historic Park
10. Kikiaola (Menehune) Ditch
11. Kōke'e Museum & Lodge
12. Hanapepe Café
13. Hanapepe Art Galleries
14. Grinds Café
15. Toi's Thai Kitchen
16. Recycling Center

2 miles

2 kilometers

1. Limahuli Botanical Garden
2. YMCA Camp Naue
3. Hanalei Colony Resort and Spa; Mediterranean Gourmet
4. Hale Ho'o Maha
5. Hanalei Inn
6. Bar Acuda
7. Papayas
8. Neides Salsa and Samba
9. Hanalei Gourmet
10. Java Kai
11. Sushi Blues
12. Polynesia Café
13. Kalypso
14. Postcards Café
15. Hanalei Dolphin
16. Princeville Shopping Center
17. Last gas station on the way to Ha'ena
18. Princeville Library
19. CJ's Steakhouse
20. Paradise Bar and Grill
21. Mauna Kai
22. Emmanlani Court
23. Kamahana Townhomes
24. Sealodge
25. The Cliffs at Princeville
26. Ali'i Kai I & II
27. Pali Ke Kua
28. Hanalei Bay Villas
29. Pu'u Poa
30. Princeville Resort and Spa; La Cascata, Café Hanalei
31. Hanalei Bay Resort; Bali Hai Restaurant
32. Kilaueu Fish Market
33. Kilauea Bakery and Pau Hana Pizza
34. Lighthouse Bistro

PACIFIC OCEAN

Kilauea Lighthouse National Wildlife Refuge

To Lihu'e & Na'aina Kai Botanical Garden

Guava Kai Plantation

Moku'ae'ae Island

Kilauea Pt.

Kilauea

56

Kilauea Rd.

Kauapea "Secret" Beach

Kalihiwai Beach

KALIHIWAI BAY

Kalihiwai

Kuhio Hwy

Princeville Airport

Anini Beach

Kalihiwai Rd.

To Powerline Trailhead

Hanalei Valley

Hanalei River

HANALEI NATIONAL WILDLIFE REFUGE

Princeville

Pu'upoa Pt.

Pu'upoa Beach

Hanalei Pier

Black Pot Beach Park

Hanalei Pavilion

Ching Young Village SC

Old Hanalei School SC

Hanalei Center

Princeville Golf Club

Hanalei Valley Lookout

Ka Haku Rd.

HANALEI BAY

Waikoko Beach

Wai'oli Beach

Wai'oli "Pine Trees" Beach Park

Wai'oli Hui'ia Church, 1912

560

Lumaha'i Beach

Waikoko

Lumaha'i River

Wainiha River

Wainiha

WAINIHA BAY

Kepuhi Beach

Waikapala'e Beach

560

Ha'ena

Maniniholo Dry Cave

Kuhio Hwy

Ha'ena Pt.

Mokua "Tunnels" Beach

Ha'ena Beach Park

Ha'ena State Park

Ke'e Beach

Kaulupaoa & Keahuolaka Heiau

Waikanaloa & Waikapala'e Wet Caves

NAPALI COAST

Hanakāpi'ai Beach

Hanakāpi'ai Stream

HISTORY

The Kaua'i Kuapapa Legacy

We were born on Kaua'i. We have been to the other islands, some here and some there, to O'ahu, to Maui, to Hawai'i, to Honolulu. Yet always did we come back to Kaua'i. Why did we come back? There must be a reason. Because we love Kaua'i. We were born here. Here we have lived. And here shall we die—unless—unless—there be weak hearts amongst us.

From Koolau the Leper, *Jack London*

Jack London was right. Kaua'i is not for the weak. With a belief system rooted in mythology, land idolatry, feudalism, natural disasters, and more recently the arrival of missionaries, revolutionists, artists, surfers, and modernization, Kaua'i people have had to cope with worlds more than anyone on *Survivor* ever will.

Measuring 25 miles wide and 33 miles long, Kaua'i is the fourth largest of the Hawaiian Islands. Located just 100 miles northwest of O'ahu, this tropical isle feels continents away from the hustle of Honolulu. Nature has isolated the island from her sisters: She's surrounded by turbulent reef breaks and home to one of the rainiest places on the planet. Only 5 percent of the island is accessible by car. You won't find Honolulu hustle or high rises here.

While in the past the treacherous seas made it nearly impossible for people to get on or off the island, now flights shuttle people in, bringing both environmental threats and economic joys. With modernization currently battling it out with Mother Nature, new changes occur daily. Big-box shopping centers, fancy condominium complexes, multimillion-dollar houses, the threat of the Superferry, and high-end resorts all challenge the simplicity of this fragile environment. The Hawaiian people, who have always lived hand in hand with nature, are now learning to deal with another set of dramatic changes in their homeland.

NATURAL HISTORY

It was believed among ancients that when Pele, the goddess of fire, gets angry, she spews lava, creating new land. So when, approximately six million years ago, a volcano deep in the Pacific erupted and created Kaua'i, the eldest of the Hawaiian chain, Pele must have had something serious to moan about. Scientists believe that the island was created by one volcano, with layers of lava packing together on the ocean floor to create this landmass. This might explain the essentially circular shape of Kaua'i and the deep valleys that stretch

The Hanalei National Wildlife Reserve is home to one of the largest taro fields in the state.

down from the central mountains of Mount Kawaikini (5,243 feet) and Mount Waiʻaleʻale (5,148 feet).

To become the abundant land that you see now took a lot of work on the part of both nature and the numerous settlers who have called Kauaʻi home. For thousands of years, the lava was broken down into cinder and dirt by water and wind. With high-iron-oxide soil, and the love affair between rain and Mount Waiʻaleʻale, the land became highly fertile. When naupaka trees floated in on the water, they flourished along the coast; and when plover birds deposited seeds, bushes and trees began growing inland. But we're not talking about a bountiful array of endemic flora in a few spins of the earth. One new plant popped up every 20,000 years. You can imagine this prehistoric Kauaʻi looking slightly like the Big Island's volcano side does now.

Fast-forward into the more recent past—say, a few thousand years ago—when because of the isolated nature of the islands (did you know the Hawaiian archipelago is the most remote chain in the world?), this once barren isle acquired only two animal inhabitants— the monk seal and bats—and a handful of plants brought by wind, water, and wings. Strangely these aren't the plants you would typically associate with Hawaiʻi. Instead, these roughly 400 native species offered only a few seeds, berries, and nuts, and rarely flowered. However, these durable plants evolved into the 6,000-plus endemic species you see now— 90 percent of them found nowhere else on the planet! To this day, most of the species growing on Kauaʻi are like its people—tough against the elements, yet gentle, without much means of protecting themselves from predators.

And so when the Polynesians arrived somewhere between AD 500 and 800, Kauaʻi's peaceful environment was rocked. Sailing across the ocean for thousands of miles meant that these explorers had to bring some food. Packed in double-hulled canoes were bread-fruit (to make surfboards, sandpaper, and instruments), coconut, bananas, taro, ti, sweet

Hawaiian Plants and Their Uses

For decades scientists have been studying the benefits of Hawaiian plants. Here is a list of some of their properties and uses.

Mulberry fig tree: From this durable tree comes one of Hawai'i's greatest resources—tapa cloth. Not only is this cloth used for paper, but until the 1800s (when the Marshall Islanders introduced grass skirts), hula dancers wore it as a skirt.

Hala: This native plant was necessary for the survival of the indigenous people. You can recognize it by the straight roots reaching into the ground from the branches (it almost looks like a giant witch's broom). Ancients made sails for seagoing boats as well as paintbrushes out of these trees.

Koa: This tall, native tree is now a hot commodity. Locals sell this wood for high-priced furniture. The reason people love it is that water doesn't rot the wood. To recognize koa, look for dark green crescent-shaped leaves.

Kukui nut tree: This Hawai'i state tree used to be a source of light. Ancients would stack nuts on a branch and light the first one. Quickly all the nuts caught fire. Thus the tree got its common name: candlenut. Kukui is also used as a laxative, but doesn't taste very good. Fishermen chew and spit the nuts into the water, causing the liquid to become oily and glassy, which helps them spot fish.

Mokihana: Though this is not a native tree, mokihana is considered indigenous. This tree produces a green nut that smells like licorice and is used to make the Kaua'i lei.

Noni: In the coffee family, this natural insect repellent smells like vomit when it is ripe.

Olenu: This turmeric plant is used in cancer prevention, to stop earaches, and to prevent Alzheimer's.

Sugarcane: Here's some irony: Hawaiians chew on sugarcane to get such good teeth.

Ti: This waterproof plant was brought over by Polynesians, and Hawaiians consider it sacred, planting it around the house to protect from evil.

'Uala: The sweet potato plant is considered a healthy choice for protein, calcium, and vitamin K. In addition, the leaves are thought to have anti-cancer, anti-bacterial, and anti-diabetes properties. Ancient Hawaiian nursing women tied leis of these leaves around their necks to promote healthy lactation.

On top of the hala tree grows what locals call a tourist pineapple.

Ti plants, a necessity to Hawaiian culture since their introduction, flourish along the Na Pali Coast.

potatoes, sugarcane, plus chickens, pigs, and rats. These plants and animals thrived on Kauaʻi and quickly became synonymous with the environment.

For the next thousand years, the Polynesians lived off the resources of the island as if the plants, birds, and trees were going to evaporate. Believing that the land was chief and the humans were the servants, they saw themselves as part of, not separate from nature. And though they used trees to make everything from canoes to spoons, weapons to sandpaper, houses to clothing, they would only use one tree at a time for fear of angering the spirit god that resided in the forest. In fact, every time they cut down a tree from the upland sacred forest, they made a human sacrifice. Unfortunately, these ancients didn't feel the same about birds. Yellow and red bird feathers, once plentiful on the island, were used to clothe royalty. It took 40,000 to 50,000 bird feathers for one cape. Thus, these resourceful tribesmen basically wiped out all the yellow native birds, and a lot of the red ones, too.

Then in the late 1700s, in sailed Captain Cook, bringing with him goats and syphilis, and the flora and fauna of Kauaʻi began a phase of dramatic change. Within the next 300 years, explorers and missionaries would bring invasive species onto Kauaʻi. These modern introductions of autograph trees, ironwood, mosquitoes, wild boars, chickens, humans, and much more have altered—staunch environmentalists would say *destroyed*—much of what was once a fragile ecosystem. And now Kauaʻi's native plants and animals are have the highest rate of extinction in all of the United States.

The newest invasive environmental issue to frustrate many locals is the arrival of genetically modified crops (GMOs). Attracted by the fertile soil, corporate giants have begun experimenting with GMO corn, soybeans, tobacco, and more. Local growers fear that these crops will contaminate what is left of the agricultural industry on Kauaʻi.

Interestingly, despite all the modern introductions of invasive species, there are no snakes or reptiles, large mammals (other than domestics and wild boars), or mongooses on Kauaʻi (this is the only Hawaiian island without them). However, though dangers aren't present on land, they are alive in the sea, where whales, sharks, rays, jellyfish, eels, and a wide array of tropical fish live off the reef. Local laws have protected this abundance of sea life by banning most motorized watercraft, including Jet Skis and motorboats, from the ocean surrounding the isle.

Another important element of Kauaʻi's natural history is the weather. Ancient people

Indigenous? Native? Or Modern Introductions?

HOW TO CHART THE MURKY WATERS OF PLANT GENEALOGY

If you visit a botanical garden, or just happen to chat with a local garden aficionado, you'll likely hear the terms *indigenous, endemic, native*, and *modern introduction* in reference to flora and fauna. Below are the Hawaiian definitions of these terms, from the National Tropical Botanical Garden.

Indigenous plants: Native to Hawai'i and other places.

Endemic species: These plants evolved in Hawai'i from indigenous plants. They are native to Hawai'i and nowhere else.

Native species: Plants that reached Hawai'i without human intervention. They also did not evolve from plants already here.

Polynesian introductions: Plants and animals brought to Hawai'i by Polynesian migrants between AD 200 and 1300.

Modern introductions: Plants and animals brought to Hawai'i by humans since Captain Cook arrived in 1778.

believed different gods controlled the sea, the rain, the volcanoes, and so on, and nowhere else can you understand why better than here, where the earth amplifies her voice often. It is impossible to talk about Kaua'i without mentioning rain. Mount Wai'ale'ale is one of the wettest places on earth, receiving an average of 450 inches of rain a year. Considering that Seattle gets an annual 36 inches of rain, you can imagine the effects of all that water on waterfalls and swamps. Occasionally the rain will find its way down to the coast and cause flooding. In 2006, for instance, it rained for 40 days straight, causing a dam to break and a number of deaths.

Over a month of rain might seem like nothing compared with a hurricane. And Kaua'i has had its share. In the recent past, the island was slammed by two major ones: Hurricane 'Iwa on Thanksgiving in 1982 and Hurricane 'Iniki on September 11, 1992. With 80 mph winds, Hurricane 'Iwa plummeted the island, causing one death and over $200 million in damages. But little did the island folks know, almost

The beautiful tiare flower might seem like a representation of Hawai'i, but in fact this member of the coffee family is a non-native species.

exactly 10 years later, they would be pounded by one of the fiercest storms in history. You'll likely hear tales of Hurricane 'Iniki while on Kaua'i. Well, the 175 mph winds caused eight deaths and almost $2 billion in damages. Though it hit hardest in Poipu, no part of the island was spared. A third of the houses on the island were destroyed, cars were buried, boats were turned upside down (major hotels are still waiting to be rebuilt). When the sun returned, however, the people of the island set out to rebuild. Together. The whole community worked to get the electricity back, to create shelter for those who lost homes; some even joke that 'Iniki was the best thing to happen to the island—it cleaned up overgrown trees and got rid of the wimps.

Two other noteworthy natural phenomena that help shape the island into what it is today are earthquakes and tsunamis. Though they are not to be taken lightly, the chances of one happening while you are visiting are slim. Kaua'i has not been affected by a major tsunami since the 1950s, when a wave generated by an earthquake in the Alaska Aleutian Islands wiped out a few north shore communities. As for earthquakes, there have been no major ones on Kaua'i in recorded history.

SOCIAL HISTORY

The First Hawaiians

The Menehune, a tribe of mythical dwarf-like people, are believed to be the first inhabitants of the island. Some say they came on a cloud, or on a floating island, or that once upon a time Hawai'i and New Zealand were connected. However they arrived, they are thought to have numbered over 500,000. Rumor has it that they constructed their buildings, aqueducts, and places of worship in the night; if they saw daylight, they turned to stone. Stories of these magical inhabitants connect them to Makana Mountain, the dry and wet caves of the north shore, Nounou Mountain, and almost every sacred site in Kaua'i.

Academics, however, think Tahitian settlers labeled the first inhabitants (thought to be Marquesas Islanders) *Menehune* because, in ancient Tahitian, that word means "commoners" or "outcasts." Nevertheless, these people, whether small in stature or power, existed on some level. We know this because of their peculiar building style found on Kaua'i and the outer islands of Necker and Nehoa. They stacked lava stones to build sturdy walls

An example of Menehune building techniques.

that still exist. Except for these structures, though, no known physical remains of these people have ever been found.

In Sail the Polynesians

Imagine an idyllic land of fertile soil, jagged peaks, enough rain to grow an abundance of food, no pesky rodents, insects, or even mammals, and no people (except little elves building aqueducts at night). This is what the first people from the Marquesas Islands must have seen when they sailed in on double-hulled canoes sometime in AD 200–300. Roughly 30 people and their goods could fit into each canoe. And what a sight these folks must have been. Tattooed from head to toe, with shaved heads and whale tooth earrings, these descendants of the tough-est (and cannibalistic) Polynesians arrived when, during certain seasons, ocean currents passed by the Hawaiian chain.

A Polynesian introduction, breadfruit is bigger than your head.

These brilliant navigators (or lucky, depending on whom you ask) had the island to themselves until approximately the 12th century AD when war-like Tahitians came to conquer. They implemented a new belief system to worship four major gods: Ku (the god of war, ancestors, sunrise, and fishing), Lono (god of rain, harvest, fertility, and peace), Kane (who created the first man), and Kanaloa (ruler of the under-world). The chief ruler also started the *kapu* system, a unified set of laws (most of which applied to commoners and were punishable by death). They also created *heiau* (sacred houses of worship) and the caste system, where people were divided into four categories: *ali'i* (royalty), *kapuna* (high priests), *maka'ainana* (commoners), and *kauwa* (outcasts). People were born into a caste and could not move freely between categories. However, if a commoner did not like his or her community, that person was free to find another somewhere else on the island. You can read more about the intricacies of this culture in chapter 5.

These new Hawaiians lived in isolation for 500 years. Worshipping nature, the people set up sustainable communities called *ahupua'a* to ensure survival. Land was sliced into triangles, extending from the top of a mountain down to the ocean and centered on a water source—a waterfall that turned into a stream and drained into the ocean. By irrigating the plants with water that drained back into the main water source, the people could feed, clothe, and shelter themselves from their slice of land. Plus these bright folks ensured that they would never run out of water. When they weren't farming, the Kaua'i people also became adept hula dancers, starting the biggest hula school in all of Hawai'i—though this type of hula is not what you see at a local lu'au. Only men danced. And the hula was accompanied by a sacred chant, instead of singing or instruments.

And Then Comes Cook and the Caucasians

On January 19, 1778, British explorer Captain James Cook and his crew docked the
Discovery and the *Resolution* in the waters off Waimea Town. Believing he was the god Lono
returning on a floating island, the Hawaiians canoed out to the ships with an abundance of
fresh food (and an array of excitable women) to offer the explorers. This proved a fateful
turning point in Hawaiian history. Not only did Cook and his crew trade iron, weaponry,
and nails for sweet potatoes and fish, but they also left a scar on the pure Hawaiian population: a nasty bout of syphilis.

Leaving weapons and sickly people behind, Cook and his crew took off for the Arctic,
dubbing the friendly islands to the south the Sandwich Islands, to honor his patron, the
Earl of Sandwich. However, the weather forced him to turn back and Cook returned, dock-
ing near the Big Island this time. Once again the party received a warm welcome, replete
with the finest foods, women, and respect. But the people soon began to suspect that this
farm boy wasn't in fact a god (since the pious didn't actually *need* women, and the crew
members broke an infinite number of *kapu*). Finally, after the ships set sail for the north
once more but were forced to return due to rough seas, the locals grew angry and started
stealing iron from the ships. Cook then made a series of unfortunate decisions, which ultimately led to a battle with the Hawaiians that killed him. Cook's crew went ballistic, burning a village and beheading natives. At last, realizing that the explorer was a highly
respected man, King Kalaniopuʻu returned Cook's bones so he could be buried at sea.

Inter-Island Drama

Besides a legacy of venereal disease, Cook and his crew left a taste for violence, with
weapons to boot, in the Hawaiians. From 1786 to 1795, war and chaos ravaged the islands.
Mostly this was because of a young warrior, King Kamehameha, who ruled the Windward
Islands and desired the Leeward Islands of Kauaʻi and Niʻihau for his empire. Prophets and
high priests warned him to be content with what he already had, but greed got the best of
him and he set out to conquer the leeward duo.

After a run of bad luck, Kamehameha had to try to gain more land with a different tac-
tic. He decided to meet with Kaumualiʻi (the king of Kauaʻi at the time). Kaumualiʻi, afraid
of the powerful Kamehameha's warring forces, agreed on a pact to join Kauaʻi to the
Kingdom of Hawaiʻi, as long as Kaumualiʻi would still be the figurehead over the island.

However, Kaumualiʻi never trusted Kamehameha's intentions and wasn't surprised
when, after his death, the king's son Liholiho kidnapped him and took him to Oʻahu. Once
there, Kaumualiʻi was tricked into marrying Kamehameha's favorite wife, bringing him
into the family. Thus when Kaumualiʻi died in 1824, the Kingdom of Kauaʻi did as well. He
might have been proud to know that his loyal people rebelled. They went to war with the
Windward chiefs, fighting for their independence. Unfortunately, they lost and their land
was split among the families of chiefs from the other islands.

Russians—in Kauaʻi?

During this time, foreigners, having heard from Cook's crew about this tropical paradise,
lined up along the coast. It started with the Russians in 1804. Georg Schaeffer, a German
doctor who was attempting to help the Russians set up a colony on the island, healed
Kaumualiʻi and his wife. In return, he was enlisted as the co-monarch of Kauaʻi. On the sly,
he and Kaumualiʻi had dreams of conquering the other Hawaiian Islands.

But what a sweet deal Schaeffer got! For arranging exclusive trade rights for Russia with Kaua'i, getting permission to make factories, and promising to protect the island from intruders, Schaeffer received land and unheard-of power. He constructed Fort Elizabeth, a lava rock fort on the banks of the Waimea River. He renamed Kaua'i places with Russian monikers; the chiefs got Russian names. He started growing tobacco, cotton, melons, and vineyards. Kaumuali'i even gave Schaeffer the valley of Hanalei *and* its 30 families.

This little cross-cultural affair lasted until 1817, when the Americans, wanting trade rights and power of their own, spread rumors about Schaeffer; they then said the United States and Russia were at war. Soon the fickle nature of even the most isolated humans appeared. Schaeffer was forced to leave. All the Hawaiian names were changed back. Forts fell. And the Russians were all but forgotten—except for the remains of Fort Elizabeth that you can still see today.

In Comes Everyone Else

The vodka and potato lovers weren't the only guys trying to get a piece of the island's resources. Americans and Chinese arrived, too, wanting a piece of the trade action. During the War of 1812, explorers from the New World began trading arms with the Hawaiians. Around the same time, the Chinese traded for sandalwood. However, the sandalwood trade hurt the workers (most of them in the commoner caste); many died of starvation and mistreatment.

In 1819, the combination of missionaries sailing in and the death of Kamehameha led to a new era. Suddenly, the *kapu* system went kaput, chiefs lost power, and the local people needed spiritual guidance. The Reverend William Ellis, who knew how to speak and write Tahitian, quickly picked up the Hawaiian language and started preaching to natives in their

This plantation-era church is the oldest in Waimea Town.

own tongue. The amazed Hawaiians then attended missionary schools, while Ellis established a written Hawaiian language. By 1831, two-fifths of the population were students. Because of a shortage of teachers and supplies, as soon as a Hawaiian could read, he or she became a teacher. And rumor has it that at least one school used surfboards as desks.

The local people, needing this spiritual structure, opened their world to the missionaries, who quickly became powerful in the construction of industry. Builders with ties to the church, like Ladd and Company, created the first sugar plantation in Koloa. Missionaries encouraged (read: forced) sugar barons to hire local Hawaiians. This type of work was a new thing for the islanders, who looked at company leaders as chiefs. Of course the once regal chiefs fought this, seeing they didn't have power anymore. But even in the tropics, money talks. So when William Hooper—in charge of Koloa plantation—created a currency to pay workers (one that was used until 1850), Koloa became a flourishing village of homes, a church, and a sugar mill—albeit a rough one. With chiefs out of the picture, the people became violent, and it was up to the missionaries and heads of the mills to stifle them.

So Kaua'i had jumped into the modernization game. Westerners visited. Chiefs and missionaries grew sugarcane. People tried growing coffee and rice. And then came the opportunists. By the mid-1800s, the native Hawaiian population had decreased because of disease and the California Gold Rush. So the Royal Hawaiian Agricultural Society, looking for staff, brought in Chinese, Japanese, Portuguese, Filipino, German, and Gilbert Islander workers. But with this new influx came opium, smallpox, leprosy, a rise in crime and rebellion, and of course resentment.

The population on Kaua'i doubled during the years around the turn of the 20th century. People moved to be near mills, creating townships near Lihu'e, Koloa, and Hanalei. However, times were tough for small farmers thanks to the moody landscape, the expensive mills, and the long time it took crops to flourish. And like everywhere else the rich got richer. When they scored sugar and rice contracts with California companies (as well as the rest of the world), they became the only businesses to survive the modernization of the island.

Koolau the Leper

The Chinese brought leprosy to the islands in 1840. Once people were known to have contracted the disease, they were carted to Kalaupapa on Moloka'i, the famed leprosy camp. Many lepers, not wanting to leave their beloved Kaua'i, hid in the Kalalau Valley. Jack London immortalized the most famous hero of this time in his true story *Koolau the Leper*.

After Koolau contracted the disease, he said he would go to Kalaupapa, but only if his wife and son could go, too. The authorities said no. In revolt, he took his family to the valley and swore never to be taken alive. Authorities came into the valley to take him to the colony, but Koolau killed a sheriff. Then a larger group of police and soldiers set into this rainy forest to round up all of the lepers hiding here. This time Koolau killed three sheriffs and ended a serious attempt to capture him.

He and his family stayed in the Kalalau Valley for years, getting supplies from friends who considered him a hero. Unfortunately, during this time, his son contracted leprosy and died in 1896. Koolau died soon after. His wife then returned to south shore and remarried. But Koolau became a symbol of resistance to the way leprosy was treated on Hawai'i.

From a Monarchy to Statehood

Though the plantation owners essentially acted as the leaders of the small societies, Hawai'i was still a monarchy—albeit a dying one. In 1887, Queen Lili'uokalani (the last monarch of the islands), believing that the United States had too much control over the islands, created a constitutional monarchy. Unfortunately for her, a coup, inspired by US planters, deposed her. US soldiers then arrived for "peacekeeping" measures and made Sanford Dole the provisional president of the Hawaiian Republic.

The provisional government set up voting rights, but only for people who had a certain amount of income and property value. Most commoners still wanted Hawai'i to stay a monarchy. But they were not permitted to vote. So the islanders had to abide by US laws whether they liked it or not. One wealthy native, Prince Kuhio, the Koloa-born great-grandson of Kaumuali'i, tried to restore the monarchy but was imprisoned (later he was elected to Congress; his birthday is still celebrated today). Other than that little wave, it was smooth sailing in 1898, when President McKinley was able to secure the annexation of Hawai'i for the United States.

Strangely, it was the Pearl Harbor attack that led Hawaiians into a movement to become more than a territory. They had suddenly become American, wanting the voting power and rights that came with being a state. Thus was the statehood movement was born, one that would take 18 years to reach fulfillment. The common people, the elites, and the American Japanese studying on the GI Bill all agreed, voting by an overwhelming majority to become a state. On August 21, 1959, President Eisenhower granted the small but desirable chain of islands entrance into the club as the 50th state.

The Ironic Twist

If you listen closely to the voice of the native Hawaiian people, you might hear the phrase *Pae'aina o Hawai'i Loa*. This indicates the growing (and persistent) movement for a sovereign nation of Hawai'i. Where once countless people voted to become a part of the United States, now indigenous people want their own nation, free from the control of the red, white, and blue.

To ensure that there are some benefits for native Hawaiians, in 1887, the Kamehameha Schools were founded to serve indigenous children and non-Hawaiian orphans. Bernice Pauahi Bishop, in her will and testament, left the lands that Kamehameha Schools are based on to those descended from citizens of the kingdom. However, in 2005, the 9th Circuit Court of Appeals voted that these schools needed to open their doors to more non-Hawaiian children. Though the schools still have ways to ensure that the majority of students are indigenous, it was a blow to the indigenous population.

There have been a number of official government gestures in response to the movement, but who in the United States really wants to part with this tropical paradise? Just in time for the 100th anniversary of the monarchy's overthrow, the US Congress extended to Hawaiians the "Apology Bill," which offers little more than its name. More recently the Native Hawaiian Government Reorganization Act, commonly called the Akaka Bill, has stirred debate. Activists claim this act threatens the sovereignty movement by making the Hawaiian people dependent on the United States for decisions on economic development, land claims, and citizenship. Supporters say the bill would help end racist actions against indigenous people and give native Hawaiians rights similar to Native Americans. In 2007, this bill passed in the House.

Though this debate rages on, this doesn't stop the Hawaiian people from recognizing their place in American culture. They vote, celebrate national holidays, and generally offer their aloha spirit freely. Still, rocky times may be ahead. With the boom in mainlanders moving to the islands and buying up precious property, indigenous people cannot afford ascending costs of modern life. Many are forced to move to the Big Island, Las Vegas, and Oregon, where property is affordable. This cultural earthquake, plus the shrinking of the native forest, is leading Kaua'i to a new stage in its dramatic history.

NEIGHBORS ALL AROUND

Ni'ihau
See chapter 9.

O'ahu
A mere 20-minute flight takes you from Kaua'i to another world. O'ahu, the heart of Hawaiian culture, boasts a unique stir-fry of hip urbanity and rural island life. With just under a million people calling O'ahu home and over five million visitors per year, O'ahu has earned its moniker *the Gathering Place*. You cannot arrive in O'ahu without passing through Honolulu. Though it's plagued by traffic, noise, and high-rises, Honolulu is also a hybrid and exciting metropolis, thanks to its location between continents. In recent years some very talented chefs have opened restaurants here that bridge the divide between California and Japanese cuisine. Downtown O'ahu has also received a face-lift, making it the heart of a unique art, music, and shopping scene. This cross-pollination of Hong Kong, Tokyo, the South Pacific, and Miami Beach has blossomed into a wealth of culture like nowhere else. Once you drive out of the crowded city, the beaches are spectacular: Hanauma Bay consistently wins awards as the best snorkeling location in the world; watching the surfers battle North Shore is exhilarating. Plus, hiking up Diamond Head to view the ocean stretched before you for endless miles is a treat not to be missed.

Moloka'i
Moloka'i, with 50 percent of its population indigenous, is home to the second highest concentration of Native Hawaiians in the world (Ni'ihau has the most). Whether because it was the home of the famous leper colony, or because the beaches tend to be rough, or possibly because there is hardly any tourist infrastructure, this oasis of rural tranquility draws a minuscule number of visitors annually. The island's business center, Kaunakakai, boasts a mere three blocks of commercial buildings and has an Old Country vibe unlike anywhere else in the islands. The rest of the isle is a combination of verdant cliffs that drop into rocky seas, the longest Hawaiian beach, rich valleys, and dry plains.

Lana'i
This sleepy island, 9 miles from the action on Maui's west shore, feels like another planet. Until recently, Lana'i only had one hotel to serve the few visitors who arrived searching for a Hawai'i far from the tourist trade. Now the Four Seasons caters to the luxury crowd, though the island still comprises dirt roads, pineapple farms, and wild farm animals. Travelers enjoy steep red lava mountains that drop into the sea, remote white sand beaches, archaeological sites, and foggy forests that on clear days offer views of almost all

the Hawaiian Islands. Lana'i City remains a tin-roofed plantation town, home to agricultural workers and their families. Though it can be an expensive trek to get here, many tourists make it a day trip from Maui.

Maui

When most people think of Hawai'i, Maui's Lahaina and Kihei neighborhoods are what they imagine: bustling resorts and condos lining spectacular beaches, while serving up all the comforts (and luxuries) of home. And Maui—named for the trickster demigod who lifted the sky so humans didn't have to walk on all fours—does indeed offer this type of pampering. But a visit to this popular isle will also get you hippie villages, windsurfing beaches, sunrise views from the top of the world's largest dormant volcano, Haleakala, and the famed drive to the remote town of Hana. Some of my favorite outdoor activities are the outstanding hikes through bamboo groves, waterfalls, craters, and beaches (where you can join native Hawaiians in their search for edible seaweed), biking down Haleakala, snorkeling on Molokini, and surfing Hookipa Beach.

Hawai'i: The Big Island

This might possibly be one of the most exciting places to visit in the world. Where else can you actually watch a place sizzle to life? The biggest (twice the size of all the islands put together) and youngest of the Hawaiian Islands is still growing, and visitors can trek out to the Hawai'i Volcanoes National Park to watch the lava waterfall into the sea. Aside from the geological fireworks, this isle is an adventurer's dream. Climates range from tropical to subarctic—yes, it has even snowed here. And visitors can find everything from waterfalls to deserts, organic food to plate lunches, the tallest mountain on the islands to cool cattle pastures; some of the land might as well be on the moon, while in other areas you'll find tropical oases dotted with resorts and multimillion-dollar homes. With 300 square miles of land to explore, I always have to remind myself to take my time and settle in to the slow pace of this unique microcosm.

2

Transportation

Holo Holo

Kaua'i's location—on the northernmost tip of the Hawaiian archipelago, surrounded by Hawai'i's largest coral reef and guarded by some of the most powerful waves in the Pacific—has not stopped visitors from getting here. Since the time of ancient Polynesians, then Captain Cook, and now with over a million tourists arriving each year, people have found ways to get here and travel around the island. The first and most popular way to get here is to fly. Another option is to arrive on a cruise ship, or the impending (and highly contested) Superferry.

Once you are on the island, the best way to get around is by renting a car. If that is out of your budget, the Kaua'i Bus has mediocre island service. Though hitchhiking is quite common, I would not recommend it—as we all know, it can be quite dangerous.

GETTING TO KAUA'I

By Plane

When you deplane on Kaua'i, traditional musicians serenade you in the open-air lobbies, pictures of hula dancers line the walls, and the sweet sticky smell of humidity fills the air. Lihu'e Airport (LIH) is far from a bustling metropolis and easy to negotiate—especially because (at press time) there are only seven major airlines serving Kaua'i. **United Airlines** (800-824-6200; www.united.com) offers direct flights from the Los Angeles and San Francisco international airports. **American Airlines** (800-433-7300; www.aa.com) has a direct flight daily from Los Angeles. **US Airways** (800-428-4322; www.USairways.com) flies direct from Phoenix. **Alaska Airlines** (800-ALASKAAIR; www.alaskaair.com) recently started a nonstop flight from Seattle.

Another option (often less expensive) is to fly in from Honolulu—a 25-minute island hop. Most major airlines fly direct to Honolulu; you then change to a local airline. The low-cost carrier **Go!** (888-367-9462; www.iflygo.com) offers daily inter-island flights, as do **Hawaiian Airlines** (800-367-5320; www.hawaiianair.com) and **Island Air** (800-652-6541; www.islandair.com) from both Honolulu and Maui.

Private planes and helicopters also use the Princeville Airport on the north shore and Burns Field in Hanapepe.

Even the cars embody the Garden Isle nickname.

By Sea

Cruise Ships

Cruise ships are now common sights around Hawai'i. Lucky you, almost all of them include stops on Kaua'i. Ships dock in Nawiliwili Harbor and usually allow guests a full day to explore each island.

Cruise ships that currently serve the island are listed below:

Holland America Cruise Line (877-724-5425; www.hollandamerica.com). This fleet sails from San Diego, Seattle, or Vancouver.

Norwegian Cruise Line (800-327-7030; www.ncl.com). Operates cruises starting and finishing in Hawai'i.

Princess Cruises (800-568-3262; www.princess.com). Offers cruises between Hawai'i and Tahiti.

Superferry

At press time, the **Hawai'i Superferry** (877-HI-FERRY; www.hawaiisuperferry.com), a new mode of inter-island transportation, was still on the table. The catamarans will enable 900 passengers to sail to Kaua'i for reasonably low rates. As I write this, the ferry only travels between Honolulu and Maui, for $44–62 per person (plus $59–69 per automobile, and an additional fuel surcharge); however, negotiations are in the works for a Kaua'i leg. Check the web site for the current schedule.

Note that many locals are upset about the newest influx of 300 cars per day, plus the rise in pollution and traffic the ferry will bring to the island. In fact, when the Superferry first began service, 300 local surfers protested by blocking its way. The fight got so intense that it went to the State Supreme Court. After three months, the judge decided to allow the Superferry to serve the island. But it is still a major point of contention (and, at press time, hadn't actually started yet). If you arrive by Superferry, I recommend not bragging to locals that you did so.

If you are concerned about your carbon impact on the island, an ecofriendly option is to take the Kaua'i Bus from the harbor to your destination. See below for information.

GETTING AROUND

Though most people who come to Kaua'i rent a car, there are alternative ways of exploring the island. However, it can be difficult to get around without a car. If you choose not to rent a vehicle, I recommend that you stay in Kapa'a or Hanalei (where you have everything you need within walking distance)—or be prepared to spend a lot of time at your resort.

By Bike

Though there are no official bike lanes, exploring the island on a bicycle is a treat. With 90 miles of coastline and a mountainous interior to explore, Kaua'i is made for cyclists. Just make sure to wear reflective clothing at night because most roads are not lit up and people drive too fast. For specific information on rentals, see chapter 7.

Horse-drawn carriages take guests on tours of the Kilohana Plantation.

By Bus

The Kaua'i Bus (808-241-6410; www.kauai.gov) offers extensive islandwide service, Mon.–Sat. Small buses with handicapped access run approximately 6:30 AM–7 PM. Fares cost $1.50 per trip (50¢ for the Lihu'e Extension shuttle), and you need exact change. There are no transfers. However, you can also get a monthly pass for $15. Bikes and small baggage are permitted, but not surfboards or oversized bags. You can get an up-to-date schedule online.

As of press time, these are the current bus routes:

100	Kekaha to Lihu'e
100E	Kekaha to Koloa to Lihu'e
200	Lihu'e to Kekaha
200E	Lihu'e to Koloa to Kekaha
400	Hanalei to Lihu'e
400E	Hanalei to Kapahi to Lihu'e
500	Lihu'e to Hanalei
500E	Lihu'e to Kapahi to Hanalei
600	Lihu'e to Kapahi to Lihu'e
700	Lihu'e Extension

By Car

The most popular and easiest way to see the island is by car. There is essentially one highway that circles the 70 miles of drivable land; however, it has numerous names and can get confusing. In Lihu'e, heading west, it is called H 50 (or Kaumuali'i Highway) and it goes past the Poipu/Koloa turnoff, all the way through Kekaha to the Polihale turnoff. From Lihu'e, heading north, the highway is called H 56 (or Kuhio Highway). It takes you through Wailua/Kapa'a, Kilauea, Princeville, and Hanalei to end at Ke'e Beach.

Other notable roads include:

H 51	Kapule Highway (in Lihu'e, from Hanama'ulu to Nawiliwili Harbor)
58	Nawiliwili Road (in Lihu'e, from Kukui Grove Center to Nawiliwili Harbor)
520	Maluhia Road (to Koloa/Poipu, through the Tree Tunnel)
530	Koloa Road (from Koloa to Lawa'i)
540	Halewili Road (Kalaheo to Ele'ele)
H 550	Waimea Canyon Drive (from Kekaha to Waimea Canyon)
552	Koke'e Road (from Kekaha to Koke'e, meets H 550)
570	Ahukini Road (from Lihu'e to the airport)
580	Kuamo'o Road (from Kapa'a around Sleeping Giant)
581	Kamalu Road (from Wailua to the Keahua Arboretum)
583	Ma'alo Road (to Wailua Falls)

In general, even though distances between towns might not be that far, you can bet that it will take you longer than expected to get from place to place. Driving from one end of the island to the other takes about an hour and a half. There are no freeways and the average speed between towns is around 30 mph. In town, you can pretty much count on traffic—the biggest local complaint. In Kapa'a, Wailua, and Lihu'e, you will see lines of cars creeping along H 56 all day long. It is best to stay off the roads in this area between 7 and 8 AM and 3 and 5 PM on weekdays.

Most people rent cars when they arrive at the Lihu'e Airport. If you don't want a car for

Mileage Information and Driving Times		
From Lihu'e to:		
Poipu	14 miles	30 minutes
Waimea Canyon	36 miles	1½ hours
Wailua	7 miles	15 minutes
Princeville	30 miles	1 hour
Haena	40 miles	1¼ hours

your entire stay, some hotels and condos can arrange rental vehicles for you. Note that in high season, it is highly recommended to reserve your car in advance. Shop around online and when you see a good deal, grab it. Especially since gas prices are consistently higher than on the mainland.

Below are car rental agencies located at the Lihu'e Airport:

Alamo Rent A Car	808-246-0646
Avis Rent A Car	808-742-1627 (also in the Grand Hyatt in Poipu)
Budget Car Rental	800-527-0700
Dollar Rent-A-Car	800-800-4000 (also in the Sheraton Koloa)
Hertz Rent A Car	800-654-3011 (also at the Kaua'i Marriott)
National Car Rental	888-868-6207
Thrifty Car Rental	800-847-4389

Island Cars (800-246-6000; 2983 Aukele St., Lihu'e) is a locally owned car rental agency with some of the lowest rates on the island.

If you do rent a car, know that there are a lot of break-ins on the island. Never leave your possessions unattended in the car. I was once told to always leave my rental car unlocked with nothing of value in it, so that if someone saw a gum wrapper they really wanted, they could open the door instead of smashing the window. This might violate your rental car contract, though, so make sure to read the agreement thoroughly. Better yet, don't leave anything of value in your car.

Also note that driving out to Polihale (or on other unpaved roads) is prohibited by your rental car contract. If you are just aching to head out there, make sure to ask your agent about four-wheel drives that can make the trek. We once got stuck along the way and had to buy a bunch of guys some beer for a tow. And even so, they laughed at us *haoles*. If you get stuck, people might not be so accommodating—and getting a tow is really expensive.

Scenic Drives

To say there are a number of scenic drives on Kaua'i seems slightly redundant, since every-where you look is pretty spectacular. One of my favorite things to do is get in the car and explore a new road that weaves through the mountains or along the coast. Still, there are some old staples not to be missed.

The Sacred Journey

H 580 (Kuamo'o Road) weaves along the Wailua River, passing many *heiau*, Opaeka'a Falls, and leading up to Keahua Arboretum. As you get higher up, you can turn off to visit the

Road Rules and Hazards

Driving in Kaua'i, though it might appear easy, can be quite hazardous. There are numerous deadly crashes each year (especially along H 56 at night), and speeding is the main reason. Police officers are out in full force to catch speeders, people who aren't wearing their seat belts, or drunk drivers. Pay close attention to posted speed limit signs, and no matter how much you like those free lu'au mai tais, make sure you always have a designated driver.

Here are some basic local driving customs to know.

- Don't honk. In Kaua'i this is considered rude.
- Let faster drivers pass, when it's safe to do so.
- Don't tailgate.
- On one-lane bridges (mostly on the north shore), make sure to stop at the white line to check if there is oncoming traffic. If no one is waiting at the line on the other side, you are free to drive. If the car in front of you is crossing (and no one is waiting), follow. However, if cars are waiting on the other side, yield to them. The general rule is if you are the fifth through the seventh car, stop and let the people waiting on the other side go.

The one-lane Hanalei Bridge.

The sacred Wailua River was once the only method of transportation; now tourists use it to kayak to Secret Falls.

Kamokila Hawaiian Village and the **Hindu Monastery** (see chapter 4 for more about both). And on your way back down, there are lovely views of the sacred Wailua River spilling into the Pacific.

The North Shore

From Kapa'a, **H 56 (Kuhio Highway)** leads you through a dramatic change in scenery: from the bustling Lihu'e and Kapa'a into the jagged peaks of Kong (look for the outline of King Kong's profile on this mountain), past Roadside Falls, and toward Kilauea. Worth to the detour: Turn off onto Kolo Road to Kilauea Road and head all the way to the end for a view of the lighthouse and nesting birds. Back on H 56, the road weaves through Princeville and Hanalei until it reaches Haena. Once there, you'll pass the **Maniniholo Dry Cave** and the **Waiokapala'e** and **Waiakanaloa Wet Caves** (see chapter 5), and then arrive at **Ke'e Beach** where the road ends.

The Wild West

From Lihu'e, take **H 50 (Kaumuali'i Highway)** south. Turn onto H 520 to pass through the **Tree Tunnel** (see chapter 5) and head into **Koloa**, where you can explore the Old Mill town. Turn onto Poipu Road and follow the signs to **Spouting Horn** (see chapter 5). Back on H 50, head west, through Kalaheo, Ele'ele, and into **Waimea**, where you can explore the historic buildings of the first known settlement in Kaua'i (see chapter 4). Back on H 50, turn onto **H 550** and weave up the mountain to the dynamic **Waimea Canyon** and **Koke'e State Park** (see chapters 5 and 7). When you get back to the coast, if you still have energy (and have a car that can take on a rough road), head west on H 50, turn left almost a mile north of the military base, and drive for 4 miles on a *very bumpy road* to **Polihale State Beach** (see chapter 7) for a spectacular sunset.

BY FOOT

Walking around Kaua'i always seems like a fantastic idea. Unfortunately, aside from designated walking paths, hikes, and a few sidewalks in Lihu'e, Hanalei, Waimea, and Kapa'a, walking can be dangerous. Especially at night. That

The Kalalau Trail makes for an intense hike.

being said, I have walked from Poipu to Koloa and from Wailua to Kapa'a numerous times. However, every time I end up walking through mud or on the grass, because cars drive really fast along the two-lane road. For detailed hikes, strolls, and walks, see chapter 7.

BY HELICOPTER

It is possible to explore Kaua'i's uninhabitable interior by helicopter tour. Just don't expect to be dropped off anywhere. Tours usually last an hour and are often the highlight of your vacation. However, there have been a recent series of tragic helicopter crashes on Kaua'i. You might want to research your tour company's safety record before booking your trip. See chapter 7 for details about tour companies.

BY TAXI

Expensive and sometimes tough to find, taxis are another option on Kaua'i—especially to and from a lu'au. There are a number of taxi companies that you can call from the hotel or restaurant. Try **Akiko's Taxi** (808-822-7588) and **City Cab** (808-245-3227) on the east shore; **Kilauea Taxi and Tour** (808-652-7247) and **North Shore Cab** (808-826-4118) on the north shore; and **South Shore Cab** (808-742-1525) in Poipu.

3

LODGING

Your Island Hale

For most of the 19th century, Kaua'i visitors sailed into Koloa, where sugar barons offered high-end lodging and a glimpse into the simple life of this remote island. It wasn't until 1890, when Charles Spitz opened the Fairview Hotel (which later morphed into the Lihu'e Hotel and finally the Kaua'i Inn you see today), that the first official hotel here was born. This, coupled with the Pan Am revolution, lured tourists westward. By the late 1960s, mainlanders had "found" the pristine beaches and lush hiking trails.

Today, with just over a million of visitors a year, there are only a small number of actual resorts and hotels on the island. These are primarily centered in the developed areas of the south and north shores. However, in the last 10 years, the east and west shores acquired their share of luxury spots as well. If budget or midrange hotel options are more your speed, you'll find these mostly in Lihu'e and Kapa'a, though you may find a few on the south and north shores.

The best deal on the island is to rent a condo. Spread throughout the east, south, and north shores, you'll find a condominium option for nearly every price range. Finding the right unit for you, though, might take a little research. There is no central booking agency for any one particular condominium complex, and decor is all over the map. For the most part, each condo unit is individually owned and operated, which means two condos right next to each other will be entirely different. Another consideration is that some complexes comprise "resort condos"—condos with resort benefits (often this means that the company

Price Codes

Inexpensive	Up to $150
Moderate	$150–250
Expensive	$250–375
Very Expensive	Over $375

Credit cards are abbreviated as follows:
AE—American Express
D—Discover Card
DC—Diner's Club
JCB—Japan Credit Bureau
MC—Master Card
V—Visa

A tiki torch welcomes the south shore sunset.

What's the Deal With All Those Chickens?

At first you might think they're cute, a novelty even. You'll take pictures at the airport or up at Koke'e or at the parking lot of your accommodation. But come 4 AM, it'll be another story. The unfortunate reality of Kaua'i is that the chickens get up before you do. The positive side is that you never need an alarm clock.

No one knows exactly when chickens were introduced to Kaua'i, but we do know that Polynesian sailors had them aboard ships for food. After Hurricane 'Iniki destroyed many of the cages of captive birds, the chickens ran wild, breeding like crazy. Now no matter where you are staying—a Poipu condo or the Princeville Hotel—chickens are a presence. So if you are a light sleeper, bring earplugs. And make sure to watch the roads when you drive. Recently, a friend came to meet me at the beach and hit a chicken on the way.

And in case you are wondering, those skinny fowls don't make good eating.

Your Kaua'i alarm clock.

will charge a resort fee; this will be noted if it is the case) like maid service, wireless, and so on. An easy way to negotiate the condo conundrum is to contact a rental agency, tell them *exactly* what you are looking for, and then ask to see specific pictures of the units they suggest. I have listed what makes each building unique. I've also included rental agencies, their policies, and generally what you can expect from their services.

Agencies also rent houses around the island. You can find anything from that dreamy little beach shack for a moderate price to a five-bedroom villa that should be showcased in *Architectural Digest*. I have included a couple of houses in this chapter, but for more options, contact the rental agencies listed.

A significant rise in B&Bs and in-house stays has recently created a political conflict. Authorities say rental units strip local people of low-cost housing options, while B&B owners claim that this service is the only way they can afford to survive since the drop in agricultural revenue. At press time, new laws were being passed about the legality of these rentals. Rumor has it that the existing in-home stays and B&Bs listed below will be grandfathered into legality. If you are looking for an in-home stay other than those listed in this chapter, contact **www.hawaiibnb.com**, which is a statewide service that connects travelers to local residents who have rooms, cottages, and condos to rent.

The price range below includes the cost of lodging based on a per-room, per-night, double-occupancy charge during high season (Dec.–Apr. and June–Aug.). Note that off-season rates can be significantly lower, while winter holiday rates can often double or triple. Prices do not include 11.4 percent tax, resort fees, condo cleaning fees, and the like.

EAST SHORE LODGING

KAPA'A/WAILUA

Aloha Beach Resort
General Manager: Ron Kikumoto.
808-823-6000 or 888-823-5111; fax 808-823-6666.
www.alohabeachresortkauai.com.
info@alohabeachresortkauai.com.
3-5920 Kuhio Hwy., Kapa'a.
Price: Inexpensive.
Credit Cards: AE, D, DC, JCB, MC, V.
Handicapped Access: Yes.

If you are looking for a traditional Hawaiian resort experience loaded with local *kapuna* chanters, myth and legend tours, Hawaiian medicinal plant tutorials, and instrument-making, Hawaiian-language, and lei-making lessons, then look no farther than Aloha Beach. They really go out of their way to share the spirit of aloha to the whole family, including plenty of kids' activities, like the one that might get your tykes to help with the dishes: a lesson on the roles of ancient Hawaiian children. Recently renovated rooms enhance the island-style decor, great deals, and friendly staff. This resort offers pools, tennis courts, a restaurant, air-conditioned rooms, and wireless in the lounge. It's just a short walk from Lydgate Beach, bringing the resort experience to you if you don't want to pay Hyatt prices.

They've obviously been doing something right here to stay in business since the early 1970s. This is a good option for families on a budget who want a resort experience but not a high-end luxurious one.

Anuenue Plantation
Owners: Harry Guiremand and Frederick Wells.
808-823-8335 or 888-371-7716.
www.anuenue.com.
lodging@anuenue.com.
6163 Waipouli Rd., Kapa'a.
Price: Inexpensive.
Credit Cards: None.
Handicapped Access: None.

Ten years ago, Harry and Fred moved to Kaua'i from the Bay Area with their cat Kitty (who has the run of the house) and built this estate in the foothills of Kapa'a. They included two spacious private rooms with bathrooms—one upstairs and one down—for guests. Rooms make you feel like you're visiting a funky uncle's pad, especially with the multicolored comforters on 1980s-style beds. Both rooms have fans and big windows (the upstairs has a view of the valley, while the downstairs has a private lanai). The guest lounge overflows with newly released movies, books, and magazines. Full breakfast (banana pancakes, omelets, fruit, and more) is served up daily, with stunning valley views of morning rainbows over Waiʻaleʻale (hence the name: *Anuenue* means "rainbow"). There is also a large windowed room for yoga/meditation. This B&B is for people who want a quiet, unique, and reasonably priced experience, 10 minutes from the bustle of Kapaʻa and Lydgate Beach. There is a two-night minimum stay.

Hotel Coral Reef Resort
Innkeepers: George and Rhonda Tandal.
808-822-4481 or 800-843-4659; fax 808-822-7705.
www.hotelcoralreefresort.com.
hotelcoralreef@hawaiilink.net.
4-1516 Kuhio Hwy., Kapaʻa.
Price: Inexpensive–moderate.
Credit Cards: AE, DC, JCB, MC, V.
Handicapped Access: Limited.
Special Features: Extended-stay, military, senior, and AAA discounts.

What used to be a dive hotel, popular with druggies and prostitutes since the early 1960s, has now, after a half-million-dollar renovation, entered the resort game, with 42-inch flat-screen cable TVs, pillow-top king- and queen-sized beds, Jacuzzi tubs, marble countertops, granite bathrooms, AC, and fans in reasonably sized rooms. A few rooms even come with kitchenettes. Almost all have lanais. Some are oceanfront, while the rest are either partial ocean view or garden. This 21-room hotel is situated on a white sand snorkel beach in the heart of Old Town Kapaʻa (one of the only hotels on this strip) with a lava rock waterfall into the pool, BBQs, and a gourmet restaurant (still in the works as of this printing). Amenities also include daily maid service, free parking, in-room safe, sauna, fitness room, laundry facilities, and lots of morning chickens. This sunrise spot can be a little loud, since it is by the street and those chickens get up before dawn. They serve continental breakfast and you can cross the street and get to one of the best coffee shops on the island for your early-morning fix. This hotel is a good option for those not renting a car who still want to be in the center of the Kapaʻa action.

Kapaʻa Sands
808-822-4901 or 800-222-4901; fax 808-822-1556.
www.kapaasands.com.
info@kapaasands.com.
380 Papaloa Rd., Kapaʻa.
Price: Inexpensive–moderate (check for deals online).
Credit Cards: MC, V.
Handicapped Access: Some.

Quite possibly the best oceanfront deal in the Kapaʻa/Wailua area, this 20-unit condominium complex once was a Japanese Shinto temple. Classic Shinto temples were built on sacred natural beauty, so you can be sure that this complex serves up delicious ocean views. Since each of the units is individually owned, the only constants are the size (studios or double-story two-bedrooms), Shinto screen doors, ocean views, full kitchens, cable, lanais, and wireless. Otherwise, the decor differs dramatically. This complex is an excellent budget option for people who want a condo experience on the beach, but are okay with smallish unit that is clean if not at all fancy. Complex amenities include a pool and a laundry room. Coconut Marketplace is a couple of minutes' walk away.

Kauaʻi Coast Resort at Beachboy
Managed by Shell Vacation Resorts.
General Manager: Jasmine Silva.
808-822-3441.
www.kauaicoastresort.com.
520 Aleka Loop, Kapaʻa.
Price: Moderate–expensive. (Shop around—you can find decent deals online.)
Credit Cards: AE, D, DC, JCB, MC, V.
Handicapped Access: Some.

One of the classiest time-share resorts on Kaua'i, with exotic landscaped grounds and blazing tiki torches at night, a lava rock waterfall into the pool and spa, overlooking the ocean. Given the proximity to Coconut Marketplace (across the street) and the relatively smaller size of the grounds (108 rooms), this is an excellent choice for people with limited mobility and families who want oceanfront resort accommodations. Since this used to be a boutique hotel, room interiors are decorated island-style, but not cheaply, with heavy wooden furniture, king-sized beds, and big windows, most with ocean views. Kaua'i Coast offers studio rooms (with no kitchen, washer, or dryer), as well as one- or two-bedroom apartments with the works: washer and dryer, pullout sofa, stocked full kitchen. Amenities include BBQs, hammocks, chairs by the ocean, a sandbox, beachfront massages, in-room AC and fans, lanais, daily maid service, Internet access (for $9.95 a day), free local calls, tennis courts, and a workout room. One of the best restaurants in Kapa'a, Hukilau Lanai, is located on the property; at night, musicians play in the open-air lobby/bar. Be aware that since this is a time-share resort, you will get phone calls to attend a time-share presentation for discounted activities. Staff are friendly, down to earth (read: not pushy), and doing something right, because during the day streams of people tour the property.

Kaua'i Country Inn

Owners: Mike and Martina Hough.
808-821-0207.
www.kauaicountryinn.com.
6440 Olohena Rd., Wailua.
Price: Inexpensive–moderate.
Credit Cards: AE, MC, V.
Handicapped Access: None.

The energetic Mike and Martina Hough have taste. After working in the film advertising industry for 17 years, they moved to Kaua'i, bringing colorful style to the inn crowd. The first things you'll notice in this 2-acre house, set in the quiet hills above Kapa'a, are the murals and the hat collection lining the walls. But it isn't until you enter your suite that you'll know you have arrived in a special place. The five executive suites and the three-bedroom cottage are spacious and decorated with exotic tiles, hardwood floors, big windows overlooking the valleys, Hawaiian-motif furniture and artwork, and big comfy beds. Units have kitchenette. Some offer lanai, fireplace, and grill. All rooms have TV, DVD, and in-room computer with DSL, plus access to Mike's film collection. Guests are invited to use the hot tub, kayaks, beach gear, and boogie boards; and if that isn't enough, guests are encouraged to attend Mike's entertaining tour of his unique Beatles Museum, packed with memorabilia, original artwork, and Brian Epstein's Mini Cooper. Even non–Beatles fans will be intrigued.

Lae Nani

Castle: 808-822-9331 or 800-367-5004; fax 808-822-2828.
www.castleresorts.com.
Outrigger: 877-523-6264 or 808-822-4938; fax 808-822-1022.
www.outrigger.com.
410 Papaloa Rd., Kapa'a.
Price: Expensive–very expensive.
Credit Cards: AE, D, JCB, MC, V.
Handicapped Access: Some.

Depending on which company rents your condo here, you might enjoy anything from a resort experience (including daily maid service) to mellow non-intrusive condo living on the ocean side of town. Once the site of a sacred Hawaiian temple, this property now beckons travelers to gather. This is an excellent choice for multigenerational families who want a central location (just a short walk to the Coconut Marketplace). A grassy central area around the large pool and BBQs, facing the small beach, is often where kids play soccer, football, and Frisbee. Spacious units are one or two bedroom, with stocked kitchen and two bathrooms. Big windows and a lanai face the ocean and pool. There is a tennis court for guests. And though these are not the classiest (or most private) condos, this is an excellent oceanfront option in Kapa'a. The folks at Rosewood rent one condo at this property; you might check with them if you are on a budget.

Lanikai

General Manager: Diane Pavao.
808-822-7700 or 800-367-5004; fax 808-822-7456.
www.castleresorts.com.
390 Papaloa Rd., Kapa'a.
Price: Expensive–very expensive.
Credit Cards: AE, DC, JCB, MC, V.
Handicapped Access: None.

This 18-unit luxury property sits on a lovely expanse of landscaped oceanfront real estate. All units have two bedrooms, with panoramic views of the ocean. Most units have been upgraded to include granite bathroom, top-of-the-line kitchen, washer and dryer, and air-conditioning. All have spacious lanais and a large bathroom for each bedroom. This property is very mellow—not for the partier, but for people who want to have some civilized oceanfront quiet time. However, since it is on the Coconut Coast, there is street noise. The fenced-in complex (one of the only gated condos on this stretch of beach) makes this a good place for children, who can't go running off toward the turbulent ocean. And because there are no elevators, make sure to ask for a bottom floor if you have limited mobility. Condos are walking distance from the Coconut Marketplace and a short drive from downtown Kapa'a and Lydgate Beach. Check online; you can get discounts.

Mohala Ke Ola

Owner: Ed Stumpf.
808-823-6398 or 888-465-2824.
www.waterfallbnb.com.
Kauaibb@aloha.net.
5663 Ohelo Rd., Kapa'a.
Price: Inexpensive.
Credit Cards: None.
Handicapped Access: None.

Mohala ke ola means "open to life" in Hawaiian. The owner, talkative Ed Stumpf, does his best to lure guests into this mantra by accepting all types of people into his health-and-healing-themed B&B. Since he is a masseur, you might feel the New Age vibe, but Ed tries his best to make sure that this three-room bed & breakfast, in a residential hillside area of Kapa'a, doesn't come off preachy to visitors. Instead, he allows the spectacular backyard views of Secret Falls, Wai'ale'ale, and the sacred Wailua Valley to work their magic. Here, visitors put their feet up and say *ahhh*. And it all starts with a breakfast, served daily in the kitchen (which guests are also allowed to use), that includes fruit, bread, cereal, pastries, coffee, and lots of island advice from Ed. Each spacious room has a private bath, cable TV, lanai, a Tempur-Pedic bed, sitting benches in the showers, and sofa beds. Guests can also make use of the washer and dryer, beach gear, books, CDs, pool, and Jacuzzi. Though Ed doesn't encourage kids, he won't discriminate; it is just not the best place for the younger crowd (or partiers, for that matter). Here you'll find people meditating on the back patio, blissed-out postmassage folks, and even the occasional Japanese monk. Make sure to check out the intense paintings by local artist Laka Morton; you might recognize his work from the Kaua'i Museum.

Outrigger Waipouli

General Manager: Dale Stetson.
808-823-8300; fax 808-823-8301.

www.outrigger.com.
4-820 Kuhio Hwy., Kapa'a.
Price: Expensive–very expensive.
Credit Cards: AE, D, DC, JCB, MC, V.
Handicapped Access: Yes.

Outrigger Waipouli scored the last ocean-front spot in Kapa'a, angering some residents and pleasing guests with the most luxurious condo complex to hit the Coconut Coast. Located within walking distance of food and shops, this "condo-tel" is an excellent choice if you want a high-end resort experience with the perks of your own apartment (without having to pay a resort or parking fee). Since each unit is individually owned and managed, you can't be sure what you'll get in terms of decor, but I can guarantee that your room will either be one-bedroom/two-bath or two-bedroom/three-bath, with top-of-the-line spacious kitchen, a lanai, cable TV, washer and dryer, air-conditioning, king beds, rich hardwood furniture, and giant master bathroom (with a Jacuzzi tub and two toilets). Both the living area and bedrooms have views of the ocean or pool/gardens. Amenities include a 2-acre landscaped oceanfront pool with waterslides and three whirlpools, a fitness center, snack bar and restaurant, concierge, and a spa. Families will love the convenience of this centrally located resort, while vacationers will be pleased with the decadence of having mai tais delivered while they laze away in the sun. Plus, the convenience of having a fancy kitchen delights the chef in everyone who stays here.

Resortquest Islander on the Beach
General Manager: Clinton Owen.
808-822-7417 or 877-997-6667; fax 808-822-1947.
www.rqislander.com.
440 Aleka Place, Kapa'a.
Price: Moderate–expensive.
Credit Cards: AE, D, DC, JCB, MC, V.
Handicapped Access: Yes.

Spread over 6.5 acres on a tropical beach in the heart of the Coconut Coast, this 36-year-old "condo-tel" offers simple rooms with views. Since this resort is located next to the Coconut Marketplace and on the ocean, it's an excellent choice for couples who don't want to rent a car, or for families (kids stay and eat free). The 178 rooms are on the smaller side (about 365 square feet) for the area, and include a kitchenette and a lanai to enjoy your morning coffee. Each unit is individually owned, though you will usually find them consistent in the decor with rattan furniture and floral-printed bedspreads. The rooms are not luxurious: You are paying for the location and the plantation-style decor of the buildings (reception is nicer than the rooms). Side units have more windows to maximize that Kaua'i breeze, but all rooms have air-conditioning that turns off when you open the door (to conserve energy). One unique perk is the web cam by the pool, allowing you to wave to your family and friends back home. Other amenities include a Jacuzzi, business center, DSL ($9.95 a day), cable TV, BBQ, daily maid service, and one of the most helpful concierges around.

Resortquest Kaua'i Beach at Maka'iwa
General Manager: Ray Blouin.
808-822-3455 or 866-774-2924; fax 808-822-1830.
info@resortquesthawaii.com.
650 Aleka Loop, Kapa'a.
Price: Expensive–very expensive.
Daily Resort Fee: $12. Includes Internet, free valet parking, local phone calls, 15 percent off spa treatments, bathroom amenities, and morning-delivery newspapers.
Credit Cards: AE, D, DC, JCB, MC, V.
Handicapped Access: Yes.

Since this resort opened in 1978, it has been through a variety of owners. Now that Resortquest is in charge, they are trying to figure themselves out (which is great for travelers, because that often means deals). After a major renovation, the rooms are simply decorated in Indonesian teak; and though they measure 328 square feet, they feel spacious and inviting. Count on cable TV, air-conditioning, big windows with ocean or garden views, a lanai, and wireless. Plus you get loads of resort amenities, including two restaurants, a morning coffee kiosk for jet-lagged travelers, an oceanfront pool and Jacuzzi (that unfortunately didn't get the perks of renovation), tennis courts, an in-house spa, live nightly entertainment in the lounge, a small fitness room, an on-site lu'au, and wedding packages (their most popular is at sunrise). And if you are looking for a place to have that seminar, they specialize in group rates and meetings. The central location on the Coconut Coast makes this a good choice for people who want to be close to restaurants and shops. Make sure to check out the lobby display of the historical voyaging artifacts of ancient King Moikeha, who landed on this shore and never left.

✪ Rosewood Inn

Owners: Rosemary and Norbert Smith.
808-822-5216; fax 808-822-5478.
www.rosewoodkauai.com.
rosewood@aloha.net.
872 Kamalu Rd., Kapa'a.
Price: Inexpensive–moderate.
Credit Cards: None.
Handicapped Access: None.

Can it be true: a Victorian-style community located in the Kapa'a foothills, just a 3-mile drive from Old Town Kapa'a and Lydgate Park? This unlikely site, reminiscent of San Francisco architecture but with island-style interiors, has been a pleasant surprise to travelers for the past 25 years. And not only because of the unusual yellow house that springs up out of nowhere. Rosemary and Norbert Smith invite guests into their home

Rosewood's yellow Victorian Cottage in the Kapa'a foothills.

and treat them like one of the family. Because of that hospitality, Rosewood Inn has grown into a full-fledged community with some of the best deals on the island. The three bunkhouses with hardwood floors, loft beds, microwave and refrigerator, shared bathrooms, and an outdoor shower—all for less than 50 bucks—make budget travelers feel just as special as the B&B crowd. The bed & breakfast rooms inside the main Victorian offer mountain views, a king-sized pillow-top bed, a private bathroom, and access to Rosemary's delicious continental breakfast (usually including fresh organic fruit from her trees). Finally the cottages make great makeshift homes for families. There's Colleen's Dream, a one-bedroom cottage with a kitchen, small living space, indoor toilet and sink, and outdoor shower. The Victorian Cottage is a two-bedroom Xerox of the main house, with a bathroom (that has an indoor shower), an outdoor shower, hardwood floors, fans, a spacious living room, a computer with wireless, a large lanai with rocking chairs, and a private garden. Finally, Shannon's Serenity is the three-bedroom ranch-like house on the back of the property, with laundry, "heavenly" beds, full kitchen, Internet hookup, and a couple of bathrooms. Plus Rosemary serves Aloha and Mahalo breakfasts for the guests staying in the cottages. During this time, chat with Rosemary and Norbert, who have raised seven kids on the island and can assist you with activities and advice. Be forewarned that there is a farm across the street, and the animals start up early. Plus their pet peacock, Pete, gets up on the roof in the morning and screams at passing cars that disturb him. Rosemary is a real estate agent who specializes in vacation rentals.

LIHU'E

Garden Island Inn
Owner: Steve Layne.
808-245-7227 or 800-648-0154.
www.gardenislandinn.com.
3445 Wilcox Rd., Lihu'e.
Price: Inexpensive–moderate.
Credit Cards: AE, D, MC, V.
Handicapped Access: Yes.
Pets: Yes.

Owner Steve Layne and his partner, Dawne Morningstar, have turned this roadside-motel-looking establishment into one of the most colorful accommodations on the island. You won't get the biggest or nicest rooms around (in fact, they can be a little cramped and dark), but what you do get is quality service, a friendly atmosphere, vibrant murals on the doors with tropical gardens to match, and a great location. One-of-a-kind artwork hangs in every room (all done by Miss Fontaine, the self-proclaimed colorful character), and all is for sale. For those of you missing your pets at home, you'll get lots of love from the cats and Dawne's standard poodle, Fifi. Steve goes out of his way to constantly keep the property clean and up-to-date with new showers, TVs, paintings, furniture, and fresh flowers. All rooms have a lanai, air-conditioning, microwave, refrigerator, coffeemaker and coffee, and free wireless and local calls. Upstairs rooms are more airy with better views. The inn offers free beach gear, camping fuel, snorkels, masks, fins, golf clubs—you name it, just ask. They even have a DVD lending library of films made on the island. The property is across the street from Kalapaki Beach and Nawiliwili Harbor (and near the airport), and there are plenty of restaurants, bars, and shops to walk to if you take the Superferry and don't want to rent a car.

Hilton Kaua'i Beach Hotel and Resort
General Manager: George Costa.
808-245-1955 or 888-805-3843; fax 808-246-9085.
www.kauaibeachhotelandresort.com.
info@kauaibeachhotelandresort.com.
4331 Kauai Beach Dr., Lihu'e.

Price: Moderate–very expensive.
Daily Resort Fee: $12.95 (plus tax). This includes the Sunset Cocktail Party, torch-lighting ceremony and Polynesian dance show, coffee/tea service, in-room safe, local phone calls, airport shuttle service, and unlimited self-parking and valet parking.
Credit Cards: AE, DC, D, JCB, MC, V.
Handicapped Access: Yes.
Special Features: Ask about AAA, AARP, military, and other discounts.

Shuffled between owners since its birth in 1986, this plantation-style accommodation was recently bought and restored by Hilton. If you are looking for a resort that is centrally located in Lihu'e, but still feels remote and simple, this is a good option. Even though there are 350 rooms, this resort's intimacy delights. It's tucked between a couple of fields in Lihu'e; the only reminders that other people are on the island are the planes flying overhead and the boats on their way to the harbor. The property is located on a rocky beach where you can walk for miles (but don't try swimming). One of the ocean-view pools has a lava rock waterfall; the other, that hard sand you find in Vegas pools. Here you can rent beach gear, get surf lessons, or have a sunset cocktail at the beach bar. The fancy Naupaka Terrace steak house opens for dinner, while the Shutters Bar offers food, music, and drinks, plus a big flat-screen TV to catch up on sporting events. Rooms are decorated with koa wood, dense island-style furniture and doors, tiled floors, and marble sinks. The decorators went out of their way to supply classy simple touches: sprawling comfortable beds, lanais with cushioned chairs, empty refrigerators to store your snacks, big windows, and air-conditioned rooms. If you want an ocean view, make sure to ask specifically what you are getting (some "ocean views" are more "pool views"). For an extra 40 bucks a night, the concierge level offers a private concierge, breakfast, an honors bar, afternoon pupus, and maid service to refresh your room every time you leave. An interesting perk to note is that if you like you room, you can actually buy it.

Kaha Lani Resort

General Manager: Diane Pavao.
www.castleresorts.com.
808-822-9331 or 800-367-5004; fax 808-822-2828.
4460 Nehe Rd., Lihu'e.
Price: Expensive–very expensive.
Credit Cards: AE, D, DC, JCB, MC, V.
Handicapped Access: Limited.

This remote oceanfront condo resort, the only one situated on Lydgate Beach Park, is perfect for families who want to be near Kapa'a but also secluded on one of the best swim beaches in Kaua'i. This is probably why they named it Kaha Lani, which means "heavenly place." Built in 1976, these one- to three-bedroom units are all oceanfront with stocked kitchens, fans, lanais, cable, daily maid service, and free local phone calls. The 74 units are all individually owned (and about half are managed by Castle), so there are inconsistencies. (Some have washers and dryers, for instance, while with others you'll have to use the on-site Laundromat.) Rooms can be dark and somewhat on the plain side, so try for top-floor units, which have vaulted ceilings and bigger windows. Hibiscus flowers and red ginger line the walkways leading guests to the pools, tennis courts, and putting green. Note that Castle has a contract with Shell Vacation Resorts, so the folks at Shell will call you to participate in presentations; if you do attend a time-share demo, they offer great discounts on activities.

Kaua'i Inn

Innkeeper: Tony McKnight.
808-245-9000 or 800-808-2330.
www.kauai-inn.com.

info@kauai-inn.com.
2430 Hule Malu Rd., Lihu'e.
Price: Inexpensive.
Credit Cards: AE, D, MC, V.
Handicapped Access: Yes.

Formerly known as the Fairview Hotel, the Kaua'i Inn is officially the oldest hotel on the island. And like most aged places in Kaua'i, it has had its share of drama. After a $3 million renovation in 1991, Hurricane 'Iniki flattened the property. Using recycled wood from the original hotel, and now spread across 3 acres, this 48-unit plantation-style hotel boasts the simple pleasures of island life—banana and bougainvillea trees, coconut palms, trade winds, a friendly staff, and a seriously mellow vibe. It's nestled in a residential neighborhood (though very close to the harbor and airport), where Nawiliwili Harbor meets Huleia River. Guests are treated like family, with free run of the fruit trees, pool, coin-operated laundry, and barbecues. All rooms have a refrigerator, microwave, fan, free local calls, wireless, air-conditioning, and a 27-inch cable TV. They're decorated with antique furniture, some with cowboy themes, some with funky rooster decor (possibly a play on the roosters hanging around the property) and lanais; the down-stairs rooms are a bit nicer, while upstairs rooms offer ocean and mountain views, but no outside space. Building 2 has the best views. But you can't go wrong here for the price. Breakfasts are a simple affair by the pool, with a spread of juices, pastries, coffee, and fruit from their trees.

Kaua'i Marriott Resort and Beach Club
General Manager: Bill Countryman.
808-245-5050; fax 808-245-5049.
www.marriott.com.
Kalapaki Beach, 3610 Rice St., Lihu'e.
Price: Expensive–very expensive.
Handicapped Access: Yes.
Credit Cards: AE, D, DC, JCB, MC, V.

If you want your Kaua'i vacation in a sprawling Vegas-style resort with a

The fit-for-ali'i columned pool at the Kaua'i Marriott makes guests feel like royalty.

Corinthian-columned 750,000-gallon pool (including five Jacuzzis), this 576-room hotel/time-share resort is your best bet. Located right on the sand, very close to the airport, harbor, and a popular locals' beach, this resort makes it possible for you to do without a car the entire time you are on the island. A wealth of restaurants and shops, as well as a business center, a fitness center, a golf course, bars, and beaches, are within a short walk. And this hotel is so large, it might feel like you are navigating an entire island. But for some, it feels like the perfect tropical place to lose yourself in. Tropical ponds and palms decorate the facility. Asian antiques, numerous sundries shops, a spa and a salon, five restaurants, yoga, Pilates, or aerobics classes, kids' activities, a doctor, a dentist, and daily activities like walks, crafts, and hula lessons might be enough reason never to leave. Rooms are reasonably sized and decorated simply in whites with a few color splashes (and the beds are really comfortable). The bathrooms are pretty tight. All rooms have lanais and air-conditioning. Note that "beach-view rooms" are often more "pool views," and they can get a bit noisy from the action below—the beach is popular with locals. The pool can get very crowded as well, especially during the continental breakfast and the evening sushi bar happy hour. There is no resort fee, but they charge for wireless and parking. This is a good place for Superferry or cruise ship passengers who want to veg out for a couple days without renting a car.

Tip Top Motel

General Manager: Jonathan Ota.
808-245-2333; fax 808-246-8988.
3173 Akahi, Lihu'e.
Price: Inexpensive.
Credit Cards: MC, V.
Handicapped Access: Limited.

Tip Top Motel and Café is an institution on Kaua'i. This red-brick building, on a quiet side street in the center of Lihu'e, offers 25 simple rooms. There is nothing quaint or cute about the Tip Top. This is a cheap place to crash at the end of an exhausting day. You basically get a bed (or two), a small TV, a shower, AC, a toilet, and a sink. You might have a chair in your room. That's it. There are no paintings, no extra frills. Check-in is 6:30 AM–3 PM (7 AM on Monday) and 5:30 PM–9 PM.

Coco Palms Resort

888-321-2626, SALES@COCOPALMS.COM

In the 19th century, the last reigning monarch of Kaua'i, Queen Deborah Kapule, lived in a sacred coconut grove on the banks of the Wailua River. In 1953, Coco Palms Resort opened on this very spot, banking on tourists' desire to feel like royalty. And they delivered. The popularity of the resort skyrocketed when Elvis Presley filmed *Blue Hawaii* on the property (the cast of *South Pacific* staying here didn't hurt, either). Soon tourists were making dutiful pilgrimages to this mysterious Polynesian resort.

Unfortunately, all was halted when Hurricane 'Iniki blew in, destroying the simple natural beauty of this landmark location. For the past 16 years, Coco Palms has been struggling to rebound. Though the resort is replanting the coconut palms it displaces, zoning laws have slowed the rebuilding process. This taxed site is slated to change from the thatched-roof huts of yesterday to a giant condo/hotel/time-share complex straddling the river and stretching deep into the palms. They also plan to have a couple of gourmet restaurants and a spa. Last I heard, the resort was not due to be opened until 2009 (though that date keeps getting extended).

WAILUA

Vacation Rentals

Castle (808-822-7700 or 800-367-5004; fax 808-822-7456; www.castleresorts .com). With headquarters on O'ahu and condo resorts scattered throughout the South Pacific, Castle has a standard for rooms that works. Amenities include daily maid freshening service and fourth-day full cleaning, on-site Castle reps, free local calls, wireless, and that corporate efficiency not often found on Kaua'i. They manage condos at Makahuena at Poipu, Poipu Shores, Kaha Lani, Kiahuna Plantation, Lani Kai, and Lae Nani. They accept all major credit cards.

Rosewood (808-822-5216; fax 808-822-5478; www.rosewoodkauai.com; rosewood @aloha.net). Local owners Rosemary and Norbert Smith offer real estate sales and vacation rentals. With 35 houses and condos for rent, plus a lovely B&B property listed above, whatever you need, they will help you find it. The personal, friendly service and knowledge of Kaua'i allow you to feel like you are getting help from friends. Rates are below average, which is great because they don't accept credit cards. There is a onetime, nonrefundable off-site cleaning fee that varies by property. All units are nonsmoking.

SOUTH SHORE LODGING

KALAHEO

✪Bamboo Jungle House
Innkeepers: Lucy and Terry Ryan.
808-332-5515 or 888-332-5115.
www.kauai-bedandbreakfast.com.
3829 Waha Rd., Kalaheo.
Price: Inexpensive.
Credit Cards: MC, V.
Handicapped Access: None.

Since buying this 22-year old bed & breakfast in 2004, Lucy and Terry Ryan have gone out of their way to create a tropical

Slippers in the breakfast area are just one of the simple touches highlighting the Bamboo Jungle House.

retreat in a residential neighborhood. As you pass through the gate and approach the green-and-white plantation house, the tropical foliage, fountains, lava rock Jacuzzi, lap pool, orchid garden, massage gazebo, and wide lanais have the power to make that long flight melt away. Plus Lucy and Terry's kind, yet distant demeanors allow for the privacy you might have been searching for here away from the crowds. Just a few miles from those famous Poipu beaches, this B&B offers three smallish rooms with mosquito-net-draped beds and high ceilings. Lucy supplies earplugs for the roosters, in-room flowers, local soaps, lotions, shampoo, and conditioner. All of the hot water in this B&B is solar powered. The upstairs Jungle and Waterfall rooms are smaller, but each has a lanai with ocean views and a telescope for whale-watching. The Bamboo Garden Room is the biggest (and most private) with a kitchenette, a lanai, a table, and chairs. In the large and beautifully decorated breakfast area, they supply you with slippers, informational literature, photo albums, beach gear, flip-flops, a store selling local arts and crafts, and an amazing breakfast (not just a continental). A word to the wise: There is only room to park a small or mid-sized car. So if you show up with an SUV, be warned that Lucy will send you back to the rental agency. Depending on the room, there is a three- to five-night minimum stay.

Kalaheo Inn
Innkeeper: Lyle Otsuka.
888-332-6023; fax 808-332-5242.
www.kalaheoinn.com.
ki@hawaiiantel.biz.
4444 Papalina Rd., Kalaheo.
Price: Inexpensive—moderate.
Credit Cards: MC, V.
Handicapped Access: None.

The Kalaheo Inn offers the benefits of a condo (meaning kitchens or kitchenettes) without the price. New Californian owners recently raised the rates, but this spot is still a steal. In the heart of Kalaheo, you'll stay in a real Kaua'i neighborhood—within walking distance of the best breakfast and pizza restaurants on the south shore. Understand that this 15-unit property is not a luxury option. The rooms, in fact, could use a serious renovation, but they are clean and a fine place to pass out after a long day of activities. Rooms are small but all include a TV, VCR, fan, coffeemaker, microwave, electric skillet or George Foreman Grill (studios and a couple of units have stovetops—ask if you really want one), lanai, and queen beds. Rooms don't have their own phone, but the office phone is available for free local calls, and if you have a laptop, you can use the wireless connection there as well. Guests have access to barbecues, beach gear, golf clubs, games, books, coin-operated laundry, and property-grown bananas. When you book, they ask for a $100 deposit and then expect you to pay in full 30 days before arrival. There is a two-night minimum stay, with discounts for longer vacations.

KOLOA AND POIPU
Since most people want their Hawaiian vacation to include the sun, they head out to the Poipu/Koloa area. Developers are banking on this. At press time, eight new developments were taking shape in the area, including a high-end resort. Chances are, because of the noise, you can negotiate for deals. So make sure to ask whether or not construction will take place next to your lodging, and consider bringing earplugs.

Alihi Lani Poipu Condos
808-742-2233 or 800-742-2260.
www.poipuconnection.com.
2564 Hoonani Rd., Koloa.
Price: Expensive.
Credit Cards: MC, V.
Handicapped Access: Limited.

An excellent choice for families, especially snorkel or scuba dive junkies, this property is across the street from Koloa Landing. These two-bedroom/two-bath condos are a great deal for the price. But they fill up fast. There are only six of them, and Poipu Connection expects a four-night minimum stay. The intimate setting creates a homey atmosphere, rare in the south shore condo complex scene. This also ensures a lot of repeat customers. Rooms are staggered so that each lanai has privacy. All units are stocked with a TV, DVD, VCR, stereo, washer and dryer, beach gear, and full kitchen. Plus guests have access to outdoor

The luxurious grounds of the Grand Hyatt Resort.

grills. Room styles vary but you can count on white-on-white kitchens, hardwood cabinetry, and pastel floral interiors. With great views of the ocean, including at the pool, this mellow vacation rental takes you out of the hustle of the big condo complexes and offers a little slice of privacy.

✪ Grand Hyatt Kaua'i

General Manager: Doug Sears.
808-742-1234; fax 808-742-1557.
www.grandhyattkauai.com.
1571 Poipu Rd., Koloa.
Price: Very expensive.
Daily Resort Fee: $15 (required). Includes an hour of tennis per day, use of the fitness room and wellness classes, parking, local calls, newspaper, and a variety of discounts.
Credit Cards: AE, D, DC, JCB, MC, V.
Handicapped Access: Some.
Special Features: Camp Hyatt (including hula lessons, shell jewelry and lei-making classes for kids), tennis courts, 18-hole championship golf course, rental car offices on the property, bank, ATM, doctor, spa, shoeshine, photo processing, shops, pools, babysitting, and bike rentals.

On at least 15 international Best-Of lists, the Grand Hyatt deserves the self-proclaimed title of the grandest resort on the island. This 602-room resort is the place to pamper yourself for a week. Guests often do not want to leave the manicured gardens, the splendid service, the 52 acres of property, the variety of world-class restaurants and pools. Upon arrival, you will be greeted with a lei and enter a breezy lobby that serves up a grand view of the ocean through the palm trees and a big hello from the tropical birds. Green rooftops and sloped architecture give this large resort an intimate essence; buildings rarely block views of the ocean or of the bougainvillea-, palm-, and plumeria-scented gardens. Typical rooms are about 600 square feet; many have king beds. All include AC, fan, well-furnished lanai, in-room safe, empty refrigerator, cable TV, and wireless access (for a daily fee). Rooms are decked out in koa wood furniture, doors (which have recently been updated to conserve energy), and moldings, plus marble sinks, large bathrooms, a couch, and a desk. At night, the trade winds and ocean breeze will rock you to sleep. But people don't stay at a resort like this merely for the rooms. It is all about the perks. Hyatt offers 24-hour pools, a 150-foot waterslide, Jacuzzis, an adult pool, saltwater pools, and access to a lovely beach all within walking distance (though if you have limited mobility, note that everything is pretty spread out). And then there are all those obscene ways to pamper yourself.

Voted one of *Condé Nast Traveler*'s Best Resort Spas for the past five years, Anara Spa is a sensory treat. With a new renovation to include a 25-yard lap pool, a wealth of spa services, classes, a salon, garden treatment *hales*, and the best fruit juices on the south shore, visiting the spa is a must. In addition to traditional Hawaiian-style *noni* fruit and red clay massage and facial treatments, one unique treatment offered is the Rock Star package for teenage girls, who can get their hair braided with a temporary dye job as well as a rockin' mani/pedi. The new exercise rooms and indoor/outdoor pavilions even got local residents excited, as Hyatt donated the old exercise equipment to local schools.

And then there is the food. What with seven restaurants and six lounges, room service, and a lu'au, some people never leave the property. And even if you find the restaurants insanely priced, know that the waste from your omelet goes to a good cause: Hyatt's restaurants reuse 670 gallons of vegetable oil each month for biodiesel. The multilingual staff and concierges go the distance to assist you. When I was here once with my mom, she was looking for a particular store. She called the front desk,

and the woman who answered told her they didn't have the store on the premises. A minute later the desk attendant called back and said, in fact, it was there and gave my mom directions how to navigate through the 12,000 square feet of retail and fine art shops (make sure to peek into the quilt store for a glimpse of some traditional folk art). Of course, all this service doesn't come cheap. The Grand Hyatt is one of the most expensive hotels on Kaua'i. Expect to pay. A lot. But also expect to be wooed by the royal treatment.

Hale Pohaku Beachside

Owner: Summer Harrison.
www.vacationrental-kauai.com.
summer@aloha.net.
808-742-6462; fax 808-742-8787.
2231 Pane Rd., Koloa.
Price: Inexpensive–very expensive.
Credit Cards: AE, D, MC, V.
Handicapped Access: No.

This vacation rental is the perfect place for family reunions or weddings—as long as everyone likes one another. The property consists of a main plantation house with four bedrooms, a side studio apartment, and a few two-bedroom cottages. Summer also rents out units individually, but if you want privacy, know that the property is compact and outdoor space is basically shared. Units are authentic and lack the frills of a lot of other vacation rentals. Each has its own BBQ and lots of windows to welcome the trade winds. The large manager's house was built in the 1950s and is well kept, tastefully decorated in island rattan and floral decor, with a big private lanai. It is great for families. The attached studio apartment shares laundry with main house and is perfect for a couple or single traveler—or those in-laws who insisted on tagging along. All other units have their own laundry. Built in the 1940s, the units are a little under the weather, but spacious.

They each face the shared pool and the tropical gardens. Cottage C is the nicest and biggest, then cottage B, and finally A. Units have games and books, beach gear, wireless, and full kitchen (including dishwasher). The property is half a block from the beach and a short drive from local restaurants and shops.

Kiahuna Plantation

Castle: 808-822-7700 or 800-367-5004; fax 808-822-7456.
www.castleresorts.com.
Grantham: 808-742-2000 or 800-325-5701; fax 808-742-9093.
www.grantham-resorts.com.
Outrigger: 877-523-6264, 808-822-4938; fax 808-822-1022.
www.outrigger.com.

2253 Poipu Rd., Koloa.
Price: Expensive–very expensive.
Credit Cards: AE, CB, D, DC, MC, V.
Handicapped Access: Limited.

Before Muir Plantation was built here, archaeologists unearthed an ancient community that had aqueducts running under houses like sewage drains. Some of the site was preserved in building this plantation, making this one of Kaua'i's sacred sites, but mostly this is now one of the grandest condo complexes on the island. During the sugarcane explosion, the Muir Plantation home (now the site of the Outrigger registration) was a serious party house. Now you can still be entertained in the Plantation Manor restaurant and visit the Moir Pa'u a Laka gardens (see chapter 4). Even better, if you want to shell out the cash, you can

The Kiahuna Plantation Resort Condominiums in Poipu.

stay in one of these stark white plantation condos surrounded by wide grassy fields, palms, and flowering trees. Since units are privately owned and managed by a variety of companies, you'll have to do some research to make sure you get the experience you are looking for. Some companies (like Grantham) rent you your condo and let you have your experience, while others (Castle and Outrigger) consider this a resort condo (which basically means you get housekeeping services, video rentals, and an in-room safe). All agencies offer large one- or two-bedroom units with stocked kitchens (some with granite or marble countertops), free parking, island-style decor, cable TV, VCR, and beach gear. Grantham units offer free wireless access, while Outrigger has high-speed Internet access for a fee. Units do not have AC, so even though there are plentiful windows, lanais and fans in each condo, it can get stuffy in summer. Partial-ocean-view rooms are a splurge for a slice of sea. All guests have access to the tennis courts and pool (across the street). Some units have washer and dryer. Again, do your research. Some may feel too close to Poipu Road here.

Koloa Landing Cottages

Innkeeper: Ellie Knopf.
808-742-1470 or 800-779-8773.
www.koloa-landing.com.
infokoloalanding@aol.com.
2704 Hoonani Rd., Koloa.
Price: Inexpensive–moderate.
Credit Cards: MC, V.
Handicapped Access: One unit.

Offering an old Hawaiian experience, across the street from the ocean, these five beautifully decorated cottages are the perfect choice for couples and families looking for something unique. Ellie has created a tropical retreat for the right price. The most popular unit is the Bamboo Boat House Studio, which used to be a real boathouse

and has high ceilings to prove it. Even though it is the smallest unit, it still feels large. The Hoonani and Tiki houses are two-bedroom cottages that feel like you are staying at traditional Kaua'i dwellings. The two-bedroom Tea House used to be the main house and is the kind of place you might want to relax in for a month to write that novel you've been dreaming about. Finally, the one-bedroom Plumeria House is a perfect place for a couple to hide away from the world for a few romantic nights. All cottages have lots of windows yet feel private, surrounded by artfully decorated gardens designed by a Vietnamese master gardener. Each has a full kitchen, lanai, wireless, a private BBQ, and plenty of funky island-style furniture. Don't expect the typical tan-colored scheme of island decor; these units, gardens, walls, and even buildings are splashed with color. They offer tons of beach equipment for guests' use and access to a coin-operated laundry. There is a three-night minimum stay. If you are a clean freak, note that recently friends stayed here and found that their cleaning fee was not put to good use: The cottage was straightened but not really cleaned.

Makahuena

Grantham: 808-742-2000 or 800-325-5701; fax 808-742-9093.
www.grantham-resorts.com.
Poipu Connection: 808-742-2233 or 800-742-2260; fax 808-742-7382.
www.poipuconnection.com.
1661 Pe'e Rd., Koloa.
Price: Moderate–expensive.
Credit Cards: AE, D, MC, V.
Handicapped Access: No.

Set atop cliffs overlooking the Pacific, this condo complex offers excellent views and a generous ocean breeze. However, sometimes the breeze is more a roar, making this spot too windy to walk straight. Units are hit or miss. Some I have seen are dazzling lofty affairs, while others are in need of a serious renovation. Makahuena, a good option for bigger parties, offers two- and three-bedroom accommodations. All of the units are open and spacious, but have no side ventilation, so it can get stuffy. Some have AC. All have vaulted ceilings, big front windows, and island-style furnishings. Some units are one floor; some are two. The key to happiness in this condo complex is to ask your rental agent to see pictures of the specific unit you are interested in. The units vary. A lot. I would also recommend getting a room closer to the ocean. Since this is the southernmost part of the island, the sunrises and sunsets are magnificent. Plus, the buildings are squeezed tightly onto the plot of land, so you have a variety of views, but if it isn't the ocean, you'll probably be gazing at the back of a building. The perk of this complex is the location. You can walk to beaches and enjoy full access to the pool, Jacuzzi, BBQ area, and the landscaped grounds. And did I mention the property sits atop the Pacific? Castle also rents pricey units here.

Nihi Kai Villas

808-742-2000 or 800-325-5701; fax 808-742-9093.
www.grantham-resorts.com.
1870 Ho'one Rd., Koloa.
Price: Moderate–very expensive.
Credit Cards: AE, D, MC, V.
Handicapped Access: Limited.

Across the street from the ocean, this simple condo complex offers a slice of the tropics without the frills. The landscaped gardens surrounding the pool are a perfect place to chill out after an eventful day. However, the 70 units vary dramatically. Some are decorated with the flair of an interior designer, dotted with worldly antiques and Kaua'i artifacts, while others look a little run down, with closet doors falling off their hinges. Make sure to communicate what you want and ask to see pictures. In general, you can count on spacious one- to three-bedroom accommodations (1,000–2,100 square feet). Most include a large kitchen and living area with expansive windows and lanai upstairs, and dark bedrooms downstairs (great for people who like to sleep in). All units come with high-speed Internet, cable TV, fans (no AC), and access to the tennis courts. The ocean-view rooms are in demand, but are also the closest to the street. Suite Paradise and R&R also have units here.

Poipu Crater

Grantham: 808-742-2000 or 800-325-5701; fax 808-742-9093.
www.grantham-resorts.com.
Suite Paradise: 808-742-7400 or 800-367-8020; fax 808-742-9121.
www.suite-paradise.com.
2330 Hoohu Rd., Koloa.
Price: Inexpensive–moderate.
Credit Cards: AE, D, MC, V.
Handicapped Access: No.

These duplexes are a hideaway in the heart of Poipu. Jungle-like landscaping accompanies these 7 acres, so that you almost expect monkeys to peel the bananas hanging around the pool, BBQ, tennis courts, saunas, and clubhouse. The tan hut-like units are spaced out from one another enough that you feel you are staying in your own retreat. Inside, units are bright (so bright it almost feels like you are outside) and airy, with lanais and skylights. All units have cable TV, VCR, DVD, stocked kitchen, washer/dryer (in most), and fans. These two-bedroom units have no AC and can get stuffy if the trade winds aren't kicking, especially in the master bedroom loft upstairs. This is one of the most remote accommodations you can get this close to the ocean. And one of the cheapest.

Poipu Kai Resort

Grantham: 808-742-2000 or 800-325-5701; fax 808-742-9093.
www.grantham-resorts.com.
Suite Paradise: 808-742-7400 or 800-367-8020; fax 808-742-9121.
www.suite-paradise.com.
1941 Poipu Rd., Koloa.
Price: Moderate–expensive.
Credit Cards: MC, V.
Handicapped Access: No.

Spread across 110 acres of land, this gigantic condo complex is the largest in the area. Split into a variety of mini complexes that spread from Poipu Road to Poipu Beach, every single unit has its own flair, style, perks, and issues. In this condo complex especially, you need to be very specific about what you want and shop around. Generally, the furniture and style of Grantham's and Poipu Connection's units are the classiest, while Suite Paradise offers the best deals. Resortquest's are quite fancy. You can get anything from a cramped (but air-conditioned) studio apartment to a five-bedroom villa. The architecture resembles mainland condo complexes, but each unit is individually owned and decorated in island-style wood or rattan (though the quality of the decor varies immensely). Rooms generally do not have AC. There are ceiling fans and lots of windows, but I have found that construction around the complex can get annoying. Kitchens are well stocked. All units have at least one private lanai; some have up to four. Most units have washer and dryer, TV, DVD, VCR, and stereo. Because this complex is so big, you can get all sorts of views: garden, ocean, even Poipu Road (which can be a little noisy). The Poipu Sands mini complex is a nice option because the condos have ocean views and are far enough off the street that you don't hear noise (though you can occasionally hear the neighbor's plumbing). Plus they have nice layouts. The grounds are well tended with palms, bougainvillea, and some Hawaiian ti plants. Each unit has access to tennis courts, a pool, the beach, the activities desk, hot tubs, and BBQ grills. Almost every rental agency on the island has a piece of this complex. All in all, it's for people who want a reasonably priced condo without much atmosphere.

Poipu Kapili Condos

800-443-7714.
www.poipukapili.com.
aloha@poipukapili.com.
2221 Kapili Rd., Poipu.
Price: Expensive–very expensive.
Credit Cards: MC, V.
Handicapped Access: Some.

The Poipu Kapili evokes the Hawaiian phrase *mea ho'onanea* (to relax). Spread across a verdant field of grass, the buildings stand in a half circle as if paying homage to the cross-shaped pool and the crashing ocean across the street. The effect of this architecture is twofold: The breeze touches each unit (which is nice because there is no AC), and even though there are 60 units, there is an essence of privacy, since there are no buildings between you and the ocean . . . just a street. The grounds contain an herb garden and a wide collection of plumeria trees and banana palms. Upon your arrival, a basket of fresh-picked bananas waits on your doorstep. And once you walk into these spacious (1,120–2,600 square feet!) condos, you will understand why these units are in such demand. It seems they have thought of everything: Each unit has more bathrooms than bedrooms; you can see whales from your bedroom-sized lanai; they offer maid service and your seventh night free. One-bedroom units have access to the coin-operated laundry, while two-bedrooms include washer and dryer. All condos, though individually owned and operated, are equipped with wireless access, cable, a CD player, pool towels, VCR, DVD, full kitchens, koa wood doors and trim, beach gear, and fans. All guests are invited to a Friday continental breakfast at the pool. You also have access to the tennis court, plus the extensive video and book collection in the office. Since you will probably sleep with your windows open to get the breeze and hear the ocean, consider opting for one of the buildings a bit back from the street.

Poipu Plantation Resort

Owner: Chris Moore.
800-634-0263 or 808-742-6757; fax: 808-742-8681.
www.poipubeach.com.
plantation@poipubeach.com.
1792 Pe'e Rd., Koloa.
Price: Inexpensive–moderate.
Credit Cards: MC, V.
Handicapped Access: No.

When you walk into the main office of this septuagenarian plantation house, lounging dogs and wide smiles greet you. Across the street from Poipu Beach, this plumeria-scented property offers B&B rooms (two standards and two suites) and nine plantation condo/cottages. Spread over an acre of property, all units offer a healthy degree of privacy with views of the ocean, Ni'ihau, the Hawaiian ti plant gardens, and, on a clear day, Wai'ale'ale. Upon arrival, you'll find a fresh bouquet of tropical flowers in your room and a wealth of information (plus beach gear) from the front desk staff. All condo units have full kitchens and are relatively spacious even though they are decorated with heavy island-style furniture. Note that these units do not have maid service. However, standard B&B rooms do. These rooms can be a little cramped, but if you need more space, there is a nice-sized shared living room with a refrigerator. This is where your full tropical breakfast (included in the price for B&B rooms) is served; hopefully Javed will whip up his guava French toast while you're here. All guests have access to the outdoor BBQ area, hot tub, coin-operated laundry, and family-style living experience. Plus, all units have wireless access (some even on your lanai) and AC. Depending on the room, there is a three- to five-night minimum stay.

Prince Kuhio Condos

808-742-2233 or 800-742-2260; fax 808-742-7382.
www.poipuconnection.com.
5061 Lawa'i Rd., Koloa.
Price: Inexpensive.
Credit Cards: MC, V.
Handicapped Access: Some.

If you are looking to save money but still enjoy the benefits of a condo, this old motel-turned-condominium takes you back to the Brady Bunch trip to Hawai'i: lush palm-shrouded gardens, a deep blue pool, a koi pond, and a BBQ area. The biggest sell (besides the price) is its location across the street from a small beach, next door to the Prince Kuhio Park and close to restaurants and hotel bars. This L-shaped building has studios (with AC), and one-bedroom units that vary in size depending on the view and location (mountain views are bigger). At press time, there are excellent mountain views, but construction is slated to start behind the units, so some views may be compromised. Rooms closest to the ocean are also closer to the street. Third-floor rooms have the best vistas. All units have a funky setup, with reasonably sized living and bedrooms, but very small bathrooms. The walls are made of cement and there are big windows leading to the lanai but no side windows, so it can get a bit stuffy in there. Especially since some of the rooms I have seen are cramped with too much pastel floral-print furniture. All units have tile floors and a lanai; most have a washer and dryer. This is an excellent choice for people on a budget who want to be in walking distance to the ocean.

Sheraton Kaua'i

General Manager: Angela Vento.
808-742-1661 or 866-716-8109; fax 808-742-9777.
www.sheraton-kauai.com.
2440 Hoonani Rd., Poipu.
Price: Very expensive.
Daily Resort Fee: $17.71. Includes Hawaiian entertainment, cultural arts and crafts, beach activity discounts, fitness center, tennis, local calls, coffee and tea, refrigerator, in-room safe, news library, use of the library computer, and self-parking.
Credit Cards: AE, D, DC, JCB, MC, V.
Handicapped Access: Yes.

This 394-room property spreads across Hoonani Road and spills out onto one of the nicest swimming and sunset-viewing beaches in Poipu. Upon arrival, guests are greeted with leis and the aroma of tropical flowers floating through the open-air lobby. Grassy fields dotted with palms, torches, and lava rocks weave through the eight four-story buildings, depositing guests at the two adult pools, two children's pools (with waterslides), or Jacuzzis. With six restaurants, a couple of bars (including the famous Point, where locals and tourists meet for nightly entertainment), a fitness room, a business center, gift shops, a beauty salon and massage center, tennis courts, guest news, libraries with newspapers and Internet, a kids' club, movie night under the stars (with popcorn), hula and lei-making classes, mai tai receptions, a beachfront lu'au, and much more, guests rarely leave the property. Rooms are 410–510 square feet and recently underwent a $15 million renovation. Now they

provide Sheraton's Sweet Sleeper two- or four-poster beds—some rooms with king-sized beds and others, two doubles. Rooms are decorated with simple touches: primary colors, dark wooden furniture, flat-screen TVs, and an empty fridge to stock up on water or snacks. Some rooms even have a door to walk through the closet to the bathroom. Bathrooms feature a towel ladder and a big tub with a curved shower rod to make the bath feel more spacious. At press time, if you want wireless access it will run you another $14.95 plus tax, per day, but there has been talk of including wireless in the resort fee.

Sunset Kahili Condos

808-742-7555 or 800-367-8022; fax 808-742-1559.
http://r7r.com/sunset_kahili.htm.
randr@r7r.com.

Sheraton Kaua'i Resort.

1763 Pe'e Rd., Koloa.
Price: Inexpensive—expensive.
Credit Cards: MC, V.
Handicapped Access: Yes.

Sunset Kahili gets to claim that it is ocean-front, even though there is a parking lot and another condo building between this old structure and the water. You'll find one- or two-bedroom units with full kitchens, partial ocean views, washer/dryer, and fans. Did I mention the pastel floral-print 1970s decor? Since this L-shaped, motel-like building backs onto Pe'e Road, there are only windows on the lanai (ocean) side of the condo, which means units can get stuffy. But the Pacific-facing carpeted lanais are a welcome retreat if you find yourself in the rooms during the hot parts of the day. The best of the 36 units are the corner rooms, with numbers ending in 1 or 8, because they have more windows. And try to be on the third through fifth floors for less obstructed views. R&R units offer weekly cleaning. They also rent snorkels, bikes, toys, and baby gear; they can book rental cars, too. All guests have access to the pool, wireless connection, BBQ grills, recreation room (with games), and free morning coffee. This is a good choice for families on a budget or people who really liked the '70s.

✪Waikomo Stream Villas
800-742-1412 or 808-742-2000; fax 808-742-9093.
www.grantham-resorts.com.
2721 Poipu Rd., Koloa.
Price: Inexpensive—moderate.
Credit Cards: AE, D, MC, V.
Handicapped Access: Some.

This might be the best value in Poipu. Located on Poipu Road, just a short walk from the ocean, this condo complex gets it right. The lush landscaped grounds bear lichee, banana, coconut, as well as plume-ria, bougainvillea, Hawaiian ti plants, and orchids. Tropical birds live in the trees and feed off the stream that winds through the property. The brown units are almost hid-den from view. These one- and two-bed-room condos are ridiculously spacious, with high ceilings and plenty of windows to keep you bright during the day and cool at night. The two-bedroom units have lofts. All con-dos, though individually owned, are consis-tently tastefully decorated and have koa wood cabinetry, moldings, and doors. There is no AC, but when I stayed here, between the windows and fans I actually got a bit chilly. Most owners consider everything in the kitchen from plastic wrap and rubber bands to guidebooks, videos, and extra blankets for late-night TV watching. Beds are kingly. The lanai is the perfect place for breakfast (though the mosquitoes are hun-gry, too). Buildings 3–5 are located off the street (which can get noisy). Buildings 2 and 3 have partial ocean views. My only big rec-ommendation is to opt for the earplugs that they sell in the office. Like most places in Kaua'i, the roosters are loud, but here there are also bullfrogs. There is a tennis court, a pool/Jacuzzi, and BBQ grills for all guests. All in all, this is a luxurious condo option for a great price, if you can stand being a couple of blocks from the ocean.

Whalers Cove Condo Resorts
Innkeeper: Marianne Martin.
800-225-2683; fax 808-742-1185.
www.whalers-cove.com.
2640 Puuholo Rd., Koloa.
Price: Very expensive.
Daily Resort Fee: $15. Includes unlimited local calls, parking, coffee, towels, Internet access (with your own computer), and a daily newspaper.
Credit Cards: AE, D, MC, V.
Handicapped Access: Limited mobility okay.

Opened in 1984, this 39-unit resort condo is one of the most luxurious condo options on the island. Hovering over Koloa Landing, guests watch dolphins, whales, and sea turtles up close from their giant lanai. This might be the closest you can sleep to the ocean without embarking on a ship. All units are owned separately, yet the standard of quality here surpasses most condo complexes. All units are decorated with bulky Hawaiian-style furniture (as one of my friends says, à la *Miami Vice*), and Premier keeps up renovations so most units recently got appliance upgrades. Grand, airy, and palatial (approximately 1,400–2,000 square feet), units have koa wood doors and trim, stocked kitchens, washer and dryer, safe, daily maid service, and dramatic ocean views from the lanai. Most have Jacuzzi tubs as well. The architecture optimizes the trade winds so that you hear them blow through the palm and orchid gardens. During most of the year, the breeze suffices, but since there is no AC in the units, July and August can get stuffy. This is probably why winter quickly sells out here at this popular resort—that and the quality of service, the privacy, the beauty, and the location. You can take advantage of the heated pool overlooking Koloa Landing and the BBQ grills. Most guests like building 1 for its oceanfront location, but I prefer building 2 with its views of the renovated pool, ocean, and an intimate glimpse of Koloa Landing. There is a 45-foot drop to the ocean right off the rocks, so whales come close. This quiet oceanfront oasis is one of Kaua'i's unique gems. Grantham also has some units here, for less than Premier.

Lawa'i

Hale Kua Guest Cottages
Innkeepers: Cathy and Bill Cowern.
808-332-8570 or 800-440-4356.
www.halekua.com.
treefarm@halekua.com.
4896 E. Kua Rd., Lawa'i.
Price: Inexpensive–moderate.

Credit Cards: None.
Handicapped Access: No.

If you would rather be in the jungle than on the beach, Hale Kua is for you. Up a long, steep driveway at the top of the Lawa'i Valley, these vacation rentals are a bit hard to find, but once you arrive, Cathy and Bill go out of their way to make you feel at home. Dogs and cats laze around the units all day, birds swoop through the trees, friends pop in to say hello. The Cowerns offer a three-bedroom cottage and four one-bedroom condo units spread across a wealth of fruit trees (make sure to try some of the star fruit—it is the best on the island). Units have views of the jungle-covered mountains, rainbows stretching across the valley, and the ocean. This is the kind of place where you will see more birds than people—often bird-watchers spot more varieties from their lanai than at Koke'e. All units have kitchenettes, access to BBQs, beach gear, laundry, extra towels and linens, cable TV, DVD, VCR, and free videos. Though units are not the most spacious, they are a good deal and decorated simply. Cathy and Bill understand that you're here for the island, and the units are set up to accentuate the views of the trees. On the property is a Bodhi tree that is a direct descendant of the one Buddha meditated beneath. Talk to Bill about his ideas on energy and conservation and you'll want to know where to sign up. Hale Kua is gay-friendly, a great place for families, couples, and friends.

Kaua'i Banyan Inn
Owner: Lorna Hoff.
888-786-3855.
www.kauaibanyan.com.
tropicaldayz@msn.com.
3528 B Mana Hema Place, Lawa'i.
Price: Inexpensive, plus a cleaning fee.
Credit Cards: MC, V.
Handicapped Access: None.

Loquacious Lorna has owned this house for 40 years and decided to turn it into an inn in 2004. She offers five suites with either kitchenettes or full kitchens. The property sits above Poipu Beach, with dramatic ocean or mountain views (though not necessarily from your room), and is surrounded by banyan and fruit trees. Since the property is in a residential area, guests find this a mellow option to play house—often staying for weeks or even months, and for this Lorna offers significant discounts. Decently sized rooms are decorated simply, with small unique touches like tiled kitchens, hardwood floors, and marble baths. All rooms have king-sized beds, fans, a DVD and CD player, a phone, a lanai, and kitchen supplies. She refreshes the room every other day. Guests have access to the hot tub, BBQ, books, and beach gear. In-room bananas and muffins welcome guests to their room, and since roosters are abundant, Lorna offers free earplugs. This country-style inn is a reasonable option where couples and families with children over 10 will feel comfortable. There is a three-night minimum stay.

✪ Marjorie's Kaua'i Inn

Innkeepers: Michael D'Alesandro and Daniela Powers.
808-332-8838 or 800-717-8838.
www.marjorieskauaiinn.com.
alexis@marjorieskauaiinn.com.
3307-D Hailima Rd., Lawa'i.
Price: Inexpensive–moderate.
Credit Cards: D, MC, V.
Handicapped Access: None.

When Marjorie created this B&B, she did it right by selecting a location perched above the National Tropical Botanical Garden, with sweeping views of the jungle, rainbows, and a wide variety of birds. Recently, she sold this property to Alexis and Mike Boilini, two experienced B&B owners, who took this property to another dimension.

No expense has been spared in adding lovely little touches, including a saltwater lap pool overlooking the valley, a Jacuzzi, lovely garden art, and a valley facing Bali hut, perfect for morning coffee or afternoon wine and cheese. Many travelers inhale a breath of fresh air when they arrive here up a steep and rocky driveway; some rarely abandon the giant lanai. Three rooms, all on the ground floor, have a full bath, kitchenette, mountain views, queen beds, artistic furnishings (no country decor within miles), and flat-screen TVs. The studio is larger with a separate bed and a couch. The huge windows bring a lot of light into the spacious kitchen/living room and often make travelers feel comfortable to watch movies, read, or chat with the innkeepers. Continental breakfast (make sure to be here on Sunday when they serve their famous waffles-and-crêpes extravaganza) includes fruit off their trees, pastries, and coffee, and is included in the price. They supply binoculars for bird-watching. Plus, they offer garden massages in the Bali Hut.

Strawberry Guava B&B

Innkeeper: Tracy Sullivan.
808-332-0385 or 808-634-5539.
www.homepages.hawaiian.net/lauria.
lauria@hawaiian.net.
4896 Z Kua Rd., Kalaheo.
Price: Inexpensive.
Credit Cards: No.
Handicapped Access: No.

If you are looking for an inexpensive B&B (under $100, including breakfast), in a house overlooking the Lawa'i Valley, just a short drive from Poipu but seemingly worlds away from the tourist scene, this is the place for you. The isolation makes this spot a bit hard to find, but once you are nestled beneath the jungle canopy, in the loving hands of the Sullivan family, you'll be glad you came. The property was

The jungly saltwater pool is just one reason to hide away at Marjorie's Kaua'i Inn.

designed to maximize the trade winds and views. Guests arrive through an open entryway, which is actually the common sitting area. The three rooms are U-shaped around the outdoor space and make a separate wing of the house. There are two small standard rooms and a larger two-room suite, decorated simply with fans, and private entrances. The only thing fancy here is breakfast. Fresh farmer's market fruit and homemade pastries with the Sullivans is a treat. Make sure to try some of the exotic fruit they serve. Tracy and Ben go out of their way to make guests feel comfortable and at home: welcome notes on your door, beach equipment, binoculars, and free wireless. This is a great choice for those of you looking for simple, clean accommodations at the best price in the area.

Vacation Rental Agencies

Grantham (808-742-2000 or 800-325-5701; fax 808-742-9093; www.grantham -resorts.com; stay@grantham-resorts .com). With about 33 rental homes and units in 12 condo complexes, this south shore vacation rental agency is one of the best on Kaua'i. Rates, though a bit higher than other agencies, are usually very reasonable, and you can be sure that their units are well taken care of and decorated with a tasteful flair. They have a five- to seven-night minimum stay in all units. They offer free local calls, stocked kitchens, washer and dryer, wireless in most units, but no daily housekeeping (if you want your linens refreshed, they will for a fee). I always find the folks at Grantham to be the classiest rental agency on the island.

Poipu Connection (808-742-2233 or 800-742-2260; fax 808-742-7382; www.poipu connection.com; poipu@hawaiilink.net). Family owned for the last 20 years by Anne, Larry, and their son, Ben Wachler. This hardworking team gives service as personal and honest as you can find on the south shore. They don't have as many units as many of the vacation rental companies, but the condos and houses they rent are taken care of and reasonably priced. The Wachlers themselves check out each property before and after guests leave. They offer amenity packages of flowers and cookies in each room. They have a four-night minimum stay (longer during the holiday season) and accept MasterCard and Visa.

Suite Paradise (808-742-7400 or 800-367-8020; fax 808-742-9121; www.suite -paradise.com; mail@suiteparadise.com). This vacation rental agency has the largest selection of condo rentals on the south shore for some of the best prices around. Unfortunately, the sacrifice is often the decor. Suite Paradise units often are decorated in floral bedspreads, wicker furniture, and the like, rather than the heavy wooden furniture you might find in other units. They offer no daily maid service, but all units generally include, cable TV, VCR, CD player, a stocked kitchen, washer/dryer, phones with dataports, voice mail and automated wake-up service, ceiling fans, and some AC. They accept American Express, Diner's Club, MasterCard, and Visa.

WEST SHORE LODGING

KEKAHA

Hale Puka Ana B&B
Innkeepers: Patrick and Jules McLean.
808-652-6852.
www.westkauaisunset.com.
info@kekahakauaisunset.com.
8240 Elepaio, Kekaha.
Price: Inexpensive—moderate.
Credit Cards: AE, MC, V.
Handicapped Access: Limited mobility okay.

Patrick and Jules opened their house to guests five years ago to cater to the REI crowd—those who want to spend lots of time hiking Koke'e but also desire 600-thread-count bedsheets. The only bed & breakfast located oceanfront in sunny Kekaka that gives the royal treatment. With Hawaiian-style framed pictures accenting simple white bedding and hardwood floors, guests find rooms comfortable, yet decorated with high-end touches. The suites each have a TV, refrigerator, fresh flowers, and a private bathroom (with lovely lotions and soaps); upstairs, guests have access to the microwave, big-screen cable TV, wireless, free phone calls, and beach gear (including snorkels and boogie boards). Since the property is a little far from the commercial area of Waimea, Patrick and Jules built a communal outdoor grill/kitchen area with views of the ocean. There is also an outdoor shower surrounded by fruit trees. When guests arrive, they are greeted with leis, a smoothie, and lots of assistance from the kind owners (who are great resources about where to surf). Each morning guests sit on the large lanai, staring across the Pacific at Ni'ihau, to eat a continental breakfast. The airy living area makes for a unique place to chill out, morning or evening. There is a three-night minimum stay, and chances are you are going to want to hang out longer than that.

WAIMEA

Waimea Inn

Innkeeper: Lorraine De Rosa.
808-338-0031.
www.innwaimea.com.
stay@innwaimea.com.
4469 Halepule Rd., Waimea.
Price: Inexpensive.
Credit Cards: AE, D, MC, V.
Handicapped Access: One unit.

A welcome addition to the Waimea area, this inn and its vacation rentals are located in the center of town just steps from the ocean. There are four spacious rooms, a suite, and three cottages decorated in modern furnishings. The inn used to be the church house and now feels like a renovated plantation. Standard rooms can fit a third person on a pullout couch; all have queen-sized beds. Nice touches like the jet tub and a king bed complement the more expensive Banana Suite. A shared large lanai, overlooking the trees and few houses on the street, is the perfect place to read a book and unwind. There is also a darkly lit communal living space where fruit is available for guests. Since there is no AC in the rooms and windows are smallish, the fans can keep the rooms cool at night, but in summer it can get hot. This is an excellent choice for people who aren't in the room much but want to stay in one of the most historical neighborhoods in Kaua'i.

✪Waimea Plantation Cottages

General Manager: Stephanie Iona.
808-338-1625 or 800-992-4632; fax 808-338-2338.
www.waimeacottages.com.
info@ResortQuestHawaii.com.
9400 Kaumuali'i Hwy., Waimea.
Price: Moderate—very expensive.
Credit Cards: AE, D, DC, JCB, MC, V.
Handicapped Access: Some.

Driving onto this 27-acre property, you magically travel back in time to where plantation cottages abound and banyan trees reroute roads. This is the most unusual property on Kaua'i. With 59 studio-five bedroom stand-alone cottages, all built between 1880 and 1940, you can easily conjure the image of sugarcane workers relaxing on lanais after a long day in the fields. Or maybe this will feel more like grown-up summer camp, with flashlights on your room key, where children play in the wide expanses of lawn, people ride around in golf carts, couples sit on rocking chairs or hammocks reading, families sing around bonfires, local *kapuna* sing to guests, and

This banyan tree at Waimea Plantation Cottages reroutes the road.

the evening is best spent on the micro-brewery's deck, sipping house-brewed beer. Waimea Plantation Cottages is committed to the integrity of each unit by continuously upgrading. Each cottage has a story passed down from the Faye family who, preserving the history of each family, decorated them fittingly with antique Hawaiian furnishings. All are private, led up to by gravel driveways, and surrounded by palms, bougainvilleas, and banyan trees. Cottages have fully renovated kitchen, cable TV, fresh orchids, DVD player, and private lanai. There is no AC in the rooms, but fans and trade winds keep them fairly cool, though it can get warm in summer. Guests have access to the black sand beach, the pool, shuffleboard, a spa, a full restaurant, volleyball courts and Ping-Pong tables, Faye Museum, and the gift shop with locally made items. Though this is not the place for everyone, I highly recommend Waimea Plantation Cottages for weddings, events, family reunions, family vacations, honeymoons, and couples who want a unique lodging experience. People tend to forget that when staying at this classic property, mosquitoes, roosters, and the occasional faulty door come with the package.

NORTH SHORE LODGING

HAENA

Hale Hoʻo Maha

Owners: Kirby Guyer and Toby Searles.
808-826-7083 or 800-851-0291; fax 808-826-7084.
www.aloha.net/~hoomaha.
hoomaha@aloha.net.
7083 Alamihi Rd., Hanalei.
Price: Moderate.
Credit Cards: DC, JCB, MC, V.
Handicapped Access: Limited.

Spunky Kirby Guyer and Toby Searles have served up funky accommodations in Haena for 27 years in one of those north shore houses on stilts that make you wonder how the heck people actually cart groceries into them. Well, Hale Hoʻo Maha has an elevator with a mural stretching the height of the house to carry you (and your bags) upstairs. This bed & breakfast rents out four suites, each with private bathroom (and double showerheads). Fruit-themed suites are decorated to showcase the owners' travels (though the Pineapple Suite is more a tribute to fruit than the South Pacific, with even a pineapple-shaped bed). All rooms have big windows, a private lanai, and TV; all but one have a king bed. Many visitors are world travelers who talk story in the large common room while enjoying breakfast treats like Portuguese sausage, blueberry-macadamia pancakes, and Kirby's favorite: Kona Chocolate Mac-Nut coffee. Guests are welcome to use videos and books, the kitchen, free drinking water and ice, BBQ, chessboards, the office computer and printer, and the ozonated hot tub downstairs. They gladly welcome children over 7.

✪Hanalei Colony Resort

Manager: Laura Richards.
808-826-6235 or 800-628-3004; fax 808-826-9895.
www.hcr.com.
aloha@hcr.com.
5-7130 Kuhio Hwy., Hanalei.
Price: Expensive–very expensive. Note: There is a car surcharge per day.
Credit Cards: AE, MC, V.
Handicapped Access: Yes, but you must inform them first.

Located near the end of the road in Haena, this rustic oceanfront resort is for people who really want to get away from it all. There are no TVs or phones in the rooms. You can occasionally get a wireless signal or watch TV in the coffee shop, but other than that you get to listen to the sound of the ocean crashing against a relatively private

Escape the world at the Hanalei Colony Resort.

white sand beach. The 40 two-bedroom/two-bath units are simple with big windows, a lanai, large sliding doors separating bedrooms, and full kitchens. Big grassy fields and courtyards wind among buildings, leading to BBQ areas and the small pool. With lots of books, games, and toys in the office and a very friendly staff, this resort feels like a summer camp with better furniture, plus a gourmet restaurant and bar with live music, day spa, and coffee shop/art gallery. Families meet for BBQs, kids play Frisbee or soccer, couples lope off to watch the sunset at Tunnels Beach. Upon checking in, guests receive a welcome basket of snacks, fruit, and fresh flowers from the housekeepers, who clean units twice a week. Other amenities (depending on the season) include weekly continental breakfast, evening receptions, and lei-making or basket-weaving classes. There is a five-night minimum stay during high season. They also perform weddings here.

HANALEI

Hanalei Inn & Hanalei Bay Inn
Innkeeper: Bill Gaus.

808-826-9333.
www.hanaleiinn.com.
5-5468 Kuhio Hwy., Hanalei.
Price: Inexpensive–moderate.
Credit Cards: AE, D, MC, V.
Handicapped Access: Yes, but you must tell them first.

If you are looking for an inexpensive place to sleep in the heart of Hanalei town, this is your only option. Hanalei Inn is actually two structures, a couple of blocks apart. The first (and more budget-friendly) is right on Kuhio Highway, a short walk from Hanalei's commercial district. These motel-like rooms are good for people who just want a place to crash. Small and dark, despite a recent face-lift, there isn't much outdoor space to kick your feet up after a long day of surfing or hiking. The second property (Hanalei Bay Inn), a house a block from Pine Trees Beach, has one- and two-bedroom units, some with ocean views. Most rooms have HD TV, microwave, dishware, bathtub, AC, fans, wireless access, and maid service (for a fee). Kids are welcome. Both properties have a mellow vibe, great for people who don't care about luxury but want something clean and simple, in the center of the funkiest town on the island.

KILAUEA

Aloha Sunrise Inn & Aloha Sunset Inn

Innkeepers: Catherine and Allan Rietow. 808-828-1100 or 800-828-1008; fax 808-828-2199.
www.kauaisunrise.com or www.kauai-sunset.com.
apt@hawaiian.net.
4899-A Waiakalua St., Kilauea.
Price: Moderate.
Credit Cards: None.
Handicapped Access: Limited mobility okay in Aloha Sunset Cottage.

These two ecofriendly cottages nestled within a 7-acre organic garden are a welcome retreat for those who want to escape it all. The Aloha Sunset Cottage has a cozy ranch-style layout. It can feel a little dark, but the homey decor livens it up with Hawaiian bark-cloth sofa and chairs, floral-printed bedspreads, wicker furniture, and hardwood floors. Photos of Hawaiian families from the past line the walls. This cottage has cable TV, a private patio area, king bed, washer and dryer, full kitchen, and lots of storage. The other cottage, Aloha Sunrise, is actually attached the garage, but the vegetable garden and abundant fruit trees (all available for your picking and eating) make the space feel more remote. This unit has a dimly lit downstairs kitchen and bathroom. Upstairs, a loft living and sleeping area with skylights makes this unit appear more spacious than the other. In both cottages guests are greeted with flowers, chocolate, a coffee and tea basket, fruit, bathroom amenities, and sundry items in the refrigerator. Neither cottage has air-conditioning, but being in Kilauea, it can get very breezy, so there are fans and lots of windows. Luxury perks include 540-thread-count sheets and organic fruit. And

for the green folks, the entire property has purified water and composting toilets. It's all located a short drive from the Kilauea Lighthouse and restaurants, plus only about 10 minutes from Princeville. Yet with the spacious yard for lounging, the friendly hosts, and the remote setting, you might not want to leave. Since cottages are small, this is really only a good option for couples and very close friends.

North Country Farms

Owner: Lee Roversal.
808-828-1513.
www.northcountryfarms.com.
ncfarms@aloha.net.
P.O. Box 723, Kilauea.
Price: Inexpensive.
Credit Cards: None.
Handicapped Access: Limited mobility okay.

The enthusiastic Lee Roversal offers two wooden cottages on her 4-acre working organic farm. Located in Kilauea, just a short drive from the town, these vacation rentals give a slice of rural living in a tropical setting. Each unit is 500 square feet with one bedroom, a kitchenette, lanai, BBQ, and indoor and outdoor showers. The Garden Cottage sleeps four, while the Orchard Cottage sleeps six (that is, if a couple people in your group are interested in sleeping on the lanai's futon—with a mosquito net—or the outdoor hammock). Cottages are decorated with dark wood walls and big windows, a queen bed, and pullout sofas for the kids. Aside from the tropical accents, you could be in a cabin in the mountains. Secluded on the land by lush palms, guests have privacy unlike most north shore offerings. The yard has a trampoline, and kids are encouraged to pick fruit from the farm. Guests are welcomed with an Aloha Breakfast basket of granola, biscotti, tea and coffee, organic milk, and fruit. Lee also runs a CSA through her farm,

Stay in a cottage in the organic North Country Farms.

so you are likely to meet some of the islands colorful characters. There is a three-night minimum stay. This is one of the best options for families on the north shore.

PRINCEVILLE

The condo rental market in Princeville is astounding. New complexes open daily. The best way to find the right condo for you is to talk to a rental agency *on the island* and research their units. Make sure to ask for pictures. At the end of this section, I have included three locally owned rental agencies working in the area along with the details about their policies—including minimum stays, amenities, and payment options.

Ali'i Kai I and II

Hanalei North Shore Properties: 808-826-9622 or 800-488-3336; fax 808-826-1188. www.rentalsonkauai.com.

Oceanfront Realty: 808-826-6585 or 800-222-5541; fax 808-826-6478. www.oceanfrontrealty.com. 3830 Edwards Rd., Princeville. Price: Moderate. Credit Cards: Policies vary; call or visit online for information. Handicapped Access: Limited Mobility Okay.

This huge condo complex offers two-bedroom/two-bath units with ocean and garden views. Some units have been upgraded (with high-end appliances and leather furniture), some haven't (with rattan sofas and old kitchens); they are priced accordingly, so ask. Some have panoramic Bali Hai views from atop a cliff (like building 4); others gaze onto grassy fields and mountains, or even the other buildings. All units have lanai, fans, low ceiling, a big master bedroom and a smaller second bedroom, a spacious open layout where the kitchen, living, and dining rooms are all one, and big windows throughout. There is no access to the beach from the property, but since this is not the most luxurious condo complex in Princeville, it is actually a decent option for families—maybe the best deal you can find on a very large two-bedroom. However, if you have young kids, consider getting a unit farther back from the bluffs. Complex amenities include tennis courts (some units have access to Princeville Tennis Club), pools, and a Jacuzzi.

Cliffs @ Princeville
Oceanfront Realty: 808-826-6585 or 800-222-5541; fax 808-826-6478.
www.oceanfrontrealty.com.
Premier Resorts: 808-826-6219 or 800-367-8024.
www.cliffs-princeville.com.
3811 Edward Rd., Princeville.
Price: Moderate.
Credit Cards: Policies vary; call or visit online for information.
Handicapped Access: Limited mobility okay.

This sprawling plantation-style condo complex is now one of the biggest in the Princeville area. As the name suggests, it is set atop the cliffs, near the Princeville golf course. This is a good option for people who want a semi-luxurious condo without the fuss of resorts. Buildings are spread across grassy fields and, though new, seem to be acquiring some wear and tear. Units are one-bedroom, one-bedroom with a loft, or four-bedroom. Condos have a compact kitchen connecting to the living room and sliding glass doors leading to the lanai. These condos are on the smallish side and are probably best for couples who won't spend a ton of time in the unit or people with limited mobility. Some units have ocean views (though there is no beach

access from this complex). Amenities include tennis courts, an on-site video store and library, pools and Jacuzzis, and BBQ gazebos.

Emmanlani Court
808-826-6585 or 800-222-5541; fax 808-826-6478.
www.oceanfrontrealty.com.
5250 Ka Haku Rd., Princeville.
Price: Moderate.
Credit Cards: MC, V.
Handicapped Access: Limited in downstairs units.

Golfers will love this intimate condo complex located right on the Princeville green. These stark white buildings with Mediterranean tiled roofs are a good option for families and older travelers who want to make themselves at home in a clean and spacious condo. However, without beach access or ocean views, you'll notice that long-term renters and owners favor this complex instead of vacationers. This results in a quiet environment where you can sit on your lanai and pretend you live on this world-class golf course. Units are bright and airy with one to three bedrooms. There is a small pool on the premises as well as covered parking.

Hanalei Bay Resort
General Manager: Jim Braman.
808-826-6522 or 800-827-4427; fax 808-826-6680.
www.hanaleibayresort.com.
5380 Honoiki Rd., Princeville.
Price: Moderate—very expensive.
Credit Cards: AE. D, JCB, MC, V.
Handicapped Access: Limited.

Walking into the open-air lobby gives guests one of Kaua'i's most striking tropical vistas: the Hanalei Bay Resort's grounds, with a backdrop of Bali Hai. This 134-room resort waterfalls down the cliff until reaching (after quite a long trek) the Pacific. Winding through palm-hidden buildings, a snake-like pool with lava rock waterfalls, tennis courts, and bougainvilleas are the one-bedroom suites. Split in thirds among a hotel, a time share, and vacation rentals, your room could need a serious remodel because of ailing rattan furnishings or could be decorated by a world-traveling interior designer. All rooms are spacious with kitchenette, king beds, lanai, views, AC, and cable TV. But people don't love this place for the rooms. The grounds and vistas make this a good place for people who want the resort experience, but don't want to pay for the Princeville Resort. Unfortunately, the staff can be a bit cold. The concierge, instead of merely helping you with activities, will try to sell you time-share ownership, and in general service at restaurants is slow. You'll have to pay extra fees for everything: local calls, the safe, wireless, lei-making classes, hula lessons, and more. This resort is like a prom queen, gorgeous on the outside, but in need of some substance to make it worth the dough. Oceanfront Realty has rooms here for a bit cheaper, so you might want to shop around.

Hanalei Bay Villas

808-826-6585 or 800-222-5541; fax 808-826-6478.
www.oceanfrontrealty.com.
5451 Ka Haku Rd., Princeville.
Price: Moderate.
Credit Cards: MC, V.
Handicapped Access: None.

These unique Princeville cottages align on a ridge overlooking the Princeville Golf course, the jungle, and Bali Hai. The two- or three-bedroom units aren't the most luxurious inside, but the privacy of having your own stand-alone accommodation makes up for the innards. Depending on the light, cottages can be dark and stuffy, and there isn't much room to move around.

Still—where else can you drink coffee on a private lanai in your own cottage and feel as if you are suspended above Hanalei? This property is not for people who are scared of heights—cottages are on stilts on a cliff. There are no amenities at the property, but it's a short walk to the Princeville Resort. In the evenings you hear frogs, chickens, and birds welcoming one of the best sunset views in town.

Kamahana Townhomes

Hanalei North Shore Properties: 808-826-9622 or 800-488-3336; fax 808-826-1188.
www.rentalsonkauai.com.
Oceanfront Realty: 808-826-6585 or 800-222-5541; fax 808-826-6478.
www.oceanfrontrealty.com.
3800 Kamahameha Rd., Princeville.
Price: Inexpensive–moderate.
Credit Cards: Policies vary; call or visit online for information.
Handicapped Access: None.

A relatively secluded condo complex located on the southwest edge of Princeville, this quiet and affordable location makes for a low-key homey atmosphere. Many people live at this complex year round, so it feels more intimate than many of the other condo options in the area. Most units offer views of the Pacific and the golf course from your lanai. And the complex is just a short walk to the Sealodge Beach trail. The buildings are set on the Princeville golf course and sometimes you can see Albatross hanging out on the green. These one-two bedroom units are on the smaller side, with vaulted ceilings and big windows that make them seem larger. Couples and small families will be comfortable here. There is a pool onsite with BBQ areas between buildings.

✪ Mauna Kai

www.rentalsonkauai.com.
Hanalei North Shore Properties: 808-826-

9622 or 800-488-3336; fax 808-826-1188.
www.oceanfrontrealty.com.
Oceanfront Realty: 808-826-6585 or 800-
222-5541; fax 808-826-6478.
3920 Wyllie Rd., Princeville.
Price: Moderate.
Credit Cards: Policies vary; call or visit
online for information.
Handicapped Access: Limited mobility
okay.

If you can handle not being on the beach,
this lushly landscaped condo complex is
one of the best deals on north shore. With
10 units per acre, the 46 hut-like buildings
blend into the palms, bougainvillea, red
ginger, streams, and hibiscus trees. Units
are spacious with a fireplace (that you won't
ever need), a private lanai, a large kitchen
(some are upgraded, so ask), a sunken living and dining room, and two or three bedrooms. Even though there are big windows
throughout, sometimes the units can feel
like you are inside a nest. This is a great
option for families or two couples who want
a comfy place to come home to, or are staying for extended periods of time. Most
units have been upgraded and are tastefully
decorated, but make sure to ask your rental
agency. Hanalei North Shore Properties
rents out Sylvia's Tower, a three-story
stand-alone unit owned by a professional
harpist, with slight ocean views, unique
decor, and simple touches like videos,
books, and a seriously stocked kitchen.
Mauna Kai has one of the biggest condo
pools in Princeville.

Pali Ke Kua Condos

Hanalei North Shore Properties: 808-826-
9622 or 800-488-3336; fax 808-826-1188.
www.rentalsonkauai.com.
Oceanfront Realty: 808-826-6585 or 800-
222-5541; fax 808-826-6478.
www.oceanfrontrealty.com.
Princeville Vacations: 808-828-6530 or
800-800-3637; fax 808-828-6529.

www.princevillevacations.com.
5300 Ka Haku Rd., Princeville.
Price: Moderate–expensive.
Credit Cards: Policies vary; call or visit
online for information.
Handicapped Access: Limited.

This old-school Hawaiian style complex on
the cliffs above Bali Hai is highly coveted. It
offers one-bedroom, one-bedroom with a
loft, and two-bedroom units with laid-back
style; vacationers sign up to stay here
months in advance. An on-site pool, Jacuzzi,
sundeck, open grassy areas for kids to play,
and beach path to one of the best snorkel
strands in the area make this the perfect
place for families or outdoorsy couples.
West-facing buildings have spectacular Bali
Hai and ocean views where, if the time is
right, you can sit on your lanai and watch
whales migrate. If you are okay with older
units, this is one of the best deals you can
get for the location. Some condos are two
floors, some are only one (go for the downstairs units, which are more spacious and
feel more homey); some have views, some
don't; some have been upgraded, some
haven't. Make sure to do your research with
the rental agency about the specific unit. At
press time, a new gourmet restaurant on the
property was in the works.

✪ Pu'u Poa

Hanalei North Shore Properties: 808-826-
9622 or 800-488-3336; fax 808-826-1188.
www.rentalsonkauai.com.
Oceanfront Realty: 808-826-6585 or 800-
222-5541; fax 808-826-6478.
www.oceanfrontrealty.com.
Princeville Vacations: 808-828-6530 or
800-800-3637; fax 808-828-6529.
www.princevillevacations.com.
5454 Ka Haku Rd., Princeville.
Price: Expensive.
Credit Cards: Policies vary; call or visit
online for information.
Handicapped Access: None.

Princeville Resort
808-826-9644 or 866-716-8110; fax 808-826-1166.
www.princevillehotelhawaii.com.
info@princeville.com.
5520 Ka Haku Rd., Princeville.
Price: Very expensive.
Credit Cards: AE, D, DC, JCB, MC, V.
Handicapped Access: Yes.

At press time, the Princeville Hotel, a grandiose resort on the bluffs overlooking Hanalei Bay and Bali Hai, was beginning a major renovation to become a St. Regis. Resort representatives claim this will be a six-month project. Since renovations will be done in phases (a new spa, the pool, rooms, and so on), the resort will stay open during this time. Which is great because the 23-year-old Princeville Resort is a tourist destination in itself, with five gourmet restaurants, a world-class golf course, a spa, shops, tennis courts, a snorkel and surf beach, a giant pool, lu'au, and panoramic views. When you enter this palatial nine-level structure that slopes down the side of a bluff, you'll notice the floor-to-ceiling windows, a classical lobby area to have a drink, play chess, or just space out watching whales migrate, and the almost Victorian decadence that might just make you okay with paying over $500 a night for a garden-view room. Because this property sits on the land named for a prince, the Princeville Hotel does a fantastic job of creating a space truly fit for a king. Did I mention how spectacular the views are from the lobby and restaurants? Because of renovations, I cannot offer comprehensive information about this property, aside from saying that you might score on good room deals if you don't mind a bit of hammering.

There is nothing, on all of Kaua'i, like the architecture of these units. The plushest oceanfront condo complex on the north shore is just a short walk from the Princeville Resort and high in demand. With the entire ocean-facing side of these two-bedroom condos made of glass (including the ceiling over the living area) and an oceanfront lanai bigger than some hotel rooms, you never want to leave the condo. Set on the cliffs over Hanalei Bay, you will spend hours staring at the sea, watching sea life frolic in the waves. A sunken living area, connected to the kitchen and dining area, faces the ocean. Set farther back (but only separated by a sliding door) is a large master bedroom and bath. The second bedroom doesn't have views. This is an excellent choice for two couples (though you might lift fists to decide who gets the master bedroom) and maybe families (though the amenities are basically views and BBQs on the lanai). There is a steep path leading to the snorkel beach. This is the perfect place to finish reading *War and Peace* and drink endless amounts of Kona coffee.

Sealodge
Hanalei North Shore Properties: 808-826-9622 or 800-488-3336; fax 808-826-1188.
www.rentalsonkauai.com.
Oceanfront Realty: 808-826-6585 or 800-222-5541; fax 808-826-6478.
www.oceanfrontrealty.com.
3700 Kamehameha Rd., Princeville.
Price: Inexpensive.
Credit Cards: Policies vary; call or visit online for information.
Handicapped Access: None.

Just part of the view from Pu'u Poa Condominiums.

These small condos in shingled, 30-year-old buildings right on the bluffs overlooking Hanalei Bay are probably the best deal on the north shore. With Bali Hai to one side and the coral-reefed Pacific to the other, you can watch sea life and sunsets from the property (and sometimes your room). Units are one or two bedrooms set among jungle-like grounds with lots of birds nesting in the lush palms. The architects, seeming to want guests to feel like they are in nature, made it a trek to get to units (especially the lower-floor ones). All condos have a small kitchen, fans, big windows, and BBQ. Some have lofts. In general the decor is not much to speak of, but where else can you stay right on the cliffs overlooking the ocean for such a steal? There is a semi-rough trail to a snorkel beach on the property. And it is a short drive to Princeville Beach, shops, and restaurants. This is an excellent option for budget-minded families who want views and can sacrifice luxury.

Vacation Rentals

Hanalei North Shore Properties (808-826-9622 or 800-488-3336; fax 808-826-1188; www.vacation-rental-kauai). Roberta Haas and Mimsy Bouret opened this local rental agency and real estate venue almost 30 years ago. What started as a dream in a garage has now flourished into them managing 60 houses, cottages, and condos along the north shore. They do not accept credit cards, but take electronic checks. A five-night minimum is required in all units. The cleaning fee varies between $115 and 275. All units have VCR or DVD, stocked kitchen, fans, free local calls, and washer/dryer. Some units have air-conditioning and wireless access. None are specifically handicapped accessible, but many are fine for limited mobility.

Oceanfront Realty (808-826-6585 or 800-222-5541; fax 808-826-6478; www.oceanfrontrealty.com). Almost three decades old, this family-owned and -operated vacation rental agency specializes in the north shore area. Owner Donna Apisa's philosophy is to encourage staff and guests to be good communicators. So make sure to tell Oceanfront what you want. They tend to be upfront with potential guests. And with 60 rental houses, condos, and cottages and real estate properties as well, they are doing something right. The friendly staff provide in-house activity booking/concierge services (with good discounts) and they allow guests to use their computers at the office if necessary. All units have free local phone calls, washer and dryer, full kitchen with a rice cooker, toaster and blender, irons, basic cable, and laundry detergent. The cleaning fee runs $95–140, depending on the property. There is a three-night minimum. They accept MasterCard and Visa.

Princeville Vacations of Coldwell Banker Bali Hai Realty (808-828-6530 or 800-800-3637; fax 808-828-6529; www.princevillevacations.com). With more than 20 years' experience renting luxury condos and houses on the north shore, Princeville Vacations is a dependable option. Owner Robert Thompson and his staff's units are often a bit pricier than their competition, yet they are also slightly more upscale. Units generally have fans, wireless (make sure to ask if you really need it), washer and dryer, dishwasher, and DVD or VCR. Some limited-mobility rentals. They do not accept credit cards, have a three-night minimum stay, and charge a $150 cleaning fee.

4

CULTURE

The Origins of Aloha

Most people arrive on Kaua'i with images of exquisite Polynesian women placing leis around their necks while muscled men wearing grass wraps serenade them with 'ukuleles. Though this still happens at lu'aus and resorts, it's not modern Kaua'i. For people deeply engrossed with natural beauty, it can be difficult to find the actual culture of the isle. This is not the place for happening nightlife or huge music festivals. Most traditional architecture has disappeared, and now Kaua'i is home to mini malls ands big-box stores. Locals dress similar to people in Southern California or Florida and drive in the same cars, listening to similar music. When you look close enough, however, you find a unique potpourri culture unlike anywhere else in the world. Here aloha is a way of life, not just a word.

ARCHITECTURE

You won't find palm-thatched huts with lava rock walls anymore unless you go to the **Kamokila Hawaiian Village** (see Museums). Other than the *heiau* archaeological sites (see chapter 5), traditional Kaua'i architecture has all but disappeared.

Now when people discuss historic buildings, they mean from the plantation era instead of the *kuapapa* times. However, most of the buildings from this era are located in the town of Waimea, where the ancients were known to have lived. On Huakai Road you'll find the oldest building in town: the New England–style **Gullick-Rowell House** (1829), located near the entrance to the hospital. Back on Kaumuali'i Highway, if you head east toward town, pass the Old Sugar Mill on your right; two blocks from there is the art deco **Waimea Theater** (1938), which still shows movies. Continue east past the

The art deco Waimea Theater.

The mountains of Allerton Gardens turn fuchsia in spring, when the bougainvilleas bloom.

Hawaiian Church (1865), which has had a congregation since 1820, and find the **Yamase** and **Masuda buildings** (1919), then head toward **Wrangler's Steakhouse** (1909) and the **Collectibles and Fine Junque Antique Store** (1890) across the street. Wander toward the center of town to check out the **Electric Power Company Building** (1907) and the **First Hawaiian Bank**'s (1929) facade-style structure. In the center of town at Hofgaard Park stands **Captain Cook's Monument**. Finally, on the hill above town on Haina Road is the oldest church in town, the **United Church of Christ** (1859).

Another way to understand the architecture of Kaua'i is to visit the plantations. Characterized by simple wooden walls and floors, these buildings are often constructed with a main house in the center and an array of smaller workers' houses surrounding it. Some traditional plantation buildings still exist, and you might note that many of the houses in Lihu'e, Waimea, and Hanalei reflect this style of architecture. For a glimpse into the original plantation of the Faye sugar baron family, in Waimea, the **Resortquest Waimea Plantation Cottages** preserved the original structure of the workers' cottages and transformed them into vacation rentals. Understanding that each cottage has a story, the Faye descendants are writing the oral histories so that the resort can then renovate each cottage to retain the history of the family who once resided there. The **Faye Museum** (see Museums) offers guided tours of the old mill, as well as some older worker cottages at 9 AM, Tues. and Sat.

Heading north, in Lihu'e, a prime example of preserved plantation architecture is the **Grove Farm Homestead** (1864) (see Museums), where you can walk through the intact homes of the Wilcox family and their workers. This plantation tour is a step back into a quieter time, where families sat on rocking chairs on the lanai and sipped lemonade, kids ran around the lawn, and cats lazed around in the sun all afternoon.

Another example of plantation architecture is Gaylord Wilcox's **Kilohana Plantation** (1835) (808-245-9593; 3-2087 Kaumuali'i Hwy., Lihu'e; www.kilohana kauai.com). Here you can wander around the 15,000-square-foot main house (or eat here—see chapter 6), or even take a Clydesdale horse-and-carriage tour of the farm, gardens, and workers' cottages. Inside the Tudor-style main house, you'll notice some of the original furniture, rugs, and artwork left from Mr. Wilcox's wife, Ethel's affection for Hollywood glamour. Also pay attention to the wooden moldings, the swooping staircase, and the 1930s

Koloa Church.

mirror near the main entranceway. There are a variety of high-end shops on the property (see chapter 8), as well as a luʻau that caters to cruise ship passengers.

If you are interested in Kauaʻi's old churches, starting in Lihuʻe, across from the Kukui Grove Shopping Center, are two examples of lava stone buildings: **Lihuʻe First Church** (1840) and the **Lihuʻe United Church**. Around where H 56 becomes H 50, take Hoʻomana Road to the **Lihuʻe Lutheran Church** (rebuilt in 1982 after it was destroyed by a hurricane to replicate the original 1885 structure), the oldest Lutheran church in all of Hawaiʻi.

Another point of architectural interest is the **Kauaʻi Hindu Monastery** (808-822-3012; 107 Kaholalele Rd., Kapaʻa; www.himalayaacademy.com). Open 9–noon Mon.–Fri., with guided tours depending on the moon cycle; call ahead for details. Located in the foothills over Kapaʻa, the rain forest garden hides two sacred Hindu temples. In the **Kadavul Temple**, visitors can glimpse the world's largest (and one of the oldest—50 million years to be exact) crystal. People who have been vegetarians for longer than a year may also enter the shrine. The **Iraivan Temple**, which is still in the works, is a hand-carved white granite structure being created by artists from Bangalore. To visit the temples, dress modestly (no shorts, tank tops, or short dresses). They will provide you with sarongs if you forget to dress to their standards.

Rich with history is the area of Koloa, where the first sugar mills flourished and hordes of workers and visitors poured into this small community each year. There are a number of old churches in the vicinity. The most dramatic is on the way from Koloa to Poipu: the **Koloa Church** (1859). Next to that are the lava rock **Koloa Union Church** and **Koloa Missionary Church**. In Koloa, the Japanese heritage of the sugar mill workers is evident in the **Koloa Hongwanji Mission** (1910) and the **Koloa Jodo Mission** (1910), which were built by Japanese woodworkers. Finally, Kauaʻi's oldest Catholic church, **St. Raphael's Catholic Church** (1856), is located just outside town. To get there, take Weliweli Road to Hapa Road (turn right) and drive until the pavement ends.

Historic Hanapepe reenacts a slice of the Wild West. Most of the buildings are made of single-wall wood construction with vertical tongue-in-groove or board-and-batten siding. The western-style **Aloha Theater** represents the art nouveau era. An effort is under way to restore this classic theater. Many of the 1920–1930s buildings are noted for their large display windows, false-front parapets, and pent roofs or awnings at their front elevation. Make sure to wander out onto the **Hanapepe Swinging Bridge**, which was constructed for people to carry water into town. The bridge swings over the river (often getting a little too creaky and swingy when more than one person is on it) and was reconstructed after ʻIniki blew the original away.

On the north shore, Kilauea houses the **St. Sylvester's Catholic Church** (808-828-2818; Kolo Rd.): an octagonal structure with a roof that looks like a rice hat. Inside check out the murals, painted by Jean Charlot, a famous island artist. Another church of interest, **Christ Memorial Episcopal Church** (1941), is where Kolo Road meets Kilauea Road. The lava rock structure is surrounded by an attractive garden.

In Hanalei, the mission hall of the **Waioli Huiia Church** (1912) (5-5393A Kuhio Hwy.) is the oldest surviving church building in Kauaʻi. Built to reflect the American Gothic architecture of New England, the shingled church has a belfry tower with an old mission bell. The green clapboard structure is still used by the public and has a fantastic choir at 10 AM on Sunday. Another notable architecture site up north is the **Hanalei Bridge**, a one-lane bridge in the Hanalei Wildlife Reserve. Finally, make sure to walk out on the **Hanalei Pier** at sunset, where locals play slack key guitar and the views are spectacular.

CINEMA

Kaua'i has three movie houses that often show films a couple of weeks behind mainland releases. In Wailua, the **Coconut Marketplace Cinemas** (808-821-2324) has two screens, usually showing major Hollywood blockbusters and horror films. The **Kukui Grove 4 Cinemas** (808-245-5055; Kukio Grove Shopping Center, 4368 Kuhio Grove St., Lihu'e) is packed on weekends. And the remodeled art deco **Waimea Theater** (808-338-0282) shows one film per night, Wed.–Sun.

For guests (and folks who happen to wander by at the right time), the **Sheraton** (808-742-1661) in Poipu has an outdoor movie night, showing kid-friendly films and offering popcorn for authenticity.

The **Hanalei Community Center's Uncle Jack's Place** (808-826-1011) offers free kids' movies Fri. 4–7 PM.

GALLERIES

Since most Kaua'i galleries are also retail shops, I have chosen to primarily list galleries in chapter 8. Below is information about a couple of arts organizations that

The Sunday-morning choir at the Waioli Huiia Church delights.

promote public exhibitions throughout the year, and the most popular weekly art and culture event on Kaua'i.

Garden Island Arts Council (808-245-2733; www.gardenislandarts.org) organizes art and cultural events around Kaua'i, including theater and musical events, art classes, poetry readings and exhibitions. The **Kaua'i Society of Artists** (www.kauaisocietyofartists.org) is a nonprofit that promotes public exhibitions throughout the year, and offers classes; they can also direct you to local artists' studios.

The Fight to Stop Big-Box Homogenization

At press time, the citizens of Kaua'i were battling over the saturation of supersized chain stores in Lihu'e. Since the island already has a Wal-Mart, Kmart, and Costco, locals question the necessity of expanding the Wal-Mart into a superstore. The fight has been going on for months in the city council, and recently the members voted against the expansion. Both sides of the argument have valid points. Local people are looking for cheaper goods (since everything is shipped in), but the arrival of big-box stores is hurting local proprietors. Seems most people I talk to wish the big-box stores wouldn't take over the marketplace; however, they admit that they still buy toilet paper at Wal-Mart.

Keikis' backpacks hang outside the classroom in Waimea.

Each Friday 6–9 PM, **Hanapepe Art Night** takes over the streets of old Hanapepe. People from all over the island come out to sell their crafts on the sidewalk, drink coffee (or beer and wine), and hear live musical performances. Often the little street becomes a block party, though I have been here a couple of times when hardly anyone showed up. Regardless, it is worth the trek to check out how the environment of Kaua'i has inspired some local artists. Though the galleries change often, below are some that seem to have withstood time, or new ones worth a peek.

Amy Lauren's gallery (808-335-2827; 3890 Hanapepe Rd.) offers one-of-a-kind oil paintings in a boutique setting. Work honors the local culture and land, with bright colors sure to catch your eye.

Arius Hopman Gallery (808-335-0227; 3840C Hanapepe Rd.) showcases this Kaua'i resident's watercolors, often painted on location. There is also a collection of his photography on display.

Joanna Carolan's **Banana Patch Studio** (808-335-5944; 3865 Hanapepe Rd.) offers easy-on-the-eyes ceramics, tiles, oil paintings, jewelry, and gifts and is located in the restored Chang Building (1926), now on the National Register of Historic Places.

Bay Area transplant Angela Headley's **Island Art Gallery** (808-335-0591; 3878 Hanapepe Rd.) showcases a fine sampling of her oil paintings, glasswork, and jewelry. They also serve wine and sweets during the art walk.

Kaua'i Fine Arts (808-335-3778; 3905 Hanapepe Rd.) shows off an impressive array of antique maps, books, wood art, and jewelry in a cluttered little house, perfect for getting lost in.

The woodsy smell of the **Kama'aina Koa Wood Gallery** (808-335-5483; 3848 Hanapepe Rd.) always makes me feel like I have arrived at a real artist's studio. Showing off a wealth of pricey carvings and furniture, you'll be hard pressed to stop the drool from running down your chin.

GARDENS

Being that Kaua'i is called the Garden Island, it makes sense that gardens are a part of the cultural fabric. You'll notice some of the richest soil both in the mountains and along the beaches, soil that breeds healthy plant life from all over the globe. For those of you who are

Kauaʻi brings out the artist in us all.

curious, there is much to be learned about the history of plant life on the island. For example, all of the colorful plants you normally associate with Hawaiʻi are actually non-native species, some of them invasive. Making a visit to one (or all, if you can) Botanical Garden is a sure highlight of your trip. You'll not only see some of the most beautiful (and colorful) landscapes on the island, but you'll learn about the history of biological life on Kauaʻi.

SOUTH SHORE

Kukui-o-lono Park and Gardens
In Kalaheo, turn toward the sea on Papalina Road; the park is on your right.
Open: 6:30–6:30.
Price: Free.

This south shore park is populated by locals and golfers (see chapter 7) but offers peaceful

Palm trees have long been a necessity for the Hawaiian people.

glimpses of the expanse of the Pacific. *Kukui-o-lono* means "light of Lono." This is where ancients lit torches for south-traveling fishermen and travelers. There used to be a giant *heiau* located here, but now there are merely a few rocks left from *kuapapa* times. In 1919, Walter McBryde donated the land back to the Kaua'i people (he is now buried at the golf course). If you want to visit the sacred site and gardens, pass the golf course and drive up the hill; just past a grove of trees is the Japanese Garden.

Moir Pa'u a Laka
808-742-6411.
Kiahuna Plantation, 2253 Poipu Rd., Koloa.
Open: Sunrise–sunset.
Price: Free.

Hugging the Plantation Gardens Restaurant, this cactus and succulent garden is a rare treat on this tropical isle. Sandie Moir created this garden in the 1930s, naming it "skirt of Laka" (the Hawaiian goddess of hula), and it has since turned into one of the most striking feats in America. After a few false tries with tropical plants, due to the low rainfall in the south shore area, Mrs. Moir finally found succulents to thrive in the region (you won't believe the size and shape of some of these plants). Both *Sunset* and *Life* magazines have lauded this unusual feat—to grow abundant succulents in one of the rainiest islands on earth—naming it one of the 10 best cactus and succulent gardens in the world. Today you'll find some rare varieties of these dry-loving plants. You'll also notice historical artifacts from the sugar mills and a dynamic orchid garden set around the restaurant. When combined with a trip to the adjoining restaurant, this garden delights.

National Tropical Botanical Gardens
808-742-2623.
www.ntbg.org.
members@ntbg.org.
Bill and Jean Lane Visitor Center: 4425 Lawa'i Rd., Poipu.
Open: 8:30–5.

Across the road from Spouting Horn is the 1920s plantation home that acts as a shop and information point for all three Kaua'i gardens under the blanket of the National Botanical Gardens. Established in 1964 as a research, conservation, and educational nonprofit, the NTBG works to preserve rare and endangered tropical species. The visitor center acts as the check-in location for two of the gardens—McBryde and Allerton. The center itself has an interesting (and small) native plant collection. But the highlight is actually going to one of the three gardens. Note that the balance of the tours is walking. You must check in 15 minutes prior to departure time. Information about each garden is listed below. For all gardens make sure to wear sunblock, and bring plenty of water and mosquito repellent.

Allerton Garden
Bill and Jean Lane Visitor Center: 4425 Lawa'i Rd., Poipu.
Guided Tours: Mon.–Sat. Trams depart the visitor center at 9 AM, 10 AM, 1 PM, 2 PM.
Reservations required.
Price: $40.

All 2 1/2-hour tours of Queen Emma's garden are guided. This O'ahu queen, who came to Kaua'i to mourn the death of her young son and husband, created this retreat. Visitors used to bring her exotic flowers and trees as offerings. Now the lasting effects of her love affair with bougainvillea are evident in winter, when the mountainous walls are draped with the fuchsia flowers. Down the cliffs of the Lawa'i Valley, you take a tram into the valley floor, tour a remote beach, and visit the artistic garden. Here you will see not only colorful flowers but also sculpture gardens, the bamboo garden, the Moreton Bay fig trees (seen in *Jurassic Park*), monkeypod trees, plus you'll get to wander through the McBryde Garden. Note that year-round the biodiversity fluctuates—some seasons you'll have a colorful visit and others you'll be greeted with green fields of giant leaves and bamboo. Tours can be a little long—especially if you happen to get a dull tour guide. But visually, this is one of the most stunning gardens on the island.

McBryde Lawa'i Garden

Bill and Jean Lane Visitor Center: 4425 Lawa'i Rd., Poipu.
Open: Trams depart from the visitor center daily, every hour on the half hour, 9:30–2:30. No reservations required.
Price: $20 adults; $10 ages 6–12; free for those under 5.

The roots of these Moreton figs (at the Allerton Gardens) are almost as tall as you.

Set among the deep rugged cliffs of the Lawa'i Valley, this array of tropical flora offers a glimpse into rare and endangered exotic species. After taking a 15-minute tram ride into the depths of the valley, you can explore the 250 acres on your own or choose to learn about the efforts being made to save endangered plants. Pay special notice to the ancient Canoe Garden, which showcases the Polynesian plants that the ancients brought with them to the island. As you meander down the stream, you will see palms, a variety of flowering trees, orchids, heliconias, coffee plants, Maidenhair Falls, chocolate and ginger plants, and the world's largest native Hawaiian plant garden. The headquarters of the National Tropical Botanical Garden horticulture facilities are located here. Because the other garden tours tend to be longer, this is a good option for families with younger children (or people with short attention spans). Note that all your money goes back into restoring the Lawa'i Valley and conserving the native species that already exist here. Call in advance; if there has been a lot of rain the garden occasionally closes.

NORTH SHORE

✪ Limahuli Garden and Preserve

808-826-1053.

Located on H 56 in Haena, 0.25 mile before Ke'e Beach.

Open: Tues.–Sat. 9:30–4.

Price: Self-guided $15 adults; free for children under 12.

Guided Tours: $25 adults. Reservations required for guided tours only.

This 1,000-acre garden and preserve (part of the National Tropical Botanical Garden) blankets a tropical valley overlooking Hanalei Bay. Guests can take either a 2 1/2-hour guided tour (well worth the money), or a 1 1/2-hour self-guided tour (the garden offers an informational pamphlet to guide your walk). You'll wander through lava rock terraces rich with still-thriving taro and native plants, stopping occasionally to view a native plover, watch whales spouting in the open sea, or just take in the giant mountainous peaks guarding the trees. Of all the gardens in Kaua'i, this one speaks not only to the biological history of the island, but also to the cultural history. This area was once the site of a sustainable *ahupua'a* (a model for a neighborhood), where the water flowing from the mountains irrigated the food, then was routed back to the original water source to continue the cycle. Noticeably, plants and food thrived here for the ancients. You can still see the remnants of an original Menehune taro field (that still produces vegetables), though it was built over 700 years ago. In 1967 Juliet Rice Wichman, a missionary descendant (who also started the Kaua'i Museum), bought the land and, with her grandson Chipper Wichman (the director of the gardens), donated the gardens to the NTBG. Now the organization is working to preserve native species and educate the public about sustainable gardening practices. They have even re-created a native mesic (moist) forest; in the wild, such forests are disappearing at an alarming rate. There is archaeological evidence of a homesite, possibly of a chief or *kapuna*. The garden provides umbrellas and recommends wearing comfortable walking shoes. Make sure to have plenty of mosquito repellent with you.

Na 'Aina Kai Botanical Gardens and Sculpture Park

808-828-0525.

www.naainakai.org.

4101 Wailapa Rd., Kilauea.

Open: Tues.–Fri. 9:30–1:30.

Price: $25–70, depending on type of tour.

Once the private playland of Ed and Joyce Doty, this 240-acre garden in the works since 1982 is now open to the public—by appointment only, that is. You'll see a variety of modern non-native introductions, designed with a clear—but manicured—eye. The garden offers six tours, varying in length (1 1/2–5 hours), price (see above), and type (stroll or covered carriage ride, formal or wild gardens, children's garden or waterfall-lagoon tours). Though quite pricey, there are 13 gardens with over 60 bronze statues often humorously placed throughout them. You can get lost in the Hedge Maze, or absorb yourself in the natural ponds, the 60,000 hardwood trees, the desert gardens, the bog house, the beaches and marshes (which are great for bird- and whale-watching), the orchid garden, or the children's garden—with a log cabin, a 16-foot bronze Jack and the Beanstalk sculpture in a pool, a train, a giant play structure, and tropical jungle. My favorite is the Wild Forest, which feels the most like Kaua'i even though none of the plants are native; here you get to see chocolate, cinnamon, ylang ylang, and nutmeg trees while birds sing and the wind blows through the palm leaves.

HISTORIC BUILDINGS

See Architecture.

LIBRARIES

Kaua'i public libraries offer a surplus of books and magazines about Hawaiian culture, story-time events for children, Internet access, teen and adult classes, film rentals, and historical information. Libraries are closed on weekends and major holidays. Call ahead for event details.

Hanapepe Public Library (808-335-8418).

Kapa'a Public Library (808-821-4422; 1464 Kuhio Hwy., Kapa'a).

Koloa Public Library (808-742-8455; located adjacent to Koloa School on Poipu Rd.).

Waioli Mission House.

Historic Walking Tours

You can get a color map to take a **Historic Hanapepe Walking Tour** (808-335-5944) for $2. Otherwise, you can easily tour the area yourself, since it is centered on Hanapepe Road. From the highway, drive over the 1938 bridge and head west; the last right is the west entrance onto Hanapepe Road. Park in town and wander past the buildings (described under Architecture), making your way toward the swinging bridge. Be sure to stop in at the **Taro Ko Chips Factory** (3940 Hanapepe Rd.) for some fresh taro chips.

An interesting stroll, offered by the Kaua'i Historical Society, is the **Kapa'a Town Walking Tour** (808-245-3373). The 90-minute exploration of the former sugar and pineapple region costs $15 for adults and $5 for children (at 10 AM and 4 PM on Tues., Thurs., and Sat.). You must make reservations. Local guides are knowledgeable about the area, Hawaiian culture, and history, plus they can tell you their favorite places to grab a plate lunch.

If you are engaged by the Waimea sugar history, you can take a guided walking tour of the once booming **Waimea Sugar Mill and Plantation** (808-335-2824; reservations required). Tours occur at 9 AM on Tues. and Sat. They last for approximately 90 minutes. It'll run you $10 for adults. Guides know a ton about the history of the area. Currently, the Faye family is working to preserve all the history of each family that lived here in a book. Not only do you get to explore the plantation, but you also see the old mill. It might help to know that your money goes to preserve this historic structure.

To learn about the historic buildings of Waimea, the **Waimea Visitors and Technology Center** (808-338-1332; 9565 Kaumuali'i Hwy.) offers free guided tours on Monday at 9:30 AM (reservations required). If you would rather go at it alone, see Architecture.

Lihu'e Public Library (808-241-3222; 4344 Hardy St., Lihu'e).

Princeville Public Library (808-826-4310; 4343 Emmalani Dr., Princeville). This is the only public library open on Saturday as well.

Waimea Public Library (808-338-6848).

Lu'au

What's a visit to Hawai'i without a lu'au? Once a spiritual event surrounding the sacrifice of a pig, cooked in an *'imu* pit overnight while tribe members chanted the hula to communicate with the gods, it's now a tourist affair. But a fun one, nonetheless. The Kaua'i-style lu'au has turned into a big business (with quite the hefty price tag). From the companies listed below, you can generally expect all-you-can-drink beer, wine, mai tais, and Blue Hawaiian bar, a hula lesson for the *keikis* willing to get on stage, a trio of musicians singing Don Ho's and Elvis's "Hawaiian" songs, an all-you-can-eat buffet including *kalua* pig, teriyaki chicken or beef, fish, taro, rice, macaroni salad, *lomi lomi* salad, *poi*, fresh fruit, *haupia*, and a variety of cakes. Plus, each lu'au has a version of the same show, which takes guests on a musical journey through the history of hula and the colonization of Kaua'i. Below are shows that I have attended and recommend for different reasons. The main draw when selecting your lu'au is, first and foremost: If you plan to drink, how close is it to your hotel? I have listed what each lu'au does well as well as those things that aren't so

A hula dancer at the Grand Hyatt Lu'au.

great so you can decide which type of experience you want. At the end of the day, they are all fun and they are all cheesy. Are they worth it? Yeah. Why not? Where else are you going to try *poi*?

EAST SHORE

Kilohana Plantation Lu'au

808-245-5608.
www.kilohanakauai.com/luau.
3-2087 Kaumuali'i Hwy., Lihu'e.
Tues. and Thurs., 6:30 PM.
Price: $65 adults; $61 teens; $35 kids.

With a new lu'au tent up and running, this giant lu'au caters mostly to cruise ship passengers. Food is prepared by Gaylord's restaurant (See chapter 6). So if you are looking for a good dining experience with a somewhat forgettable show, this is a good option on the east shore. They do have an *'imu* ceremony and, unlike the other lu'aus, they actually cook the fish in the pit as well. Located on the Kilohana Plantation property, you will be taken back in time to the plantation days, with a nice outdoor setting.

Smith's Family Garden Lu'au

808-821-6895.
www.smithskauai.com.
Wailua Marina State Park, Wailua.
Mon., Wed., Fri., 5 PM. Summer: Mon.–Fri.
Price: $63 adults; $27 ages 7–13; $17 ages 3–6.
Special Features: Seat reservations for parties of six or more.

This is the Las Vegas of lu'aus. It's set on big beautiful grounds, filled with peacocks, Japanese gardens, a false Easter Island head, a lake, and marked flora. They urge you to wander through the property before gathering in the shadows of Sleeping Giant Mountain to learn about the traditional *'imu* ceremony. Then guests are herded into the tent (go early to get a seat if you are a group of four or five and want to sit together) to be entertained by a family of musicians. Since there are so many people crammed into the tent, it might take a while to line up for dinner—but when you do, the food is decent and plentiful. Make sure to try the rice pudding, which they cook in the hearth with the pig. The show then takes place in a pavilion to which you are directed after dinner. Unfortunately, the performance is not the best for kids. While most lu'au shows are interactive, I always find this one is too long with not enough personality to it. In fact, it is pretty boring compared with other shows. Yes, they have the fireworks and the big lava with fire, but in terms of the music and dancing, there are much better choices. This is, however, a good option for people staying in the north or east shores.

Tihatu Hiva Pasefika Lu'au

808-823-0311.
www.resortquest.com.
Resortquest Kaua'i Beach at Makaiwa, 4-484 Kuhio Hwy., Kapa'a.
Nightly (except Mon.), 5:45 PM.
Price: $68 adults; $45 teens; $35 children.

Compared with other lu'aus, this company serves up a unique experience. Guests meet at a cocktail hour on the beach while musicians play, kids learn hula and get their faces painted, and the pig is presented (but not dug up). They then lead you (sort of like cows) through the hotel and into a circus tent in the parking lot (the lu'au used to take place in the Luau *Hale*, before the fire dancer burned it down). Guests are immediately led to the buffet line, which unfortunately is not the best (vegetarians: eat beforehand). Though they offer traditional takes on *kalua* pork, mango chicken, *lomi lomi*, and *poi*, the fare just wasn't tasty the last time I attended. Luckily, this lu'au is smaller, more intimate, and gives everything a visitor to Kaua'i might want—complete with coconut bikini tops, grass skirts, and a cheesy emcee who does costume changes and gets the audience involved. The show is almost the exact same as the Hyatt's (though cheaper), and is very entertaining with quality dancers.

SOUTH SHORE

Grand Hyatt Lu'au

808-742-1234.
www.kauai.hyatt.com.
1571 Poipu Rd., Koloa.
Sun. and Thurs., 5:30–8 PM.
Price: $75 adults; $65 ages 13–20; $37.50 ages 6–12.

Probably the largest lu'au on the island, the Grand Hyatt *Tihatu* Luau can seat up to 1,000 people. And since it takes place either in the garden (which is a million times better) or in the ballroom (which makes it feel like a bar mitzvah), you might want to call in advance—especially since this is one of the most expensive lu'aus on Kaua'i. A big bummer is that there is no *'imu* ceremony. That being said, staff are playful and make sure their energy and humor infect the room. Quickly, with the help of a free mai tai, beer, or wine, the room becomes a big party. This is necessary since, compared with the rest of the lua'us, the buffet is not the highlight. What makes this an experience is the show—maybe the best on Kaua'i. This big production, with great costumes and dancers and lots of drums, is great for kids and people who want a *show*. And worth the price of admission is the chance to watch the fire knife dancer, Benjy Keala Daliva Pomaika'i, who is the best I have ever seen,

Sheraton Surf to Sunset Oceanfront Lu'au

808-742-8205.
www.sheraton-kauai.com.
2440 Ho'onani Rd., Poipu.
Mon. and Fri., 5:30 PM.
Price: $75 adults; $37 ages 6–12.

Sheraton Kaua'i knows how to host a *lu'au*. They've got the location: on the beach; the food: some of the best selection and quality around; and an entertaining show (mostly this is because of the hysterically cheeseball emcee). Though there is no *'imu* ceremony, they make up for it in location. With only about 300 people lined along the beach, this is an excellent choice for both families and couples. Kids can play on the sand; new couples can take a sunset stroll; longtime couples can get silly on stiff mai tais. A highlight is the dinner musicians, who are easy on the ears. FYI: if you aren't interested in paying for the food and drinks, you can walk on the beach and get a free show.

Lifting a pig out of an 'imu pit is tradition for a luau.

Princeville Hotel Beachside Lu'au
808-826-9644.
www.princevillehotelhawaii.com/de_luau.
5520 Ka Hoku Rd., Princeville.
Mon. and Thurs., 6–8 PM.
Price: $99 adults; $90 teens and seniors (65-plus); $45 ages 5–12.

The only lu'au option on the north shore, set in the pool area of the Princeville Hotel, just a few steps from the ocean, make this an excellent choice for people staying up north. Though the show could use a lot of work (it actually was quite boring at times), the *'imu* ceremony and the buffet are the best on the island. Offering historical information throughout the evening, this is a good option for adults or people on honeymoons—especially since it is the perfect place to watch the sunset. Rumor has it that when the hotel is going through renovations, the lu'au won't operate as frequently, if at all.

MUSEUMS

Since rain on Kaua'i is guaranteed (a sorry fact, but true), having a number of museums to explore can keep you entertained until the sun returns. Kaua'i is not known for its world-class art exhibits (for modern art, see Galleries, and chapter eight); rather, most of the museums reflect historical information, from sugar plantation tours to tracing the path of native inhabitants. In this section, I have included farm and plantation tours. Though they might not be considered museums, they do offer rare glimpses into the cultural history and modern workings of the island.

EAST SHORE

Blair Estate Organic Coffee Farm

808-822-4495.
www.blairestatecoffee.com.
6200-B Kawaihau Rd., Kapa'a.

Movie Tours

Driving around Kaua'i, you might have a sense of déjà vu. That mountain might seem familiar, or that beach, seascape, or rope swing may give you the nagging feeling you've seen it before. Well, that's probably because you *have* seen it, in a movie. Kaua'i has been (and still is) the set for the many films listed below (and much more). Often it stands in for South America, Vietnam, or fictional lands. If you are interested in a comprehensive history of films on Kaua'i, pick up Chris Cook's *Kaua'i Movie Book*. Here are some films and their set locations that are easy to recognize or visit.

Raiders of the Lost Ark—Kong Mountain and the Wailua River act as South America.
Honeymoon in Vegas—Lihu'e Airport and 'Anini Beach.
Fantasy Island—You'll recognize Wailua Falls from the opening credits.
Hook—Kaua'i plays the fictional Never Land.
South Pacific—Lumaha'i Beach is where Mitzi Gaynor washed that man out of her hair; and Hanalei Bay was the backdrop of the fictional Bali Hai—you might recognize Makana Mountain.
Blue Hawaii—Coco Palms.
Jurassic Park—Manawaiopuna Falls was the entrance to the park.
Outbreak—Kamokila Hawaiian Village plays Africa.
Gilligan's Island—Moloa'a Bay is where the pilot was filmed.
King Kong—He lived on the Na Pali Coast.
Flight of the Intruder—Kaua'i played Vietnam.
Lilo and Stitch—Okay, I know it's a cartoon, but Hanapepe plays a large role in the film.
    If you want a guided movie tour of Kaua'i film sets and their history check out:

Hawaii Movie Tours

808-822-1192 or 800-628-8432.
www.hawaiimovietour.com.
P.O. Box 659, Kapaa.
Price: $111 adults; $92 children. Includes lunch, hotel pickup and drop off (though they joke that if you don't sing, you won't get back).

This outfit offers 4x4 tours of the famous movie sights of Kaua'i. Not only will you watch the films as you are driving from location to location, but you are also given a fairly all-encompassing tour of Kaua'i. It is a good way to learn the layout of the island (if you can take a bunch of people singing TV show tunes). Highlights include a trip out to Hanalei Bay, Moloa'a Bay, and a visit to Elvis's Coco Palms bungalow.

Open: Tours Mon., Wed., and Sat., 9 AM, by appointment only.
Price: Free.

Though this farm is not open to the public for retail sales, visitors can tour the property for free and learn about the rigorous trials of growing organic coffee on Kaua'i. Les and Gigi Trent opened this coffee farm in 2001. And though it is a small working farm (which means you should not drop by unannounced), it is the only organic coffee farm on the island. Learn the process of harvesting coffee and of course taste some of the varieties.

Grove Farm Homestead

808-245-3202.
P.O. Box 1631, Lihu'e.
Open: Tours Mon., Wed., Thurs., 10 AM and 1 PM. Reservations recommended.
Price: $10 donation.

Coffee as it grows on the tree looks more like a cherry than a bean.

History buffs will love this trip into Kaua'i's past with an intimate view into G. N. Wilcox's 1864 plantation. These well-preserved artifacts are a living museum of the sugar baron and his extended family. *Wilcox* is a name you will see around the island a lot, and after going on this tour you'll understand why. You learn about the history and growth of sugar in Kaua'i, as well as how Nawiliwili Harbor (finished in 1934 because G. N. wanted a way to ship sugar) came to be; why the hospital is named for one of the Wilcox sisters; and much more. This two-hour tour, led by well-informed volunteers, takes you through the working farm (which has lovely fruit and vegetable gardens, chickens, pigs, and goats) and gives you an intimate tour of the plantation houses. The three houses are in amazing condition and show how people lived in the late 1800s and early 1900s. You see G. N. Wilcox's simple abode, the main house that he donated to his brother's family (which has the largest collection of Hawaiiana books on the island, in addition to some unusual artifacts—an original shave ice maker, a coffee grinder, and a rain gauge), and a plantation worker's home. Plus, you'll be invited into the kitchen to taste some delicious sugar cookies baked in the original wood-burning stove. As one of the oldest sugar plantations left on the island, this entire property is rich with history, from the train tracks that guard the front entrance to the kamani tree in front of the main house.

Kamokila Hawaiian Village

Off H 580, on your left, just after Opaeka'a Falls.
Open: Mon.–Sat., 9–5.
Price: $5 adults; $3 children.

The Wilcox Legacy

It seems everywhere you look in Kaua'i, the name *Wilcox* pops up—on the hospital door, in the news, on schools. One of the first missionary families to arrive in Kaua'i, the Wilcoxes quickly integrated themselves into the culture by living in the Waioli Mission House, offering church services, schooling kids and adults, and becoming active presences in the community.

However, it was G. N. Wilcox, the son of Lucy and Abner Wilcox, who made the biggest splash in island life. His vision and financial backing made it possible for him to create one of the most lucrative sugar plantations on Kaua'i—Grove Farm. Not only do the sugar fields, plantation houses, and gardens spread through the heart of Lihu'e, but until Steve Case of AOL fame bought the land, the Grove Farm Company also owned the length of Maha'ulepu Beach. Mr. Wilcox was the spearhead for creating the Nawiliwili Harbor as the major port of the island. Plus, he was a prominent member of the Kaua'i government.

However, he was also a generous and humble man who passed these traits to his extended family. He invited his brother's family to his plantation and gave them the main house while he lived in a small, simple cottage next door. The six children of this family, learning from their generous uncle, grew to be entrepreneurs, teachers, nurses, and prominent members in society. The youngest of the sons, Gaylord, ran the Grove Farm plantation until he created the Kilohana Plantation a couple of miles away. Now Gaylord's son owns Hukilau Lanai, a popular restaurant on the Coconut Coast. Elsie Wilcox opened a public health office on the grounds; later, the Wilcox Hospital was named for her. Mabel, a teacher, was responsible for keeping the legacy of the family alive by preserving the Grove Farm Homestead and Waioli Mission House, then creating a nonprofit organization to bring visitors to honor her uncle.

The Grove Farm Plantation tour treats visitors to a glimpse of the past.

Built on the site of an actual *ali'i* (or king's) village, right on the Wailua River is this re-creation of an ancient community, including birthstones, eating huts, medicine quarters, sleeping huts, and an assembly hall. The interiors of the grass huts show off tools, cooking utensils, and possible room layouts. Make sure to try your hand at the athletic games along the river and you'll surely respect the strength and ability of the ancient spear throwers. Pick up the information sheet about each site, including local plants and fruit found here. The family who owns and runs the village are very helpful and will answer any questions you may have about ancient culture. I recommend visiting after you explore the Kaua'i Museum, so that you understand a bit of ancient Kaua'i history. I once brought friends who didn't know anything about this island's rich legacy, and they weren't as impressed as I always am at this detailed exhibit of ancient life and times. However, they had seen the film *Outbreak* and were impressed to note that this is the site of the African village in the start of the movie. You can also rent kayaks here to meander down the Wailua River, past the rope swing, and all the way to Secret Falls.

Kaua'i Historical Society

808-245-3373.
www.kauaihistoricalsociety.org.
4396 Rice St., Lihu'e.
Open: 8–4 weekdays, by appointment.
Price: Free.

If you have become infatuated with Kaua'i history and want to do some research, or view an extensive array of archival material including photographs, maps, and ancient objects, visit Kaua'i's historical society. This organization works hard to preserve historical sites. Then they present their knowledge to the public in a variety of local educational programs. No other organization has worked harder to retain the cultural history and integrity of this island and her people.

✪ Kaua'i Museum

808-245-6931.
www.kauaimuseum.org.
4428 Rice St., Lihu'e.
Open: Mon.–Fri., 9–4; Sat., 10–4. Free the first Saturday of each month.
Price: $7 adults; $3 teens; $1 children.
Special Features: No cameras or cell phones allowed. Handicapped accessible.

On your first couple of days on the island, I recommend a stop at this small but interesting museum. The building itself is a

Though not an actual ancient village, Kamokila Village is built on the site of actual remains.

relic from 1924 that served as the main public library until 1970, when Juliet Wichman created the museum. With only two buildings and a friendly staff (who offer free guided tours with the price of admission at 10:30 AM on Tues., Wed., and Thurs.), you'll probably get through the museum quickly. They often have interesting rotating exhibits in the first main building, but the permanent exhibit on Kaua'i natural and social history is not to be missed. Incorporating film, pictures, paintings, and real artifacts from native culture, the exhibit showcases Kaua'i's entire history. It begins with how the land was formed, explaining the geographic regions, coral formations, weather patterns, and native species. Turn the corner and you immerse yourself in the social history, from native weaponry to jewelry, canoes, paintings of famous kings and chiefs, and a fun instrument section where they encourage kids and adults to play. You'll glimpse artifacts of colonization, including excerpts of Captain Cook's diary and artifacts from the Russian influence. Upstairs offers a look into missionary living, the rise and fall of the sugar industry, and a re-creation of how sugar plantation workers lived. The museum also has one of the best gift shops on the island, which you can enter for no charge.

WEST SHORE

Faye Museum
808-338-1625.
Waimea Plantation Cottages, 9400 Kaumuali'i Hay., Waimea.
Open: Daily 9–9.
Price: Free.

This small collection of artifacts, maps, and photos transports you into the history of the Faye family and life on their sugar plantation. H. P. Faye was a Norwegian immigrant who came to Kaua'i in 1880. He grew his small sugar mill into one of the largest sugar companies in Kaua'i: Kekaha Sugar. He also created an innovative ditch system and drainage canals, rerouting water back into swamps. The museum probably isn't worth a special trip out to Waimea Plantation Cottages, but if you happen to be in the area and are interested in archives of a time gone by, take a peek.

Gay and Robinson Sugar Plantation Tours
808-335-2824.
www.gandrtours-kauai.com.
2 Kaumakani Ave., Waimea.
Open: Mon.–Fri., 8 AM–4 PM. Tours run at 8:45 AM and 12:45 PM, Mon.–Fri.
Tours: $30. *Olokele* Tours: $60. Reservations required for both.

Driving down the dirt road to the Gay and Robinson Sugar Plantation headquarters, you'll travel back in time to what the majority of the west side must have looked like before the slow death of the sugar industry: lines of small plantation workers' homes, shady trees, kids playing outside, and everything covered by a layer of red dirt. The Gay and Robinson families must have done something right. They are the sole survivors of the Kaua'i sugar industry. Not only do they run this still-operating sugar mill, but they also own the illusive Ni'ihau (see chapter nine). The visitor center/gift shop has a decent selection of sweet products, plus a concise description of the cultivation of sugar. For a more in-depth exploration and understanding of the process churning out that sweet white powder, take a fascinating two-hour tour of the mill. You must wear long pants and closed-toed shoes; and

The Death of Agriculture on Kaua'i

The agricultural community of Kaua'i is experiencing a slow creeping death. It started with the rice industry soon after it began in the late 1880s, and has now worked its way through the majority of farming communities on the island, including sugar, coffee, guava, pineapple, koa wood, and other food products. Once a rich agricultural and self-sustaining land, the Kaua'i people now rely on tourism to keep the dollars coming in.

Some say the easy cure is for the population to embrace tourism (which it has). Many farmers turned their farms into unlicensed bed & breakfasts to survive; however the state now wants them to shut their doors and make room for low-income housing (an ongoing debate that at press time was still being fought). Unfortunately, when farmers turn their farms into tourist destinations, indigenous people lose jobs and cannot afford to live here. And even worse, some argue, is that the cost of land is rising so high that local people cannot afford to buy property. It is a tragedy when native Hawaiians are run off their own land because they can't sustain an income.

An even greater travesty, some say, is the arrival of corporate giants growing genetically modified crops. The topic is *hush-hush* around the island. No one really knows specifically who's here or what they're growing. But rumor has it the Monsanto crew (and a few other big guns) grows GMO corn, soybeans, and maybe even tobacco. Organic farmers are pissed; they say runoff infects their crops, destroys the soil, and generally taints the growing conditions.

On a positive note, you can still visit some of the old plantations listed in this chapter. And supporting local agriculture is as easy as stopping on the side of the road to buy papaya from a family farm.

make sure whatever you wear, you don't mind it getting covered in red dirt. The best time to visit is when the mill is actually working, April through October. For the more adventurous, Gay and Robinson Tours offers an ATV tour of their large property ($99–145, reservations required), leading you up to a mountain pool, where you can wash that red dirt off your face.

Kaua'i Coffee Estate

808-335-5497.
www.kauaicoffee.com.
1 Numila Rd., Kalaheo.
Take H 540 and follow the signs to the estate.
Open: Daily 9–5.
Price: Free.

The largest coffee plantation in the United States (3,400 acres) offers a self-guided tour of the grounds. Here you can wander through the 0.5-mile coffee-processing maze and learn about the cultivation of coffee from the plant to the cup. Easy to navigate and offering lovely views of the Pacific past the lines of green coffee trees, the estate is worth a stop for coffee lovers. Especially because you can sample all the free coffee you want and be buzzing around the lanai and gift shop until closing time. The museum itself is small and disappointing, especially after you've wandered through the hands-on mock coffee plant. But it is doubtful that you'll get out without buying some of this great coffee.

Koke'e Natural History Museum

808-335-9975.
www.kokee.org.
Koke'e State Park.
Open: Daily, 10–4.
Price: Donations accepted.

This is the best place to learn about the natural history of Kaua'i. The 55-year-old non-profit museum has an interesting exhibit showcasing native birds and plants, as well as material focusing on weather patterns on the island, including an intense visual display about Hurricane 'Iniki. You'll also notice the artifacts of ancient Hawaiian culture—which, if you haven't made it to the Kaua'i Museum, will be an interesting glimpse into how native Hawaiians used to cook, hunt, and create art. The museum staff are very knowledgeable about the park. You can get detailed trail maps here, plus they have an extensive book and craft shop. The nonprofit hand of the organization also works to reduce the impact of invasive plant and animal species in this fragile environment.

West Kaua'i Technology and Visitor Center

808-338-1332.
www.wkbpa.org/visitorcenter.html.
9565 Kaumuali'i Hwy., Waimea.
Open: Mon.–Fri., 9:30–5.
Price: Free.

In addition to offering free **Historic Waimea Walking Tours** (see the sidebar), this technological museum exhibits the history of sugar in Waimea Town, plus the impact of technology on the area. They sell books, lead lei-making classes, and host community events. The nonprofit leg sponsors the oldest event on Kaua'i, the Waimea Town Celebration (see Seasonal Events). You can also get online for free here.

NORTH SHORE

Ho'opulapula Haraguchi Rice Mill Tour

808-651-3399.
www.haraguchiricemill.org.
P.O. Box 427, Hanalei.
Tours: Summer Thursdays, 10 AM. By reservation only.
Price: $65, including a taro-heavy lunch.

This is the only legal way to enter the Hanalei National Wildlife Refuge. And since it's the only remaining rice mill in Hawai'i, touring the facility is quite a treat. The mill, owned by the Haraguchi family, is listed on the National Register of Historic Places and dates back to the late 1880s. On the tour, you will learn about Hawai'i's agricultural and cultural history by viewing endangered native waterbirds, exploring the cultivation and uses of taro, plus, of course, wandering around the historic rice mill. Tours are intimate and led by one of the Haraguchi family members. Though the cost is steep, know that your money goes to keeping this nonprofit historical site alive. Plus, not many people get to brag about seeing the birds inside the refuge.

Kilauea Point National Wildlife Refuge & Lighthouse
See chapter 7.

Waiʻoli Mission House Museum
808-245-3202.
4050 Nawiliwili Rd., just behind the green Waiʻoli Church.
Tours: Mon., Wed., and Thu., 10 AM and 1 PM.
Price: Free (donations gratefully accepted). Reservations required.

The first missionaries to arrive to Kauaʻi—the Alexanders—built this missionary house in 1837. Nestled in the center of town, in the shadow of giant mountains with waterfalls streaming down their edges, you can't miss the New England–style buildings, or the expansive green lawn that beckons you to sprawl out. The mission house was the home of Abner and Lucy Wilcox (see the sidebar), whose family later created the nonprofit organization that preserves and presents this historical property to the public. Restored in 1921, the house is still outfitted with Wilcox furnishings: books, pictures, paintings, furniture, dishes, and artifacts from a time long gone.

NIGHTLIFE

Unlike Oʻahu and Maui, Kauaʻi nightlife is pretty uninspired. That is not to say that late-night fun doesn't exist, but I have heard friends boast that the most happening night on the island is '70s Night at the Point. So if you are looking for nightclubs and rockin' shows, head to another island, but if you want a civilized place for a drink and some live music, here are some places to explore.

For traditional island-style music, find the weekly **Slack Key Guitar** show presented by Aloha Plenty (808-826-1469). These are usually fun local events held in community centers or restaurants. Check local papers or the *Essential Kauaʻi* for listings. Names to look out for are Sandy and Doug McMaster (who play twice a week in Hanalei) and Ken Emerson (who usually plays at the Princeville Resort). Or on Friday evenings, the **Hanapepe Café** (808-335-5011) presents local musicians (like Cindy Combs and Hal Kinnaman) on slack key or ʻukulele.

For other live music performances, the **Kauaʻi Concert Association** (808-245-7464; www.kauai-concert.org) offers shows year-round at the Kauaʻi Community College Performing Arts Center. Occasionally they will get some big names to appear, so check local listings.

If you don't want to splurge for a luʻau, there are a variety of free hula shows throughout the week at the **Coconut Marketplace** (Wed. 5 PM), **Kukui Grove Shopping Center** (Fri. 7 PM) and at the **Poipu Shopping Village** (Tues. and Thurs. 5 PM).

The east shore nightlife scene most deftly combines local culture with tourism. In the Coconut Marketplace, you'll likely hear the karaoke before you spot **Tradewinds** (808-882-1621), a local dive bar with drink specials and lots of TVs (plus outdoor mall seating). Here you might also visit the **Kauaʻi Hula Girl**, a peppy bar and grill that presents local rock bands, serves beer, cocktails, and Hawaiian food, and attracts a local rock scene.

A favorite, serving up live entertainment with great food in an open-air back garden, is **Caffe Coco** (808-822-7990; 4-369 Kuhio Hwy., Wailua); bring your own beer and wine.

Another civilized place for a drink and live music is the **Hukilau Lanai** (808-822-0600; Kaua'i Coast Resort at Beachboy), which is set in an open-air lobby of the hotel, with local musicians serenading you while you sip on creative cocktails. Or you might pop into **Coconuts** (808-823-8777; 4-919 Kuhio Hwy., Wailua) for a nightcap.

The **Kuhio Lounge** (808-823-6000; Aloha Beach Resort, 3-5920 Kuhio Hwy., Wailua) serves tropical drinks and often has local bands performing in a laid-back atmosphere. For a touristy affair, complete with fried food, a beach view, and a fake lava rock waterfall, head to **Duke's Barefoot Bar** (808-246-9599; Kaua'i Marriott Resort, Kalapaki Beach), where they sometimes have live music and always serve big tropical drinks.

On the south shore, the **Grand Hyatt Resort** (808-742-1234; 1571 Poipu Rd., Koloa) presents nightly live music, torch-lighting ceremonies, and hula shows at its **Seaview Terrace** cocktail bar. Often you'll catch local musicians performing during the sunset. Another place to hear live music with cocktails in hand is at their **Stevenson's Library**. Here you can eat sushi, explore live jazz, and play pool or chess. Lacking the giant windows elsewhere in the resort, this lounge feels like it could be anywhere in the world.

Talked about as the place to be on the south shore, **The Point** (808-742-9488; Sheraton Kaua'i, 2440 Ho'onani Rd., Poipu) offers a variety of entertaining nights, from '70s Disco Night to modern DJs. Friday nights tend to be the rowdiest. The cover varies, depending on the entertainment. There is also an outdoor area, which is my favorite place on the island to have a sunset cocktail.

For other restaurants with bars, check out the **Beach House** (808-742-1424; 5022 Lawa'i Rd., Poipu), where you can drink in the open-air bar and stare at the setting sun or surfers. Locals love **Keoki's Paradise** (808-742-7535; Poipu Shopping Village), where you can drink reasonably priced tropical drinks in a tropical setting and order good fried pupus.

The only worthy watering hole on the west shore is the **Waimea Brewing Co.** (808-338-9733; Waimea Plantation Cottages, 9400 Kaumuali'i Hwy.). This brewery serves up locally made beers on a wooden terrace and is open late on weekends.

The north shore vibe mellows out a bit and separates into two camps: classy tourist lounges and funky surfer spots. A popular nightspot is **Sushi Blues** (808-826-9701; Ching Young Village), where you'll often find live jazz and blues pumping out of the open-air upstairs restaurant. Another local favorite, popular with sports enthusiasts and those who like loud rock music (often performed by local bands), is the **Hanalei Gourmet** (808-826-2524; Hanalei Center).

An institution in Hanalei is **Tahiti Nui** (808-826-6277; Tahiti Nui Building on the ocean side of Kuhio Hwy.), open daily 11 AM–2 AM. Since 1964 tourists have come for impromptu lu'au shows, local music, and good food (which currently includes Chinese food and pizza). Now that the original owners have passed away, there isn't much left of the lu'au culture . . . except for loud drunk people, traditional food, happy hours, and live music, which I suppose is a lu'au without the glitz.

In Princeville, the **Happy Talk Lounge** (808-826-6522; Hanalei Bay Resort) offers some of the best views to drink by. Often they will have live Hawaiian music, and they serve food off a bar menu. At the Princeville Hotel, the palatial **Living Room** (808-826-9644) offers guests an indoor view of Hanalei Bay with plenty of expensive drinks, chess sets, and mellow musicians to keep you entertained. And if you want to keep the party going, head over to the **Landing Pad** (808-826-2788; Princeville Airport, 3541 Kuhio Hwy.), where you'll find live music, karaoke, or DJs spinning late into the night.

When the sun sets, head out to a beach bar to toast the end of the day.

If you are staying in Haena, you might want to visit **Mediterranean Gourmet** (808-826-9875; Hanalei Colony Resort) after dark, where they have live music and a couple of fun belly-dancing nights, drink specials (like half-priced bottles of wine), and spectacular views of the Pacific.

THEATER

Though people don't often come to Kaua'i for the theatrical events, there are a few interesting troupes performing live theater. The **Kaua'i Community Players** (808-245-7700; www.kauaicommunityplayers.org) serves up children's and adult theater performances year-round. The **Hawai'i Children's Theater** (808-246-8985) offers performances fit for the *keikis*. And the **Kaua'i Community College Performing Arts Center** (808-245-8270; www.kauai.hawaii.edu/pac) has year-round events on the college campus. Often local libraries offer story time for kids as well.

The Hilton Kaua'i Beach offers the **South Pacific Dinner Show** (808-246-0111) on Mon. and Wed. at 5:45 PM. This all-you-can-eat buffet and show will run you $83 a person. If you are aching to revisit the Bali Hai–themed playbook, look around in local tourist magazines and brochure; you'll be able to find discounted tickets.

SEASONAL EVENTS

As in most tight-knit communities, Kaua'i's seasonal events celebrate local heritage, with an emphasis on Hawaiian arts, crafts, and history. Families use these events as excuses to get together and talk story, and of course eat a ton. These events are pretty low-key and always act as a reminder of how small the Kaua'i community really is.

January
Kaua'ian Days
808-338-0111.

This weeklong festival honoring the diversity and unity of the Kaua'i people takes place at various locations around the island. It's packed with plenty of entertainment, Hawaiian games for children, sporting events, workshops, dinners, and cultural festivities—Kaua'i pride at its finest.

February
Waimea Town Celebration
808-338-1332.
www.wkbpa.org/visitorcenter.html.
9565 Kaumuali'i Hwy., Waimea.

This two-day event brings over 10,000 people to the town of Waimea to celebrate the rich history of the area. Presented by the West Kaua'i Technology and Visitor Center, this event is held on the Friday and Saturday following the President's Day weekend in February. The oldest festival on the island presents live music from local musicians, 'ukulele and ice-cream-eating contests, tons of food and drink. Plus there is an outrigger canoe race, a

"Fun Run," softball tournaments, and cowboy events. Local nonprofits and schools hold fund-raisers here, and you are likely to get to sample some excellent local-style food. Like most Hawaiian events, the party is likely to get rowdy later in the day.

March

Prince Kuhio Celebration of the Arts
808-240-6369.

All the *keikis* get the day off school to celebrate the birthday and birthplace of the first Hawaiian state representative. The ceremony at Prince Kuhio Park is full of flowers and song. And afterward, organizers re-create an ancient Hawaiian village to explore. All week leading up to the event, a variety of concerts and art exhibits are held. During this time, beaches tend to get crowded with locals barbecuing.

Garden Island Orchid Society Annual Spring Fantasy Show
In Hanapepe, the Orchid Society presents an exquisite two-day showcase of orchids and crafts. Local artisans and gardeners are there to chat with. Usually the event takes place at the same time as the Art Walk and makes for a festive evening.

April

Royal Pa'ina
808-245-3373.

The Kaua'i Historical Society celebrates the multi-ethnic heritage of the island with local entertainment and food.

May

Lei Day Celebration
808-245-6931.
www.kauaimuseum.org.
Kaua'i Museum, 4428 Rice St., Lihu'e.

May Day is Lei Day at the Kaua'i Museum. You'll get to sample local food, marvel at the vibrant colors and tropical fragrances of the leis on display, and purchase handmade crafts.

Mother's Day Orchid Show
This two-day orchid show brings together hundreds of varieties of these unique flowers to view and purchase. Expect lectures and demonstrations about orchid care and biology. It's held at the Kukui Grove Shopping Center on Mother's Day weekend.

Kaua'i Polynesian Festival
808-335-6466.
www.kauai-polyfest.com.

This four-day Memorial Day weekend event features a Polynesian dance competition and exhibitions, cultural workshops, plus arts and crafts. The whole event starts with a giant lu'au;

throughout the weekend you'll see Samoan fire knife dancers, Poi Ball, and Hawaiian hula workshops with house drummers. There is always a wealth of food and crafts to sample.

Banana Poka Round Up

808-335-9975.
www.kokee.org.
Koke'e Natural History Museum, Koke'e State Park.

The annual forest education fair, featuring Hawaiian music, environmental exhibitions, forest craft workshops, and family activities, is a treat. What better way to spend a part of your Memorial Day weekend than up in the mountains celebrating the beautiful landscape and eating a ton?

June

Taste of Hawai'i

808-821-0259.

They should call this Yum-Fest. Over 50 of Hawai'i's most famous chefs prepare innovative dishes while guests are entertained at Smith's Tropical Paradise in Wailua. All money supports local Rotary projects.

Kamehameha Day Parade and Ho'olaule'a

808-586-0333.

The grandiose floral parade features entertainment, arts and crafts, and island-style food favorites to celebrate the birthday of King Kamehameha.

A courting peacock at the Smith Family Garden in Wailua.

Kauaʻi Hula Exhibition
808-335-6466.

An annual evening of Polynesian history presented through dance. Guests will watch some of the island's best hula dancers while learning about cultural chants and history, plus sampling some great food. Held at the Kauaʻi War Memorial Convention Hall.

July
Concert in the Sky
808-245-7727.

Every Fourth of July, residents and visitors gather at Vidinha Stadium 3–9:30 PM. Sample local food from Kauaʻi's top restaurants and hotels, enjoy live entertainment, and watch an aerial fireworks show set to music.

Koloa Plantation Days
808-822-0734.
www.koloaplantationdays.com.

This nine-day festival on Kauaʻi's south shore celebrates the rich history of Koloa, the once shimmering sugar plantation town. The festival offers free family-oriented sports events such as tennis, softball, rodeo, and sailing canoe races. Plus there are historic walks, block parties, a craft fair, Polynesian dancing, watercolor workshops, entertainment, and, as at all Kauaʻi festivals, a slew of food.

August
Kauaʻi Music Festival
www.kauaimusicfestival.com.

This four-day event puts on songwriting workshops, panel discussions with professional producers and musicians, and concerts each night. People come from all over the world to participate in the festival. Visitors can purchase tickets for nightly concerts or attend one of the nightly open-mike nights.

Kauaʻi County Farm Bureau Fair
808-828-2120.

A four-day family event held at Vidinha Stadium in Lihuʻe each year. This celebration of agriculture is packed with floral and cooking demonstrations, hula exhibitions, a petting zoo, and tons of fresh local food.

September
Aloha Festivals
808-634-5352; to purchase a program guide, call 808-589-1771.
www.alohafestivals.com.

If you are planning to be on the island in late August through mid-September, consider ordering your Aloha Festival Ribbon. Not only do you help fund the statewide music, dance, and culture festival, but you also have free access to all events. The festival organizes luʻaus, storytelling events, and art exhibits islandwide.

Annual Kaua'i Mokihana Festival
808-822-2166.
www.mokihana.kauai.net.

This popular annual weeklong event features a variety of local and ethnic demonstrations, concerts, and competitions. Honoring the seed of Kaua'i's island lei, you'll get to experience the Kaua'i Composers Contest, a hula competition for men and women, beauty contests, lectures and workshops on Kaua'i's heritage, and excellent handmade arts and crafts. With a variety of venues and admission costs, you will want to check local listings for event details.

Matsuri Kaua'i
808-822-5353.

At the end of September, Kaua'i celebrates its Japanese lineage with a full day of Japanese cultural exhibits, music, and dance. Both island residents and special guest performers from Japan (often Taiko drummers) showcase *mochi* pounding, kimono dressing, and the traditional tea ceremony. Also bunches of games, crafts, and delicious food.

October

Coconut Festival
808-651-3273.
www.kbakauai.org.

If you like coconuts (or coconut products), you don't want to miss this popular two-day festival honoring the hardheaded fruit. Held in the heart of the Coconut Coast at Kapa'a Beach Park, this festival emphasizes the cultural, historical, and social significance of the coconut: Crafters sell products, chefs prepare delicious coconut dishes, musicians perform all day, and kids and adults can participate in crafts, contests, and games.

Aloha Festivals Hawaiiana Festivals
808-240-6669.

This four-day festival, held at the Grand Hyatt Kaua'i Resort & Spa, celebrates all things Hawaiian. From crafts to demonstrations, educational displays to a lu'au complete with traditional food and entertainment, this is a fun (and fancy) way to learn more about the cultural history of the Kaua'i people. You'll get to observe lauhala weaving, stone carving, lei making, and more.

Eo'e Emalani I Alaka'i
808-335-9975.
www.kokee.org.

For the past 20 years, hula *halaus* from all over the state have tramped up to the meadows in Koke'e State Park to participate in this large dance festival. Not only will you be immersed in nature, but you'll also get to watch some of the most talented dancers around. This free event also offers a royal procession, entertainment, crafts, and cultural demonstrations.

November

Hawaiian Slack-Key Guitar Festival
808-239-4336.

Hawai'i's traditional folk music, performed by the best slack key guitar musicians in the state, is honored in this five-hour festival. A free event, held at the Kaua'i Marriott Resort in Lihu'e, it offers a rare glimpse of all these great masters together in one room.

Hawai'i International Film Festival
808-528-FILM.
www.hiff.org.

This film festival features filmmakers from Asia, the Pacific Islands, and the United States. For the first two weeks in November, you'll get to watch movies with cross-cultural themes—plus this is the only time you can brag that you are watching films on Kaua'i before anyone else. This event usually takes place at the Old Waimea Theater.

PGA Grand Slam of Golf, Poipu, Kaua'i
800-PGA-TCKT or 808-742-8711.
www.pga.com.

The Poipu Bay Golf Course has hosted the PGA Grand Slam of Golf for the last decade and a half. All eyes are on Kaua'i as the winners of the major championships (the Masters, the US Open, the British Open, and the PGA Championship) compete for the million-dollar prize.

December

Lights on Rice Parade
808-828-0014.

On the first day of December, the holidays arrive on Kaua'i. Even though there is no snow and you have spent the day on the beach, at night one of the most festive occasions anywhere takes place: a parade of lights down the center of Rice Street in Lihu'e. The opening ceremony brings thousands of people downtown, so make sure you get there early enough for good seating. During the month of December, it seems the entire island is shimmering with lights.

Holiday Hula Celebration
808-335-6466.

This evening of hula with the *Na Hula 'O Kaohikukapulani* is guaranteed to be a festive event. Combining traditional dance with holiday cheer, plus a silent auction and pupus, this mid-December fun evening kicks off the holiday cheer.

New Year's Eve Celebration
Fireworks on New Year's Eve are a Hawai'i tradition. You'll hear and see fireworks exploding from every beach (and neighborhood) around. Even better, the Poipu Beach Park presents a large-scale fireworks show at midnight.

For more information about events, contact the **Kaua'i Visitor Bureau** (800-262-1400; 4334 Rice St., #101, Lihu'e).

5

SACRED SITES AND NATURAL WONDERS

Na Pana Kaulana o Kaua'i

Ancient Kaua'i was a rich society: awash with mythical (and entertaining) legends, innovative agricultural and sewage technology, and organized (though quite barbaric) leadership. The Polynesian islanders believed that the land was rich with gods and goddesses, and created sacred spaces to honor them. Forests, rocks, trees, waterfalls, caves, and the sea were manifestations of these gods. The ancients built temples to worship them, and you'll find evidence embedded within the landscape throughout the island. Today there are a variety of sacred spaces you can visit in Kaua'i, namely the *heiau* and natural wonders. All carry religious and spiritual power for the Kaua'i people and should be treated with the greatest respect (see the sidebar for guidelines to visiting a *heiau*).

HEIAU AND ANCIENT SACRED SITE LOCATIONS

EAST SHORE

Many of the ancient Kaua'i people settled along the Wailuanuiaho'ano, the great Wailua River basin, in the ancient kingdom of Puna. Religious, social, and political events took place in the stretch between Wailua Bay and Mount Wai'ale'ale, with mountains and waterfalls hugging the kingdom to the north and south. Along this stretch are seven *heiaus* that were reserved exclusively for the use of *ali'i* and high priests. Most of these are visible from the H 580 roadside, or a short walk off it. In 1962, the Wailua Complex of *Heiau* became a National Historical Landmark.

Visiting a *Heiau*

A *heiau* is an ancient temple built of rectangular lava rocks, fit together so adeptly that many walls still stand today. They used to be filled with palm leaves, wood, grasses, and sacred objects. Though they may look like a pile of rocks to you, often overgrown by brush or seemingly forgotten, remember that these are religious sites, sacred to Hawaiians. They are fragile and cannot be replaced. So please honor the suggestions listed below.

- View the *heiau* from the exterior. Do not climb on or over the rock walls; they may collapse.
- Do not excavate, destroy, or alter any historic site on state land or you will be fined $10,000.
- Do not leave offerings or trash at a *heiau* structure. Coins, candles, incense, and similar items cause long-term damage.

An example of a heiau-type rock formation at Limahuli Garden.

Kukui *Heiau* (oceanfront on the Lae Nani condominium property). Once the Kukui *Heiau* was a departure and arrival point for travelers. At night, fire torches (made of kukui nut trees) pointed out the way for canoes. Now this once bustling port is little more than stacked lava rocks on a beach overlooking the grand Pacific.

Hikina Akala *Heiau* (on the ocean side of Leho Dr. and H 56). The name translates as "rising of the sun," which is a beautiful symbol for all this *heiau* represents. Anyone who had broken a *kapu* (taboo) could safely enter this place of refuge without the pursuer following. The wrongdoer could then make offerings to the gods and, after a few days, resume her or his life.

Malae *Heiau* (on the mountain side of H 56, along the Wailua River, near the Leho Drive turnoff). Anthropologists believe this is the first recorded Menehune *heiau* because of the type of stonework here, uncommon in other parts of Hawai'i. This is one of Kaua'i's largest *heiaus*, with walls reaching up to 13 feet high. Unfortunately, the site is overgrown and uncared for. There is talk of incorporating this site into the Wailua River State Park.

Holoholoku (off H 580 on your left, just past the boat launch). This *heiau* name means "to travel here and there at will." This is the oldest known *heiau* not built by Menehune. Originally, this structure was built to honor the *ali'i* Mo'ikeha's marriage and be the space where his children would be born. In the *heiau* are two boulders, which constitute the Pohaku Ho'ohanau Birthstone. Royal women gave birth here, and all children born in this *heiau* became chiefs. After the birth, the umbilical cord was wrapped and wedged into the rock. The fate of the child depended on what happened to the cord. For example, if it was carelessly handled and rats ate it, the child would grow up to be a thief. Another known use for this *heiau* was as a place of human sacrifice to the gods.

Ancient *Kapu*

Ancient Kaua'i people had many *kapu* (taboos) that commoners could be killed or punished for breaking. They might seem ridiculous to our modern society, but the system provided a unified way to rule the tribes, make sacrifices to the gods, and have something to believe in. This belief system lasted until 1819, when King Kamehameha II ended the *kapu* system of law by eating with women. Afterward, the Kaua'i people, left with a spiritual void, turned to Christianity.

Some examples of *kapu* actions:

- It was forbidden for men and women to eat together.
- A commoner could not touch the food of a chief, or enter his house.
- If the shadow of a commoner fell across the chief (or chief's shadow), it meant death for the commoner.
- If people were in a house when someone died, they had to leave immediately; they became contaminated and could not enter another house, eat another's food, work, or touch anyone.
- Anyone who interrupted or created even a small disturbance during a ceremony was sent to die.
- During hula training, it was *kapu* to eat sugarcane, taro tops, some types of seaweed, or squid. Also, sex was prohibited. Fingernails could not be cut, hair couldn't be trimmed, and men could not shave.
- Women could not prepare any food but sweet potatoes.

Poliahu *Heiau* (off H 580, just before Opaekaʻa Falls). On a bluff above the Wailua River Poliahu is one of the largest remaining *heiau* on Kauaʻi. It is thought that the Menehune built this acre-big walled structure. Because of the size and location, local people believe that this *heiau* was the home for ceremonial items. There was also a three-floor tower where the head priest prayed for advice from the gods.

Pokahu-kani "Bellstone." (Off H 580, just after Mile Marker 1, is a dirt road heading back toward the ocean; follow this road to the end. The bellstone is 100 feet past the guardrail.) This rock had many uses for ancient Kauaʻi people. Because of the clear loud sound it made when struck, chiefs could communicate between *heiau*. One major function was to ring the bellstone when a royal woman gave birth.

Alekoko "Menehune" Fishpond (in Lihuʻe, take Waapa Rd. south to Hulemalu Rd.; the lookout is on the hill). This expansive waterway was built by the Menehune at the request of Chief Alekoko and his sister Chiefess Kalalalehua. During the erection, the little people ordered the royals not to look while they worked. But they did. In punishment, the Menehune dropped their unpolished stones in the water and washed their bloody hands there, leaving the dam unfinished and contaminated.

South Shore

There are numerous sacred sites on the southern shores of Kauaʻi, but hardly any designated as *heiaus*. New archaeological findings at Poipu Beach and Kiahuna Plantation have rekindled an effort to find ancient relics in this area. For more information, contact the Koloa History Center in Koloa.

The Alekoko or Menehune Fishpond.

Opaeka'a Falls.

Shipwrecks Beach (at the eastern edge of the Grand Hyatt property in Poipu). Occasionally this rough beach mellows out and offers a rare glimpse of a petroglyph carved into the sandstone—though usually it's buried beneath the sand. Keep walking east along the beach, and hopefully you'll be one of the lucky ones to spot it. I have been here a ton of times without a glimpse.

Ho'ai *Heiau* (in Prince Kuhio Park on Lawa'i Rd. just north of Prince Kuhio condos). The *heiau* can be found in this monument to Prince Kuhio, Hawai'i's first delegate to US Congress. The fishpond and house platform near the statue constitute the *heiau*. On Prince Kuhio Day in March, people bring flowers and celebrate the life of this famous Hawaiian leader.

Maha'ulepu Beach. (Pass the Grand Hyatt, drive down the 2-mile unpaved—and very bumpy—Poipu Rd., turn right on Maha'ulepu Rd., and continue until it ends.) *Maha'ulepu* literally means "falling together." This name refers to the land and sea battle of the 1300s when King Kalaunuio-Hua tried to become ruler of all the Hawaiian Islands. He failed, which is partially why this area is so sacred to local people—it represents the strength of the Kaua'i people. Another reason indigenous people fiercely protect Maha'ulepu is because this is one of the last beachfront areas in Poipu to avoid development (though there is talk). For more information see the Beaches section in chapter 7; you can also visit www.malama-mahaulepu.org to learn about preservation efforts.

WEST SHORE

Though there are many historic buildings (see chapter 4) and monuments in the area, most relics of ancient times have been displaced or ruined.

Menehune Ditch (in Waimea, take Menehune Rd. inland; when you see the swinging bridge, look left). This ditch is a brilliant pre-contact engineering feat. A stone aqueduct made of rocks smoothed and squared into a tight wall for water to flow through, it's said to have stretched up to 25 miles inland. Now most of the ditch is covered by road, but you can still see a 2-foot section. Interestingly, the ditch still irrigates taro patches below.

Polihale *Heiau.* (Off H 50, pass Kekaha, then turn left onto the dirt road 200 yards past the Missile Facility. Drive the 4 bumpy miles to the beach and walk to where the cliffs meet the sea.) This beach houses one of the oldest and most sacred *heiaus* on Kaua'i. This four-ter-raced structure that once measured almost 100 feet was paved, and built when the god Ku fell in love with Chief Polihale's daughter. When the chief refused to give Ku his daughter's hand, Ku took the shape of a black dog and started killing people. Chief Polihale prayed to Kane and Kanaloa, who arrived as birds to defeat the canine. This *heiau* became the lovers' first Hawaiian home.

NORTH SHORE

The northern coast of Kaua'i has a number of historical sites built specifically to honor the natural beauty of the area. All are seeped in legend, and for a great mythical explanation, read Frederick Wichman's book *Kaua'i, Ancient Place Names and Their Stories*.

Kaulu-o-paoa *Heiau* **and Kaulu-o-laka Platforms** (at the end of Kuhio Hwy., walk along the shoreline trail from Ke'e Beach). These platforms are associated with the goddess of fire, Pele, her sister Hiiaka, and their lover Lohiau. Hula troops trained here, graduating students came to trace their genealogy, and visitors marvel at the panoramic seascape. Modern hula *halau* still leave offerings for Laka along the cliff.

Though not much to see aboveground, the Menehune ditch is an intriguing look at ancient irrigation methods.

House of Lohiau (in Haena, where the coast narrows and there are only sheer cliffs beyond). What looks like a mere stone wall overlooking Ke'e Beach is actually home to a rich and passionate story (see the sidebar). Using your imagination, you might visualize how Lohiau and Hiiaka once lived on the flat section above the sea, singing songs and eating taro.

Makana "Bali Hai" Mountain (the peak that towers over Limahuli Valley—best seen at Limahuli Garden). *Makana* means "gift" in Hawaiian, and this mountain has been welcomed as one. Ancients once celebrated hula graduations from atop this jagged peak with a fire throwing ceremony. Fire throwers climbed the steep hill, waited for nightfall, then set the *hau* or *papala* logs on fire and threw them into the ocean. Canoes waited in the sea to watch the glowing ancient fireworks show. Some say that men waited in canoes to catch the burning spears to prove their love to a particular woman by branding themselves with the burning tip. Many of you will recognize this mountain from the movie *South Pacific* where it served as the famed Bali Hai.

Pohaku-o-Kane (in Limahuli Garden, face the ocean near the hala tree at view spot 35; look for the large rock on the edge of the east side of the mountain ridge). Here you will find evidence of the legend of Pohaku, a rock determined to climb to the top of the mountain to watch the world below. The god Kane helped the rock ascend in exchange for Pohaku promising to be his lookout. Kane decided that when Pohaku chose to leave his spot, the waters of the ocean would rise to his level. Local folklore thus holds that when Pohaku-o-Kane disappears, so will Kaua'i.

The Legend of a Fiery Goddess: Pele

Pele arrived on Ke'e Beach during a hula ceremony. Here she first laid eyes on Lohiau, king of Kaua'i, while he pounded a drum. She fell in love with him immediately. And it wasn't hard for this gorgeous woman to woo the king and get him to consent to live with her, but first she had to find a proper place to live, near fire. After searching for what seemed like ages, she found the perfect spot—on the Big Island. She sent her younger sister, Hiiaka, to bring her lover to her, warning Hiiaka not to kiss Lohiau and that they must return within 40 days. Or else.

After a tough journey, Hiiaka arrived at Haena, where Lohiau's sister explained that the king had died. Hiiaka could see the spirit of her sister's lover soaring over the mountains and captured it in a flower. In an amazing feat, she worked the spirit back to his body and brought him back to life.

By this time, it had been more than 40 days, but Lohiau and Hiiaka made it back to Pele! Overjoyed, Hiiaka threw her arms around Lohiau and kissed him. Seeing this Pele, the fiery goddess, shrieked until lava covered her lover, all the while cursing love and her sibling. Hiiaka and Pele's battle concluded with Hiiaka igniting Kilauea (the active volcano on the Big Island).

During the battle, Pele's brothers found Lohiau's body sticking out of the lava and brought him back to life once more. They took him back to Haena, where Hiiaka joined him in his house. They lived happily together in Haena until his mortal death.

NATURAL WONDERS

The ancient Hawaiians did not worship nature for nothing. Kaua'i is home to some of the most unusual and stunning geological elements of the Hawaiian Islands—some are accessible and some aren't. Below you will find information about the ones you can physically get to, by either car, foot, or boat.

Makana Mountain is the peak of an ancient ahupua'a community in Haena.

EAST SHORE

Nounou "Sleeping Giant" Mountain (off H 580, before Opaeka'a Falls). Using your imagination, you might see the profile of the sleeping giant in the mountain. One legend says that the giant Puni was sleeping when O'ahu warriors attacked. The Menehune threw rocks at him to wake him, but they bounced off his stomach and flew into the sea, scaring off the warriors. When the Menehune went to wake him the next day, they realized that some of the rocks had gotten into his mouth; he had choked on them and died.

Opaeka'a Falls (visible from H 580; there is a parking lot on your right). This 40-

No photo can do the dynamic Waimea Canyon and Waipoo Falls justice.

Look closely and you will see the outline of a Sleeping Giant in Nounou Mountain.

foot cascade in a Wailua residential area might seem out of place among the large houses. But remember that this was once the site of a sacred ancient community. Now it is a hot tourist attraction. Often tour buses crowd the parking lot, and the closest you can (and should) get is the gated path along the road. In 2006, two hikers died trying to access the falls. Please do not hike down here; this is *not* a trailhead and can be very dangerous.

Wailua Falls (from Lihu'e, take Kuhio Hwy. north; turn left onto Ma'alo Rd., and drive 4 miles until the road ends). Once kings jumped over this 100-plus-foot waterfall for sport. Now it is too dangerous. Half the water flow has been rerouted for irrigation. Still, whenever I am here, I see people attempt to climb down the slippery rocks to the cascade. As inviting as it looks, know that a number of people have been seriously injured here. This is an excellent waterfall to view from above and take pictures of, but then I strongly urge you to find another hiking trail around the Wailua River complex.

SOUTH SHORE

Spouting Horn (in Poipu, near the end of Lawa'i Rd., on the ocean side). Every time I arrive here, I am awestruck by the simplicity of this lava tube. Water shoots through it, 25 to 60 feet into the air (depending on surf conditions—high tide is best), creating a sound like a large groan right before it spouts. Spouting Horn was created by waves that cut through soft lava rock layers to make a hole in the harder layer. Today you can see where the waves rush in and funnel to the fountain. Please use caution here. You will see locals fishing near the gap, and often tourists, thinking it safe, walk all the way to the lip of the rock. Every time, they get knocked over. Ancients used to believe a sea monster lived beneath the tube and sucked people into the sea whenever they got too close to the edge. Try to keep this wisdom in mind when you're tempted to head down there.

Tree Tunnel (at the turnoff on Kaumuali'i Hwy., toward Poipu, on Maluhia Rd.). Okay, this might not count as a sacred site, or even a natural wonder, but it is a unique site on the islands: a mile-long tunnel of eucalyptus trees for you to drive through. The trees were brought from Australia by sugar barons to stabilize the soil; they now provide a bit of cool shade and menthol aromas to the south shore.

WEST SHORE

Kalalau Overlook (at the end of Koke'e Park). This elusive view spot often gets fogged in before noon, so make sure to head up here early for an amazing sight. Here the Na Pali cliffs yawn, spilling into the ocean. The color scheme below feels like it was created by an artist, whose use of blue, green, brown, and red cannot be matched anywhere else.

Waimea Canyon State Park (in Waimea, drive up the windy H 550). A 13-mile-long, 2,500-feet deep gaping hole lovingly dubbed the "Grand Canyon of the Pacific" by Mark Twain. Unique from the Grand Canyon of Arizona, this four-million-year old lava rock offers Christmas-like color schemes, with the plentiful **Waipoo Falls** spilling over the green-and-red horizontal cliffs. The best viewing spot is at the **Waimea Canyon Overlook,** clearly marked on the main road. For detailed hiking information, see the Hiking section of chapter 7.

Spouting Horn is a natural wonder that causes viewers to catch their breath.

Make your way into the Koloa/Poipu area by way of the mile-long eucalyptus Tree Tunnel.

NORTH SHORE

Maniniholo Dry Cave (across from the parking lot at Haena State Park). This huge ancient sea cave was named for the head fisherman of the Menehune when the little people were preparing to leave the island. They left half of their fish on Haena Beach, but when they returned, the fish were all gone. It is said that the Menehune dug out the cave to find and kill the thieves. Today you can wander deep into this humid cave and hear the water dripping down the sides.

Waiakanaloa and Waiokapala'e Wet Caves. (Park at the lot just after the Limahuli Garden, cross the street, and hike up a 150-foot trail to the first wet cave. To get to the second cave, keep walking toward Ke'e Beach from the parking lot; it's just off the road on your left.) What a site these ancient sea caves, formed from higher sea levels approximately 4,000 years ago, must have been when locals used to swim and fish in them. Legend has it that the caves were dug by Pele when she was looking for fire. Today the water inside fluctuates with the tides; swimming is not permitted.

Na Pali Coast (see chapter 7 for detailed hiking, helicopter, and boating information). *Na Pali* literally means "cliffs." These seven sharp 4,000-foot ridges, separated by narrow valleys, are the symbol of Kaua'i's bounty. Whitewater smashes into the cliffs, verdant trees hug waterfalls, and seabirds and animals are abundant. There is no access to this area by car, so you must hike, boat, or fly over the coast. Along the Kalalau Trail are turnoffs to waterfalls and beaches, including Hanakapi'ai Falls. This 300-foot waterfall was named for a chiefess who died in childbirth. If you make it here, do not swim under the falls—rocks and trees often fly over the lip without notice.

The Waiakanaloa *and* Waiokapala'e *Wet Caves aren't for swimming, but they look refreshing.*

6

RESTAURANTS AND FOOD PURVEYORS

'Ono Kine Grinds

When the Polynesians arrived on ships carting taro, coconut, breadfruit, sweet potato, banana, sugarcane, chickens, pigs, and dogs, the Hawaiian menu took a considerable turn for the better. Prior to their arrival, the only edible objects here were fish and berries.

Today these Polynesian goods are the main staples of the Hawaiian diet. Of course you can find all types of food on the island, but there are some local specialties you might want to taste. If you go to a lu'au, generally you can assume you will eat *kalua* pig, the most traditional Hawaiian food. To make this dish correctly, you need time and an *'imu* pit. In the pit, ti and banana leaves are placed over hot stones, and then the pig (stuffed with more of these hot stones) is placed on top of the leaves. Often other food like seafood, *haupia*, or vegetables are wrapped in ti leaves and placed near the pig. Everything is covered with more leaves, some mats, and dirt; then the whole shebang is left to bake for up to eight hours. What you get is a smoky, tender meat, unlike anything you've ever experienced.

In addition to *kalua* pig, other Hawaiian staples to try are plentiful, filling, and acquired tastes. Chances are you'll start with *poi*, a pounded paste of cooked taro and water, and end after a spoonful. It is helpful to remember that taro is sacred to Hawaiians: Hawaiian legend claims that the gods created taro to nourish humans for as long as humans harvest and care for taro. Also try traditional Hawaiian foods like *loco moco* (a beef patty covered in a fried egg over two scoops of rice, smothered in gravy), *laulau* (seafood, pork, or chicken wrapped in a ti leaf), *lomi lomi* salmon (salted salmon with onions and tomatoes), saimin (a Hawaiian-style noodle soup), and *haupia* (a very sweet coconut pudding).

With the rise of tourism, plus an influx of hippies migrating to Kaua'i during the 1960s and '70s to live off the grid, foodies, vegetarians, and organic food lovers will not go wanting. You'll find an abundance of Pacific Rim fusion and high-end restaurants, organic take-out joints, and even a gourmet vegan restaurant. The trick is to locate eating establishments that are actually good enough to warrant the cost of the food. Yes, the talk is true: Food on Kaua'i is expensive. Sometimes it is worth it; other times it's not. Remember that most of the food on the island is imported (which often makes for bland-tasting vegetables). Below I have indicated when restaurants use locally grown produce, are locally owned, or serve sustainable and organic food to warrant the high prices. I have also included economical restaurants for those of you traveling on a budget.

Price Codes

Since food portions on the islands tend to be bigger than most mainlanders can handle, I have made my price codes cover entrées only. I have found that in almost every restaurant, when I ordered a pupu to share and an entrée, I was unable to make a dent in my dinner plate (and I researched this book while pregnant!). Also note that breakfast and lunch cost less than dinner, which is why I will occasionally indicate a price range (say, "inexpensive–moderate"). Occasionally there will be one menu entrée priced considerably higher than the rest. If this is the case, I list the general prices only.

Inexpensive	Up to $10
Moderate	$10–19
Expensive	$20–29
Very Expensive	$30 and over

Credit cards are abbreviated as follows:

AE—American Express
D—Discover Card
DC—Diner's Club
JCB—Japan Credit Bureau
MC—Master Card
V—Visa
B = breakfast, L = lunch, D = dinner.
SB = Sunday brunch, SSB = Saturday and Sunday brunch.

My favorite part of dining in Kauaʻi is that you can wear flip-flops in almost every single restaurant listed—in fact, I think I have. Only a couple of high-end establishments ask you to wear resort wear—which basically translates to a collared shirt (like a Hawaiian print one) for men, and a summer dress for women. What this really means is no swimsuits or cutoff shorts, but flip-flops are okay.

Families will be glad to know that children are welcome in all restaurants. Almost every eatery has kids' menus, booster seats or high chairs, and management that doesn't get too put off with the little ones running around (I have noted the spots that have the most space for the *keikis* to play).

It is my intention to mainly include reasons why you might enjoy particular restaurants, however, I felt that occasionally it was necessary to highlight when a popular restaurant was not up to standard. If you have a different experience, feel free to contact me, as I am a bit of a food snob.

EAST SHORE

Between Lihu'e and Anahola you will find the most populated stretch of Kaua'i, which also means the most food choices. In Lihu'e, most restaurants serve local food for the work crowd, starting early and closing even earlier. In the Wailua/Kapa'a areas, you can find some exquisite high-end restaurants, the best breakfast spots on the island, great takeout, and a vast array of organic and local food. Once you get out of Kapa'a, your options peter out.

ANAHOLA

✪ Duane's Ono Charburgers

808-822-9181.
A little shack on the ocean side of H 56 in Anahola.
Open: Daily.
Price: Inexpensive.
Cuisine: Burgers.
Serving: L.
Credit Cards: MC, V.
Handicapped Access: Yes.

You might be wondering why a self-proclaimed food snob chose to put a little red burger shack on the side of Kuhio Highway as a must-go pick. I wondered the same thing when one of my foodie friends on Kaua'i told me I had to go here. But this spot is a find. You step into line, order, then sit at one of the few dirty picnic tables, watching local kids chase ducks, chickens, and cats . . . and before long you know why locals and tourists wait for up to half an hour for a burger. Options include the Local Girl (with Swiss cheese, teriyaki, and pineapple), blue cheese, teriyaki, avocado, or a hefty veggie, fish, or chicken burger. Even with the limited choices, this is one of the tastiest restaurants on the east side. The fries are great, and the shakes are a perfect addition—try the marionberry, which goes perfectly with a big burger. If you are in a hurry, you might want to call in your order, especially on summer days.

KAPAA/WAILUA

✪ Blossoming Lotus

808-822-7678.
www.blossominglotus.com.
4504 Kukui St., Kapa'a.
Open: Daily.
Price: Inexpensive–moderate.
Cuisine: Vegan world fusion.
Serving: D, SB.
Credit Cards: AE, D, MC, V.
Handicapped Access: Yes.
Reservations highly recommended.
Special Features: Outdoor dining.

This hidden delight, just off Kuhio Highway, is sure to convert even the most determined carnivore into a vegetable lover. With huge airy windows, local art, a helpful staff, and the best fresh food on the island, you'll understand why this restaurant consistently wins awards, including the Best Restaurant Award from *Honolulu Magazine*. Health-conscious eaters and foodies will breathe a sigh of relief upon entering this vegan restaurant. An array of organic beer and wine accompanies live

Chefs at Blossoming Lotus turn vegetables into art.

music each night. The big question is how to decide what to order. All food is organic and sustainable. The chefs prepare unique takes on traditional vegetarian dishes. Kaya's Cosmic Cornbread (made of spelt) is a treat for a starter, as is the mung dal (Blossoming Lotus is one of the only places on Kaua'i where you can find Indian dishes). If you are dying for something green to balance out the wealth of carbohydrates you find around the island, try the Sea Vegetable Salad. For entrées, you can't go wrong with the Senorita Bombia's Enchilada Casserole (it truly looks like a work of art), Lakshmi's Live Lasagne (a "living" version of the Italian specialty made of locally grown vegetables and cashew "cheeze"), or Super Shakti's Spanakopitta. Though dinner delights, my favorite time to go here is for brunch. The spelt cinnamon raison French toast should be illegal. The inexpensive vegan scrambles, crêpe of the day, and fruit parfait are also favorites. Make sure to check out their impressive tonic, tea, and juice list.

Caffe Coco
808-822-7990.
4-369 Kuhio Hwy., Wailua.
Open: Tues.–Sun.
Price: Inexpensive–moderate.
Cuisine: Pacific Rim fusion.
Serving: D.
Credit Cards: MC, V.
Handicapped Access: Yes.
Special Features: Outdoor dining.

Set amid the trees in the back of a parking lot on Kuhio Highway, this little spot is a unique courtyard dining experience. Diners order at the counter and then sit outside at sarong-covered plastic tables, with Christmas lights strewn above and local entertainers playing music, performing hula, or telling jokes. This is the place to unwind and forget that you're in the middle of Kaua'i's busiest town. And the food is divine: health-conscious Pacific Rim–influenced dishes with elements of Italian, Greek, and Moroccan thrown in for spice. You can't go wrong with anything you order. They offer large Greek salad, 'ahi, pork or tofu wraps and sandwiches, pizza, or gumbo as lighter fare. But for a treat, try the Pacific Rim Platter (a light and sweet take on 'ahi and tofu served on a silver noodle salad), the Charmoula (a Moroccan-spiced 'ahi), or the pasta bella (a penne with Gorgonzola cream sauce). Since everything is homemade, the service and food arrival isn't very speedy, so order accordingly. You might want to bring your own beer or wine to bide the time (there is a $5 corkage fee). Or check out the art gallery in the main building while you are waiting. Make sure to bring mosquito repellent with you, as the little buggers camp out under the tables.

Coconuts
808-823-8777.
4-919 Kuhio Hwy., Wailua.
Open: Mon.–Sat.
Price: Moderate–expensive.
Cuisine: Island seafood.
Serving: D.
Credit Cards: MC, V.
Handicapped Access: Yes.
Reservations accepted for parties of five or more.
Special Features: Outdoor dining.

As the name implies, everything here is decorated with parts of the coconut palm—from window shades to the ceiling, tables, chairs . . . everything but the utensils, plates, and cups. Even though you are on Kuhio Highway, what with the decor and Hawaiian music, the top-shelf liquor and wine, and the sweet food, you feel like you are in a well-deserved vacation destination. As you might have guessed, chef James Daw pays homage to the coconut. Pupus are some of the most creative on Kaua'i, including lobster ravioli with coconut *liliko'i* sauce, coconut shrimp, coconut-seared seafood cigars, coconut shrimp turnovers, crabcakes with a big salad (which is enough for a meal), and a decent calamari. Garden salads with local organic greens, key lime scallop salad, and goat cheese salad are great options for healthy eaters. Entrées are meat and seafood based (not very veggie-friendly) and range from the big *kine* spice-cured grilled pork chop in pineapple-vanilla chutney to tempura-dipped *ono*, coconut-crusted salmon, and wasabi-crusted *'ahi*, plus burgers, sandwiches, chicken, and steak. This is a good choice for families, honeymooners, and couples, and is one of my favorite places for a fancy drink and dessert. Unfortunately, service can be spotty and actually downright spacey—seems as if everyone would rather be surfing than serving.

Eggbert's
808-822-3787.
Coconut Marketplace, 4-484 Kuhio Hwy., Wailua.
Open: Daily.
Price: Inexpensive.
Cuisine: American, Hawaiian.
Serving: B, L.
Credit Cards: MC, V.
Handicapped Access: Yes.
Special Features: Outdoor dining with hungry chickens.

Since 1978, Richard and Keala have served up some of the most popular breakfasts on the east shore. With country-style decor, fast, friendly service, open windows with views of the mountains, and pictures of the owners' family all over the walls, this restaurant offers a slice of down-home Kaua'i. The menu (also covered in pictures of their children) is gigantic, meaning you will probably come back more than once. How can you possibly decide among the nine varieties of omelets, the three types of

The folks at Eggbert's make you smile like their logo.

Benedicts, *loco moco*, the plethora of egg dishes, plus fish, rice, and the ridiculously fluffy pancakes with fruit and coconut syrup? In addition, the mellow atmosphere, quick service, and Hawai'i-style portions at cheap prices make this a worthwhile breakfast stop. You can also get a variety of lunches here, but breakfast reigns supreme at this classic institution.

✪ Hukilau Lanai
808-822-0600.
Kaua'i Coast Resort at Beach Boy, 520 Aleka Loop, Wailua.
Open: Daily.
Price: Expensive.
Cuisine: Contemporary Pacific Rim.
Serving: D.
Credit Cards: MC, V.
Handicapped Access: Yes.
Reservations recommended.

This is an excellent choice for families or couples who are on a budget but want to splurge for a nice night out—that is, if you can manage not having an ocean view. Instead you will spend dinner looking at the landscape gardens and pools of the hotel. Owned by the same folks as Gaylord's restaurant in Lihu'e, this establishment is the dependable rock of the higher-end spots on the east shore. Down to earth with accessible and hardworking staff, fresh locally grown/caught food, and a mellow atmosphere, this is where the locals go to celebrate special occasions. Live music in the bar and tiki torches around the outdoor patio make this a romantic spot (make sure to get a seat on the patio, because inside the atmosphere isn't as sweet). Start with wine from their decent list (including a list of 20 international and domestic wines for under $20) or one of the supersweet cocktails. Then settle in, because the food is the star—as long as you like your food a tad on the sweet side. Starters are unusual—sweet potato ravioli, a heaping plate of 'ahi poke nachos, creamy lobster curry bisque, calamari with coconut sauce, or the Kona Kampachi seviche (marinated in coconut juice). For entrées, stick with the fish; it is what they are known for: sugarcane-skewered shrimp, the Hukilau Grill (their menu's star made up of a trio of fish and risotto), or sweet twists on locally caught opah and mahimahi. Each entrée comes with soup or salad, so chances are you won't leave hungry. But if you have room for dessert, the waiters will try to tempt you with some chocolate decadence that will make you drool.

Kaua'i Hula Girl
808-822-4422.
Coconut Marketplace, 4-484 Kuhio Hwy., Kapa'a.
Open: Daily.
Price: Moderate–expensive.
Cuisine: American.
Serving: L, D.
Credit Cards: MC, V.
Handicapped Access: Yes.
Special Features: Live music.

If you are looking for a restaurant-bar with live music and a festive atmosphere, stop at the Kaua'i Hula Girl. The draw here isn't the food, or the service, or the prices. What keeps people coming back is the atmosphere—that beer smell, sassy servers, and loud local music. They offer a hearty selection of local-style food, complete with meat, seafood, and heaping portions of pasta. Light eaters can enjoy an array of salads, soups, and pupus. Since the last few times I visited the food was seriously overpriced (and not that good), you are likely better off heading to one of the food stalls in the Coconut Marketplace to dine, then coming here for drinks.

✪Kaua'i Pasta
808-822-7447.
4-939B Kuhio Hwy., Kapa'a.
Open: Tues.–Sun.
808-245-2227.
3142 Kuhio Hwy., Lihu'e.
Open: Mon.–Sat.
Price: Inexpensive–moderate.
Cuisine: Italian.
Serving: D.
Credit Cards: MC, V.
Handicapped Access: Yes.
Special Features: Takeout and catering available.

Locals line up each night here for giant plates of pasta. And rightly so. The price is right. The portions are huge. The food is fresh (they might have the best Kamuela tomatoes on the island). And Kaua'i Pasta is very accommodating to both children and adults. An array of salads, pupus, and creative specials every night might tempt your palate, but look around and you'll see that the pasta is the highlight. The marinara and pesto rock! And both are big enough for two. Don't let the sampler pasta, advertising a hearty portion, fool you; the regular size is hearty enough. They also serve paninis (the grilled portobello or chicken Florentine are popular) and excellent salads—the baby green is my favorite. Be sure to sample some of their garlic bread. Probably the best deal on the island is their take-out pasta dinner for 30 bucks, which comes with salad, pasta, and garlic bread for four. With a bunch of tables cramped beneath a bamboo-molded ceiling, kids running around, and the nicest wait staff in town, this might not be a haven of fine dining, but it's still one of the best meals on Kaua'i. A cozy Lihu'e location in the Yasuda Building opened in 2004, but caught on fire in January 2008. At press time, there was no news about whether or not they would rebuild.

Kintaro Restaurant

808-822-3341.
4-370 Kuhio Hwy., Wailua.
Open: Mon.–Sat.
Price: Moderate–expensive.
Cuisine: Japanese.
Serving: D.
Credit Cards: AE, D, DC, MC, V.
Handicapped Access: Yes.
Special Features: Reservations required for teppan tables. For sushi, reservations only taken for parties of six or more.

Locals and tourists love this place. It is huge and loud. You always have to wait (though there is a huge bar with great cocktails to tide you over). The staff can be swift and kind, but lately I have found them too busy to actually give great service. The draw is sushi. Their rolls are huge, fresh, and quite good. They serve some funky sushi, like the Cajun Roll, Bali Hai Bomb, and Kamakazi, which tend to primarily star eel and salmon. If you are celebrating your birthday, you might want to do as the locals do and reserve a rowdy teppan table, where you can have a private chef prepare meat or fish at your table. Other options are udon, tempura (which can be greasy), and dinner

combos consisting of soba salad, fish or sashimi and tempura, teriyaki, or pork cutlets. If you are looking for a high-end Japanese restaurant, you can do better than Kintaro. In fact, the last time I was here, there was a little insect problem.

Kountry Kitchen

808-822-3511.
4-484 Kuhio Hwy., Kapa'a.
Open: Daily.
Price: Inexpensive.
Cuisine: American, Hawaiian.
Serving: B, L.
Credit Cards: MC, V.
Handicapped Access: Yes.

As you might have guessed from the name, Kountry Kitchen feels like it belongs in the outskirts of Milwaukee, rather than in the center of downtown Kapa'a. Maybe that's why locals gather here every morning to talk story, read the newspaper, and gorge on gigantic plates of local-style and traditional American breakfast. No matter how early you arrive, servers always seem perked up on coffee and ready to chat. The large breakfast menu offers omelets, deliciously fluffy pancakes, French toast, fruit plates, Benedicts, fish and eggs, and *loco moco*. Servings are Hawaiian-style, so order accordingly. Vegans will be happy because they serve Egg Beaters in creative ways. This is the place to get the best local-style breakfast in downtown Kapa'a.

Mema Thai Chinese

808-823-0899.
4-369 Kuhio Hwy., Wailua.
Open: Daily.
Price: Inexpensive–moderate.
Cuisine: Thai/Chinese.
Serving: L (Mon.–Fri. only), D.
Credit Cards: MC, V.
Handicapped Access: Yes.

If you are in the mood for traditional Thai dishes of Hawaiian dimensions—the summer rolls are fist sized—this is the place for you. Located in a strip mall in Wailua, Mema Thai Chinese doesn't mess around. Portions are gigantic and food is fresh, with a true tropical twist (no canned coconut here). When you walk in, you might feel like you have stepped into another country, with antique statues and Thai music taking you away from the bustle of Kuhio Highway. Some of my favorite dishes are the fresh coconut curries—these might be the creamiest I've ever had—and the meat and vegetable dishes served up with pineapple, basil, or cashew. This is the best option for good Thai food. Unfortunately, the service can be spotty; sometimes servers are very helpful and at other times, I have been ignored for long stretches. Since food can get pricey, remember that servings are large and you don't need to order as much as you might on the mainland.

Mermaid's Café

808-821-2026.
4-1384 Kuhio Hwy., Kapa'a.
Open: Daily.
Price: Inexpensive.
Cuisine: Organic island/pan-Asian.
Serving: L, D.
Credit Cards: DC, JCB, MC, V.
Handicapped Access: Yes.

Though this local favorite appears to be nothing special—just a few plastic tables in the center of downtown Kapa'a—it is one of the best places to grab a quick healthy lunch or dinner for a great price. Serving up excellent organic food, Mermaid's Café has become an institution on the island. The food is always great. Whether you want the heaping 'ahi nori wrap, the fresh focaccia sandwich, the tofu or chicken satay plate, or just a large organic salad with a slew of vegetables, you can't go wrong. Vegan and vegetarian items are always available. And make sure to try one of their home-brewed teas—organic spearmint-lemongrass, tropical hibiscus—or the hibiscus lemonade.

Olympic Café

808-822-5825.
4-1354 Kuhio Hwy., Kapa'a.
Open: Daily.
Price: Inexpensive–expensive.
Cuisine: American.
Serving: B, L, D.
Credit Cards: MC, V.
Handicapped Access: No.

Over half a century old when demolished by Hurricane 'Iniki, this Kapa'a mainstay acts as the watch guard over downtown. At this open-air bird's nest above Kuhio Highway, diners can sip a *mai tai,* eat nachos, salads, or omelets, and listen to live music while checking out the happenings in town below. The wooden chairs and tables give the restaurant a cozy atmosphere, even though it is very spacious and always packed with locals. People love this place because the portions are huge and the prices are reasonable. You will not leave here hungry. And because they use organic vegetables and herbs, you can guarantee that you are getting some quality food. Breakfast offers *kalua* pig and eggs, 'ahi and eggs, a huge selection of omelets, pancakes (like my favorite, the coconut-pineapple), Mexican scrambles, and Hawaiian-style scrambles. Vegans will rejoice here, because every egg dish can be substituted for tofu. Lunch serves up local favorites like giant salads and sandwiches, which are both big enough for two. Also popular are massive plates of pasta or fish with a dash of the tropics. Their potent cocktails liven up this place as the afternoon settles in.

Ono Family Restaurant

808-822-1710.
4-1292 Kuhio Hwy., Kapa'a.
Open: Daily.
Price: Inexpensive.

Cuisine: American.
Serving: B, L.
Credit Cards: AE, D, DC, MC, V.
Handicapped Access: Yes.

Because it lacked atmosphere, I avoided this place for years. Then one morning, I stumbled in and wanted to kick myself for having passed up the chance to experience this local breakfast spot. First off, no matter what you do, if you even sort of like coconut, you must order some sort of griddle fare—macadamia nut pancakes, waffles, et cetera—so you can try their sinful homemade coconut syrup, served piping hot. Enjoy it while you are on the island because even though they sell it to go, the syrup is impossible to bring back to the mainland—it'll spoil. If you can't muster up a taste for some tropical pancakes with fresh fruit, then the wealth of omelets, Benedicts, or fruit plates will be sure to get you ready for your day. Food tends to be on the greasy side, but this is a diner . . . in Hawai'i. And though the spot is slightly worn down, servers treat you like family and go out of their way to make sure you have everything you need.

Wahooo Seafood Grill and Bar

808-822-7833.
4-733 Kuhio Hwy., Wailua.
Open: Daily.
Price: Expensive–very expensive.
Cuisine: Island seafood.
Serving: L, D.
Credit Cards: AE, MC, V.
Handicapped Access: Yes.
Reservations recommended.

The interior designers of this restaurant understand that high-end diners deserve a unique atmosphere—especially if they do not have an ocean view. Wahooo Seafood Grill and Bar has one thing going for it: a beautiful interior. Draped tan cloth on the ceilings and bamboo accents along the walls offer diners an Asian tropical experi-

You'll find more than veggies at Sunshine Markets.

ence. Coupled with soft Hawaiian music and an outdoor dining area facing Bette Midler's coconut grove, and you almost forget you are right on Kuhio Highway . . . almost. However, not being on the water, this place needs to try a little harder. They do not give you enough food for the price. And what they do give is beautifully presented, but too sweet, or too awkwardly constructed to carry the entire meal. Some ambitious starter options are the king crab guacamole martini (which you can skip), shrimp cocktail gazpacho, oyster shooters or steamed oysters (a treat on Kaua'i), or escargots. Soups and salads include traditional fare like a Caesar, plus bouillabaisse and cioppino. Dinner options are heavy on seafood pastas and sandwiches, or fish dishes like *ono*, mahimahi, Kona Kampachi and volcano-spiced wahi. There are some steak and chicken options, but nothing for vegetarians. It is unfortunate that the small portions are not priced accordingly, but if you are staying on the Coconut Coast and want seafood, it is worth a try. Service is laid-back but still elegant, and staff will offer up some suggestions (though usually the most expensive items on the menu).

LIHU'E

Café Portofino

808-245-2121.
www.cafeportofino.com.
Kaua'i Marriott, 3501 Rice St., Lihu'e.
Open: Daily.
Price: Expensive–very expensive.
Cuisine: Italian.
Serving: D.
Credit Cards: MC, V.
Handicapped Access: Yes.
Reservations recommended.

For years, Giuseppe Avocadi owned a small restaurant around the corner catering mostly to locals. Since he created Café Portofino, his vision has turned into one of the most popular restaurants on the island. Consistently winning awards for serving the best Italian food on Kaua'i, this breezy open-air restaurant overlooking Kalapaki Beach is a favorite with cruise ship passengers and loyal locals. Candles and live harp music, a decent wine list, and excellent service give this restaurant a southern Italian feeling. Like most island high-end locations, this restaurant is pricey for the portion sizes. However, it is a dependable place to get fresh meat, fish, and vegetables (often a rarity on Kaua'i). Pasta dishes are the most popular, emphasizing traditional favorites such as linguine with pesto, meat or vegetable lasagna, penne with broccoli and spinach, and linguine alla carbonara. Unfortunately, desserts—caramel flan, gelato (that doesn't taste much like gelato)—are only fair. But because of the ambience, you'll probably want an excuse to hang out here longer.

Duke's Canoe Club

808-246-9599.
www.dukeskauai.com.
Kaua'i Marriott, 3610 Rice St., Lihu'e.
Open: Daily.
Price: Moderate–expensive.
Cuisine: Island steak and seafood.
Serving: L, D.
Credit Cards: AE, DC, D, JCB MC, V.
Handicapped Access: Yes.
Reservations recommended for upstairs dining.

If you want to feel like you are on vacation in an American city, visit the now legendary Hawaiian chain of Duke's Canoe Club and the Barefoot Bar and Grill. Split-level dining on Kalapaki Beach brings cruise ship passengers and tourists to this energetic restaurant. Upstairs, dinner is served nightly in an open-air atmosphere overlooking the harbor. Servings are huge. Pupus tend to be fried seafood, great for sharing. Their salad bar is one of the biggest on the island. And for main entrées (if you still have room) Dukes offers large plates of chicken, meat, or six preparations of local fish with bread, salad, and vegetables. The downstairs Barefoot Bar and Grill is a lively affair, decked with a beachfront terrace, a lava rock waterfall inside the restaurant, and harried waitresses in mini skirts serving gigantic fruity drinks. Open for lunch and dinner, this is a cheaper place for cocktails and fried pupus with a slight island, Mexican, or Asian twist. They also serve salads, pizza, sandwiches, fish, chicken, or meat dishes. Basically you can get almost any type of food here, with a great view, and be surrounded by other tourists. If this is your scene, you might want to stop by on Taco Tuesday for cheap alcoholic drinks and tacos, or Tropical Friday for discounted drinks and live music.

Gaylord's

808-245-9593.
www.gaylordskauai.com.
3-2087 Kaumuali'i Hwy., Lihu'e.
Open: Daily.
Price: Moderate–very expensive.
Cuisine: Island Continental.
Serving: B, L, D, SB.
Credit Cards: AE, DC, D, MC, V.
Handicapped Access: Yes.
Reservations recommended (and often required).

Gaylord Wilcox built the Kilohana Plantation house in 1935, and now you can pretend you are an honored guest in their mansion, complete with some of the original furnishings purchased at Gumps of San Francisco. Dining in the 16,000-square-foot house, beneath paintings of the Wilcox family, surrounded by artifacts of 1930s-era California design, is a must. Locals come here for holidays and special occasions, and rightly so: The atmosphere, food, and service are impeccable. Tables look out over the expansive grassy fields of the once booming sugar plantation, giving guests an open-air dining experience—which is great when it rains, you can still sit outside and watch the downpour. The best times to come here are for dinner or Sunday brunch, when the cooks go out of their way with creative takes on traditional American favorites: farm-raised venison or slow-roasted prime rib with *liliko'i* sauce. Sunday brunch serves up all-you-can-eat breakfast fare for a hefty price, but it is a great place for kids to run around on the lawn while Mom and Dad sip mimosas. However, if you want to experience dining here and don't want to fork over the cash, lunch is a good deal, with a decent selection of sandwiches, salads, and soups.

✪ Hamura's Saimin Stand

808-245-3271.

2956 Kress St., Lihu'e.
Open: Daily.
Price: Inexpensive.
Cuisine: Local.
Serving: B, L, D.
Credit Cards: None.
Handicapped Access: Yes.

An almost 60-year institution here on the island, Hamura's Saimin is a must-go experience. The Aikos bought this little shack in the 1950s and turned it into one of the most famous places in all of Hawai'i. Year after year it gets voted as one of Kaua'i's best restaurants in *Honolulu Magazine*. That being said, the spot is nothing special: yellow walls, a few low counters, shared tables, and 35 wooden stools (always packed with locals and tourists). This is the place to get saimin, and everyone knows it. Which is why you get few choices: small, medium, large, or extra large. Most people go for the saimin special, which includes a few more types of meat, hard-boiled egg, and some

Though it doesn't look like much, Hamura's Saimin serves some of the best food on the island.

veggies. The draw here is the noodles, which are still made by the original owners' son and will force you to continue eating until way past the point you should have stopped. If you want a bit of variety, you can order teriyaki meats (which your waitress grills herself) or udon. But make sure to leave room for the fluffy *liliko'i* pie (which often sells out). Because of the price, the quality of the food, and the family vibe, most people come back here more than once. I have a friend who eats here every day when she is on the island.

SOUTH SHORE

✪ Beach House Restaurant
808-742-1424.
www.the-beach-house.com.
5022 Lawa'i Rd., Koloa.
Open: Daily.
Price: Very expensive.
Cuisine: Pacific Rim.
Serving: D.
Credit Cards: AE, DC, MC, V.
Handicapped Access: Yes.
Reservations required, sometimes days in advance.
Special Features: Available for weddings, private parties, and catering.

If you have the cash for one nice dinner, go to this epic south shore institution. Here is a place where the laid-back Hawaiian vibe complements the taste and decadence of gourmet dining. Open air, and right on Baby Beach, diners hear the waves crashing and feel the salty air while they eat. People propose right out on the patio, overlooking the sea, with the lit-up palm trees and one of this spot's delicious tropical drinks (try the mango mojito) or fantastic wines (they have one of the best wine lists I have seen on the island). Chef Todd Barrett goes the distance with both preparation and presentation. Appetizers like the shiitake-crusted

mussels, fish nachos, and mac-nut crab salads are almost too beautiful to eat. The watermelon salad or *'ahi* Caesar are popular choices. But make sure to prepare for the main event. Tropical fare like the layered risotto is a worthy option, if you don't eat seafood. But to be frank, the fish is the star. The macadamia-crusted fresh island catch in miso is a new twist to this local favorite. And the Yamase's grilled fish (named for the fisherman who catches all the fish for the restaurant, and who always orders this unique dish) is the local catch over a tropical couscous and tomato salad, drizzled with pesto then topped with a shrimp relish. If you have any space left in your belly after all that, the Molten Chocolate Desire, always individually made and taking about 20 minutes to prepare (they recommend ordering it with your meal), is a respectable sweet ending. Ask your waiter to describe this decadence and you'll be hard pressed to deny yourself. Other stars are the sorbetto trio and the *liliko'i* sponge cake. They have a nice selection of tea, coffee, and dessert wine. Staff are friendly and down to earth, not afraid to chat about surf spots, their kids, and so forth. If you don't want to fork over the cash for a full dining experience, the bar is an excellent place to watch the sunset with a pupu and tropical beverage.

Brennecke's Beach Broiler
808-742-7588.
2100 Hoone Rd., Koloa.
Open: Daily.
Price: Moderate–very expensive.
Cuisine: American.
Serving: L, D.
Credit Cards: MC, V.
Handicapped Access: No.

Perched on a second floor across the street from Poipu Beach, this has been an institution for mai tais and pricey bar food since 1983. If you want a Tell-Your-Friends-At-

Home-About-It meal, or even reasonably priced bar food, this is *not* the place for you. When you eat here, you are paying for the views. Paying a lot, I might add. It'll cost you over 10 bucks for shrimp cocktail (with only four shrimp) at lunch and almost 20 for a crab sandwich. At press time, a scoop of ice cream was $4.50. Lunches are a greasy affair of sandwiches or salads. However, the general manager and chef, Dave Boucher offers creative dinner preparations of steak, seafood, and pasta. I like coming here for happy hour, when the drinks and pupus are on special and the sun is setting over the beach. The owners Bob and Christine French also own the deli downstairs, where you can get sandwiches for a more reasonable price.

Brick Oven Pizza
808-332-8561.
2-2555 Kaumuali'i Hwy., Kalaheo.
Open: Daily.
Price: Moderate–expensive.
Cuisine: Italian.
Serving: L, D.
Credit Cards: MC, V.
Handicapped Access: Yes.
Special Features: Takeout.

Don't bother with any other pizza restaurants. This is the best on the island by almost everyone's standards. Owned by the Demas family since 1989, it is always packed with locals and tourists—in fact, people have to park on the street because the lot is usually full. The vibe inside, with giant murals on the walls, collections of license plates hanging on the walls, and families laughing over pizza and soda, almost gives this place an Alpine feel, except for the way the baking hearths heat it up. Don't bother with a salad. Just go for the pizza. It is big, filling, and cooked just long enough to make your stomach growl. The crust is made from cornmeal combined with either white or wheat flour; they can

dust it with garlic butter if you'd like. Then it's smothered with homemade sauce and the toppings of your choice. Though some of the vegetables are canned, the pizza still tastes fresh. They also serve beer and sandwiches. One of my favorite things to do is get a pizza and take it to the beach to watch the sunset, though often the pizza is gone long before the sun.

Casablanca
808-742-2929.
At Kiahuna Swim and Tennis Club, 2290 Poipu Rd., Koloa.
Open: Daily.
Price: Moderate–expensive.
Cuisine: Mediterranean.
Serving: B, L, D, tapas.
Credit Cards: D, MC, V.
Handicapped Access: Limited.
Reservations recommended for dinner.

A welcome addition to the Poipu area, this casual open-air Mediterranean restaurant will add some spice to your day. Set inside the Kiahuna Swim and Tennis Club, overlooking both recreational areas, Casablanca feels festive yet relaxed. Breakfast is as good as it gets with varieties of eggs Benedict, scrambles, and waffles. At lunch you might find it loud, with kids playing in the pool and the music bumping, but the palm trees and bougainvilleas shading the area gives the restaurant a mellow feel. Lunch relies heavily on sandwiches, a Greek salad, and gazpacho. But don't miss the tropical tacos, the Moroccan skewers, or one of the refreshing smoothies. The bar usually has a nice crowd (especially at happy hour, when the food and drink prices can't be beat). The tapas selection draws the after-work local crowd to feast on calamari, olives, cheese plates, garlic shrimp, or crêpes. But dinner is the star. Locals love to come here for *zarzuela* or North African lamb, among a wealth of meat and fish delicacies.

Casa Di Amici

808-742-1555.
Behind Nihi Kai Condos, 2301 Nalo Rd.,
Koloa.
Open: Daily.
Price: Expensive–very expensive.
Cuisine: Fusion.
Serving: D.
Credit Cards: D, MC, V.
Handicapped Access: Yes.
Reservations required.

In 1988, the owners turned this breezy
island-style house into a one-of-a-kind
romantic restaurant that has been busy ever
since. You'll want to make a reservation
about half an hour before you actually want
to sit, because usually you still have to wait
(yes, even with a reservation). The best
seats are on the patios, though they are
hard to come by. But if you are placed
inside, it is okay, because on Saturday a
pianist plays in the main dining room.
Despite the name, this is not your traditional Italian restaurant. Chef Randall Yates
deems his food eclectic. Sure you can get
marsala, fettuccine (which is fantastic), or
Caesar salad, but their specialties are
sometimes awkward Japanese-Mexican or
Thai-Italian fusions. To start, order a small
appetizer like garlic bread or share one of
their large tropical salads, because the wait
for your meal can be epic. Every night chef
Yates rotates his specials page, so there is
always something to marvel at. I have seen
Yucatán risotto, Japanese mahogany
salmon, Thai-spiced risotto, and Hawaiian
risotto. Tastes are complex and sometimes
confused. If you don't like exploratory dinners, stick with traditional Italian, which
they do quite well. For most entrées you can
get a half order. And if you still have room,
desserts favor the southern states with
bananas Foster and bread pudding.
However, the baked Hawai'i and *haupia*
sorbet are good light and local choices. One
note on the service: Though my experience

with the staff has been very nice, a friend
refuses to return here because she has had
more than one rude server.

Dondero's

808-742-1234.
www.kauai.hyatt.com.
Grand Hyatt Hotel, 1571 Poipu Rd., Koloa.
Open: Daily.
Price: Expensive–very expensive.
Cuisine: Italian.
Serving: D.
Credit Cards: AE, D, DC, MC, V.
Handicapped Access: Yes.
Reservations required.
Special Features: Resort attire required.
Private dining room for up to 12 people.

The last couple of times I have eaten here, I
couldn't hide my disappointment. Rumor
has it that this place is getting a new chef,
but it seems the chemistry that works at the
other Grand Hyatt high-end restaurant
isn't intact at this overpriced (and quite
full-of-itself) Italian eatery. Sure, it is fine
dining experience with stuffy waiters and
creative presentations, but at the end of the
day, I always wonder if my small plate of
pasta is worth over 40 bucks. When you sit
down, the waiter brings a *boccacilli* (which
translates as a "small bite," usually of
seafood) and bread. The extensive wine list
offers international wines at six times the
retail cost. And the waiters often only recommend the most expensive things on the
menu (the $17 appetizer, or the three
entrées priced over $40). However, if you
are staying here or are interested in trying
out this classic Poipu restaurant, note that
the soups and salads are large enough for
two people to share and then split a meal.
Plates are known to have rich sauces and
heavy pasta. When the food arrives, it is
presented artistically—I have seen people
photograph their meals here. Since they
only use seasonal ingredients, entrées
change often. To give you a feel for the

dishes they create, I once had a lobster pistachio dish that was richer than my chocolate cake. There are some outdoor seats with nice views (which I recommend). It's reasonable to come here for wine, an appetizer or some port, and vanilla crème brûlée to save some big money.

Ilima Terrace
808-742-1234.
www.kauai.hyatt.com.
Grand Hyatt Resort, 1571 Poipu Rd., Koloa.
Open: Daily.
Price: Moderate–expensive.
Cuisine: Continental.
Serving: B, L, D.
Credit Cards: AE, D, DC, MC, V.
Handicapped Access: Yes.
Dinner reservations recommended.
Special Features: Breakfast buffet.

Though the open-air setting—surrounded by lava rock waterfalls and pools, with birds flying around and bougainvilleas dangling over the roof—is lovely, there are much better places to have breakfast. In fact, you can run up to Sueoki's, get some pastries and coffee, then sit by the pool and enjoy the same view for a quarter of what it'll cost you to eat here. That being said, my parents love the breakfast buffet (they'd better for almost 30 bucks a person). They like rolling out of bed and helping themselves to a generous selection of omelets, crêpes, bacon, eggs, potatoes, juice, smoothie shots, cereal, fruit, pastries, coffee, pancakes, waffles, French toast, and more. Families might opt for breakfast entrées like the lox and bagel, eggs Benedict, or *loco moco*. You might even dare to order a cup of the Starbucks French press coffee for $7.25. They also serve standard American fare for lunch and dinner.

Joe's on the Green
808-742-9696.
2545 Kiahuna Place, Koloa.
Open: Daily.
Price: Moderate–expensive.
Cuisine: American, Hawaiian.
Serving: B, L, D.
Credit Cards: MC, V.
Handicapped Access: Yes.

Go here for breakfast. Their eggs Benedict and *loco moco* are priced just right, and they're not so huge that you'll feel like you'll lapse into a food coma. Staff are friendly, knowledgeable, and quite good looking actually. Diners get great views of the golf course as they sit in the open-air restaurant, with glimpses of the ocean in the distance. The owners, Caroline and Joe, have taken the idea of a homegrown business to a new level, encouraging regulars to call them at home when a staff member is rude, or excellent. One of the owners is always there, so if you liked your meal, say hi. Since Joe is a sports fanatic from Ohio, there are usually sporting events playing on the TVs and a festive air. The big bar (with a nice selection of pub food) and the laid-back local flavor are obvious hits with locals, who frequent this restaurant often (which is why there is usually a wait for weekend breakfast). They are also open for lunch and dinner.

Keoki's Paradise
808-742-7534.
www.hulapie.com.
Poipu Shopping Village, 2360 Kiahuna Plantation, Koloa.
Open: Daily.
Price: Moderate–very expensive.
Cuisine: Pacific Rim.
Serving: L, D.
Credit Cards: AE, MC, V.
Handicapped Access: Yes.
Reservations recommended for dining room dinner.

Owned by the same people who bring you Duke's, Keoki's has made a name for itself on the south shore. You might notice birds making themselves at home in the pond, palms, and banyans swaying in the center of this expansive jungle-themed restaurant, and like most locals, you'll feel the kitsch and probably love it. The local secret is to head to the bar, where food is considerably cheaper and just as good. In fact, this might be one of the best places on the south shore for pupus and tropical concoctions. Pupus have a Mexican and Asian influence—coconut shrimp, Thai shrimp sticks, and nachos are some favorites. All day you can get sandwiches and burgers in the bar as well. In the huge open-air restaurant, panko-crusted scallops, mu shu pork, and crabcakes are typical pupus. Entrées such as the orange-ginger-baked opah, coconut chicken, or *kalua* pork ribs are popular. Whatever you choose, all the plates are gigantic and include Caesar salad and fresh-baked bread. And though the vegetables are not the freshest for the money, this is a decent dinner selection. Another option is to grab four friends, sit at the bar, and share the gigantic Hula Pie—as they say, it's "what the sailors came home for."

✪ Plantation Gardens Restaurant and Bar

808-742-2121.
www.pgrestaurant.com.
Kiahuna Plantation, 2263 Poipu Rd., Koloa.
Open: Daily.
Price: Expensive.
Cuisine: Pacific Rim.
Serving: D.
Credit Cards: AE, DC, MC, V.
Handicapped Access: Yes.
Reservations recommended.
Special Features: Private dining area for private parties and receptions.

This historical plantation manager's cottage is where the sugar barons used to party. Now surrounded by the Moir Gardens, this restaurant-bar offers up one of the most romantic dining experiences on the south shore. Open-air dining, with thick thatched fans, low Hawaiian music, and candles—

Plantation Gardens knows how to serve up a well-rounded dining experience. The chefs, Teri McLeod and Thomas Connolly, prepare unique offerings of old plantation Hawai'i cuisine in a large open kitchen using herbs and vegetables from their own organic garden. Start with a drink: They actually use some of those home-grown ingredients in the cucumber mojitos, the lichee and Asian pear cosmopolitan, or the *liliko'i* lemonade for nondrinkers. They also have a healthy wine and beer list. I always find the staff friendly and up front about the food. And because this restaurant isn't right on the water, the food is actually reasonably priced for what you get. Plus, there are no gourmet-sized portions here. Everything is large, heavy, and delicious (I often end up taking half my meal home with me). Menu items change with the season, but hopefully you will be on the island when the menu is featuring seafood *laulau* (locally caught fish and vegetables are wrapped in a ti leaf) or bouillabaisse (seafood and vegetables in a coconut curry broth). If not, make sure to try some meat or fish prepared on a kiawe wood grill, which gives the food a mesquite flavor unique to plantation-style cooking. Desserts often feel a bit too ambitious in scope, but by that point you'll probably be too full to think of more food.

Shells; Naniwa; and Amore

808-742-1661.
Sheraton Hotel, 2440 Hoonani Rd., Poipu.
Open: Daily
Price: Very expensive.
Cuisine: Steak and seafood; Japanese; Italian.
Serving: B, D.
Credit Cards: AE, D, DC, JCB, MC, V.
Handicapped Access: Yes.
Reservations recommended.

Three gourmet restaurants in one room overlooking Poipu Beach might sound

Plantation Gardens Restaurant sits inside the Moir Pa'u a Laka gardens.

Romantic dining at Tidepools in the Grand Hyatt Resort.

divine to some. Especially when you consider that no matter which restaurant you have a reservation for, you can order off any of the menus. Seems like the Sheraton understands family travel. What makes this place great is that if Grandma wants steak and little Tommy wants sushi, they can get it, while still enjoying a fine-dining experience in one place. Located in the center of the three, Shells overlooks the lava rock shores of Poipu Beach and showcases local produce, steaks, and seafood with an Asian influence. Starters that shine are the panko-crusted crabcake and the Asian shrimp salad. Entrées like the pistachio-crusted 'ahi with mango and the Hokkaido scallop-stuffed chicken are the most tropical offerings on the three menus. This is the only restaurant of the three that also serves American and international-style breakfast. At Naniwa you can find good sushi options at steep prices (two pieces of *nigiri* or a tuna roll will run you over 10 bucks . . . each), plus a few seafood plates and rice bowls. Finally, Amore Ristorante Italiano serves up traditional Italian fare with a tropical infusion. Entrées are similar to Shells with a pistachio-crusted *opaka-paka*, sugar Sambuca salmon, vegetarian pastas, steak, and chicken. Though the views are stellar and the food is good, the prices are a bit more than the food deserves. Your fine-dining dollars might be better spent elsewhere.

✪ Tidepools

808-742-1234.
www.kauai.hyatt.com.
Grand Hyatt Hotel, 1571 Poipu Rd., Koloa.
Open: Daily.
Price: Very expensive.
Cuisine: Pacific Rim.
Serving: D.
Credit Cards: AE, D, DC, MC, V.
Handicapped Access: Yes.
Reservations required.

If you are looking for the most romantic dining establishment on the island, and are willing to part with a nice chunk of cash, go to Tidepools. It has won *Honolulu Magazine*'s *Hale 'Aina* Award for fine dining—and the critics are correct, this is by far the finest restaurant on Kaua'i. Chef Ryan considers his restaurant contemporary Hawaiian fusion. And the whole package is surely a sensory pupu platter. Set over a koi pond, this thatched-roof, torchlit hut gives a sense of privacy to each table. The wind and water combine to engage the senses before you even sample the cuisine. And from the moment you sit down, you know you are in for a treat—the servers are dynamic, friendly, and correct in their recommendations. The menus are woven into wood; the salt and pepper shakers are works of art; in fact, every detail seems attended to. You'll want to start with one of their unique cocktails, a smoothie, or a glass of wine off their decent (and heavily Northern California influenced) wine list. Pupus are unique: seared yuzu scallops in filo, tofu *poke*, mango and lobster crabcakes. My favorite starter is the coconut lobster cappuccino (a fancy lobster bisque). Vegetarians have a lot to appreciate here in the entrée department: a baked tofu or veggie medley (though I have found veggies to not be their strong point, so go for the tofu). Other entrées are the oven-roasted *hapu'upu'u*, sautéed *opakapaka*, pineapple and mac-nut crusted chicken, grilled swordfish in a habanero-papaya butter, and—my favorite—the seared *opah* in a Tahitian vanilla hollandaise (this might be the best fish I have ever had). If you spared any room in your belly (which you'd better), the lava cake, the chocolate peanut butter cake, or the trio of crème brûlées are all decadence at its finest. Two people will probably not get out of here for under $100, but it is an experience not to be forgotten.

Yum Cha/Poipu Clubhouse

808-742-1234.
www.kauai.hyatt.com.
Poipu Bay Golf Course, 2250 Ainako,
Poipu.
Open: Daily (dinner Tues.–Sat. only).
Price: Moderate–expensive.
Cuisine: American and Asian fusion.
Serving: B, L, D.
Credit Cards: AE, D, DC, MC, V.
Handicapped Access: Yes.
Reservations recommended for dinner.

This large, brightly lit building on a world-class golf course is essentially two restaurants. During the day, it is a clubhouse, serving breakfast from 5 AM to eager golfers and early risers, then American-style lunch (with Hawaiian influences) at big prices. Some lunch dishes that make tourists smile are the grilled cheese, the *kalua* pork spring rolls, the *da kine* fries (covered in beef and cheese), and the Portuguese bean soup. You can find cheaper places to eat lunch (or places that actually serve portions worth the hefty price tag). But dinner is another affair altogether. Ever since chef Romel Begonia was trained in Beijing and Vietnam, Yum Cha has gotten a lot of press. Yum Cha offers Asian fusion cuisine at more reasonable prices than the clubhouse's grilled cheese. You might want to try some of their unique cocktails: a lichee and pomegranate martini, sake with passion fruit, or the large selection of Asian beer and wine. This complements the delicious combinations of Japanese, Thai, Vietnamese, and Chinese foods that chef Begonia has created. He offers some unique twists on pad Thai, soba noodles, ma po tofu, and moo shu pork. For dessert, save room for the Jasmine Tea-Ramisu, an Asian take on the Italian specialty. There are many teas to sample as well, including flowering teas, where the tea actually re-blooms in your teapot.

WEST SHORE

✪ Hanapepe Café

808-335-5011.
3830 Hanapepe Rd., Hanapepe.
Open: Mon.–Fri.
Price: Moderate–very expensive.
Cuisine: Tropical Italian.
Serving: L (Mon.–Thurs.), D (Fri. only).
Credit Cards: MC, V.
Handicapped Access: Yes.
Reservations strongly recommended for
Fri. nights.

When, on Friday evenings, Hanapepe turns into a bohemian enclave, this is the place to be. A spacious old house turned art gallery and restaurant, Hanapepe Café is a local favorite. Three years ago this vegetarian spot got a face-lift from its new owner, Andrea Kaohi, and now the dinner menu is primarily locally caught seafood and cheesy pasta (though they give recommendations on how to make your meal vegan). The shift in ownership brought a new crowd into the Friday-night event; now the wait is even longer. Luckily, you can tour the Hanapepe galleries, or listen to live slack key guitar music while you wait. This is by far one of the freshest meals you can get on the island. Pupus range from thick purees of locally grown organic vegetables to huge salads of organic greens. Entrées change weekly; I have had the pleasure of eating their wild mushroom risotto, grilled *opakapaka*, and four-cheese lasagna. Everything I have ever tried has been outstanding. And even though the plates are huge, you must save room for homemade dessert: mac-nut crème brûlée or hot apple pie with ice cream. On Fridays the service can be a bit slow, but the wait staff are friendly and accommodating. Bring your own beer and wine, since they don't have their license. Lunch offers a great selection of salads, sandwiches (their veggie burger won't even make you miss meat), and pastas at reasonable prices.

Shrimp Station

808-338-1242.
9652 Kaumuali'i Hwy., Waimea.
Open: Daily.
Price: Moderate.
Cuisine: Seafood.
Serving: L.
Credit Cards: AE, MC, V.
Handicapped Access: Yes.

Not much diversity here: shrimp or kosher hot dogs, though shrimp is the diva of this dive (it's located in what looks like a carport). Select from a small menu then, through a sliding glass window, tell the friendly chefs. Pick your variety of shrimp: peel and eat with your choice of garlic, Cajun, Thai, or sweet chili garlic; fish-and-chips style, beer battered, coconut fried, shrimp tacos, or patted into a burger. Servings, especially the tacos, are Hawai'i

The Shrimp Station serves up giant shrimp at small prices.

style (read: *large*). This is a funky spot to hang out on picnic tables and soak up the mellow vibe of Waimea after a day of wandering around Koke'e.

Toi's Thai Kitchen

808-335-3111.
4469 Waioli Rd., 'Ele'ele.
Open: Tues.–Sat.
Price: Moderate.
Cuisine: Thai.
Serving: L, D.
Credit Cards: AE, MC, V.
Handicapped Access: Yes.

Located at the back of the 'Ele'ele Shopping Center, this locally favored Thai restaurant serves up reasonably priced food with a simple vibe. Though you don't come here for the ambience, this is a worthy stop if you're a fan of Thai food. Toi's is owned and run by a family who put lots of love into the food, including growing many of the ingredients on the menu. Traditional Thai appetizers like spring rolls, hot-and-sour soup, and papaya salad populate the menu. Main dishes rely heavily on locally grown basil, coconut, and tropical fruit mixed with seafood, meat, or tofu. One of my favorites is the Toi's Temptation, a mellow version of a curry. Other favorites are *nua*, stir-fried vegetables with your choice of meat, and satay. Most dishes come with rice (brown, white, or sticky) and salad. They don't serve alcohol here, but their Thai iced tea is pretty tasty.

Waimea Brewing Company

808-338-9733.
Waimea Plantation Cottages, 9400 Kaumuali'i Hwy., Waimea.
Open: Daily.
Price: Moderate–very expensive.
Cuisine: American/Hawaiian.
Serving: L, D.
Credit Cards: AE, D, MC, V.
Handicapped Access: Yes.

Beer lovers head to Waimea Brewing Company.

Don't come here expecting German-style beers, or even Pacific northwestern microbrews. Though this crew brews their own, these are not the best libations on the planet. Not even on the island. Still, this is an excellent place to park yourself on the outdoor terrace to quench your thirst after a long day of hiking with a Captain Cook IPA, *na pali* pale ale, or *liliko'i* light ale. They also have a full bar. For pupus, try the goat cheese taro dip, the gigantic nachos, the coconut shrimp, or the garlic fries. Entrées are the typical bar food you'll find island-wide: burgers, sandwiches, humongous salads, and plates of *kalua* pork, *'ahi*, or *ono*. Service can be spotty; the last time I was here my waitress was slow and inexperienced, having not tasted one thing on the menu.

Wrangler's Steakhouse
808-338-1218.
9852 Kaumuali'i Hwy., Waimea.
Open: Daily.
Price: Moderate–expensive.
Cuisine: American.

Serving: L (Mon.–Fri. only), D.
Credit Cards: AE, MC, V.
Handicapped Access: Yes.

Whenever I walk into Wrangler's Steakhouse, I imagine the Kaua'i cowboys sauntering in for a beer and tin of steak. This 100-plus-year-old building in the center of Waimea Town has a deservedly great reputation. Owned by Colleen Faye (of the Waimea Plantation Cottages Fayes), the large house, museum, and veranda have managed to retain that rustic olden-days feeling. This, combined with the great food, is why there is always a wait to eat here. Locals and tourists gather in the gift shop (see chapter 8) or outside, waiting to eat on the lanai or inside at the dark tables. Plates are quite hefty (as you might imagine from a place that has been serving *paniolos* for decades). Appetizers like the shrimp cocktail, crabcake, or sizzling steak are good starters, but know that each entrée comes with a visit to the salad bar and a heaping portion of meat, fish, or vegetables. Specialties include the pistachio-crusted salmon salad with sour *poi* dressing, sizzling steak, kiawe-grilled steaks, and—at lunch—the "Kau Kau" tin lunch (beef teriyaki, shrimp and vegetable tempura, and kim chee). There is also a decent selection of seafood dishes and a couple of vegetarian items. For dessert, if you can't decide between the mud pie, *liliko'i* dream pie, or custard flan, you can get a sampler.

Regardless of whether you are a steak lover, a stop in Wrangler's feels like a step back in another time; it's definitely worth checking out.

NORTH SHORE

Haena

Mediterranean Gourmet
808-826-9875.
Hanalei Colony Resort, 5-7132 Kuhio Hwy., Haena.

Open: Mon.–Sat.
Price: Moderate–expensive.
Cuisine: Mediterranean.
Serving: L, D.
Credit Cards: AE, DC, D, MC, V.
Handicapped Access: Yes.

Though this beachfront restaurant has had many incarnations (it has been five different restaurants), the newest owners may have hit on a winning combination. Great views, big windows, an airy atmosphere with a big bar, good food, and nightly entertainment seem to be exactly what this mellow town needed. Some people come because the entertainer, Charo, owns the building (though she never comes to shake her thing), but the real reason to head out here is to see if *Honolulu Magazine* is right about Mediterranean Gourmet being the best restaurant in Kaua'i in 2006. Even if you have never tried Mediterranean food,

The historic Wrangler's Steakhouse in Waimea.

this is a good place to learn about the intense spices and delicate combinations. It's one of my favorite lunch spots on the north shore, and it allows you to space out on the waves hitting the remote beach without paying half the cost of your room for a sandwich. Lunch highlights are the giant falafel wraps, salads (try the Summer Bliss—a combination of lettuce and fruit—or the Greek salad), kebabs, and lettuce wraps. For dinner, you might want to start out with the hand-rolled *fatayer* (like a Mediterranean egg roll), the saffron rice cakes, or *dolmas*. For an entrée, the rosemary rack of lamb is a popular option. And if you can muster up more room, the coconut baklava is one of the tastiest desserts you'll find on the north shore. If you are in the mood for a drink, they offer everything from mojitos to mango margaritas, and even some decent wines (one night a week, they offer half-price bottles of wine). The skylights and airy atmosphere, combined with live nightly jazz or belly-dancing performances, make this bar a great place for a drink. They also serve milk shakes and smoothies for refreshers after a day at the beach. Try to get here in the early evening when the sky is electric, which always makes your food taste better.

HANALEI

✪ Bar Acuda

808-826-7081.
5-5161 Kuhio Hwy., Hanalei.
Open: Tues.–Sun.
Price: Expensive–very expensive.
Cuisine: Tapas.
Serving: D.
Credit Cards: MC, V.
Handicapped Access: Yes.
Reservations recommended.

Foodies on Kauaʻi let out a cheer when San Francisco chef Jim Moffat opened this sustainable, organic tapas spot in the heart of Hanalei. This is not your typical Hawaiian restaurant with big portions to justify the outrageous prices. Here, plates are small (owning to the Spanish tapas tradition) and combinations are more like California cuisine—with occasional fusions of unthinkable items, and delicate flavors emphasized by local ingredients. On first passing through the torchlit lanai to enter the open-air restaurant, diners often think they could be in a big city: big blue couches serve as dinner seats, and ambient-lit modern furniture emphasizes the full bar and open kitchen. Diners have the choice of sitting in the dimly lit inside, outside with views of the mountains, or at the bar. The extensive (and expensive) wine list (or the good selection of English beer) is sure to get your palate ready for some of the specialties that never change, like the warm olives, the *banderillas* (steak with a coffee/cocoa rub), and the Marshall Farm Honeycomb (served with Humboldt Fog goat cheese). Everything else on the menu changes with the season, but there are always lots of vegetarian, seafood, and meat small-plate choices. For the people who don't like a vast selection of tastes, there are three nightly big plates. Know that this is an expensive meal, considering all you have to order to get full. But it is worth it, if only for the plethora of tastes chef Moffat serves up using some of the best-quality ingredients on the island. Be sure to leave room for dessert, which is just as creative as the main courses. Once I had a lemon ricotta cheesecake with pine nuts and thought I was in heaven.

Hanalei Dolphin Restaurant

808-826-6113.
5-5016 Kuhio Hwy., Hanalei.
Open: Daily.
Price: Very expensive.
Cuisine: Seafood.
Serving: L, D.
Credit Cards: MC, V.
Handicapped Access: Yes.
No reservations accepted.

Lanai dining at Bar Acuda.

Since Hanalei Dolphin Restaurant is the only place in Hanalei to actually enjoy "waterfront" dining, it's been a tourist haven for the past three decades. Outdoor picnic tables line the Hanalei River, and the lanai offers lovely views as well. The actual restaurant is designed like the inside of a ship with wooden walls, funky windows, and lots of artwork. The ambience, however, comes at a hefty price. Everything here is offered at tourist prices, from the wealth of funky tropical drinks like the Hanalei Dreamsicle or the Tiki Torch (or even the nonalcoholic smoothies), to the generous portions of food. Pupus worth a try include the artichokes, *poke*, seafood chowder, and fried shellfish. However, if you are here for dinner, pupus are not necessary because everyone gets a big bowl of family-style salad with the entrée. The seafood is what they are famous for, so go for that. The best way to soak in the atmosphere of this north shore institution is to just get the bread and salad for 10 bucks,

with some seafood chowder for a starter. Unfortunately, the last couple of times I have been here, I've found the entrées overpriced for the quality of the food. Families find this a great place to bring the *keikis*, since there is lots of room for the little ones to run around. They also have a decent fish market, serving ready-to-cook shrimp and beef sticks, sushi rolls, and salads, and a gift shop to peruse while you wait for your table.

Hanalei Gourmet

808-826-2524.
5-5161 Kuhio Hwy., Hanalei.
Open: Daily.
Price: Inexpensive–very expensive.
Cuisine: American/Hawaiian.
Serving: B (limited), L, D.
Credit Cards: AE, D, DC, MC, V.
Handicapped Access: Yes.

Every time I come to this hole-in-the-wall in the Old School Building at the Hanalei

Picnic tables along the Hanalei River make the Hanalei Dolphin the only waterfront place to eat in Hanalei.

Center, I feel like I have found the true heart of Hanalei. Locals always line the bar, watching sports and sipping pints, while loud music pounds through the speakers; servers always seem to know the patrons, making jokes and laughing loudly; and staff always go out of their way to make guests feel welcome. Murals line the walls. Tables are close together. It smells like beer and fried food. This is not some fancy spot to have a romantic dinner and watch the sunset. Hanalei Gourmet (despite the name) is where you go for homey food and good prices. Breakfast is a quick take-out affair from the window to the right of the restaurant. For lunch you have two choices: Order sandwiches and salads from the take-out counter (they are pretty big for a reasonable price), or sit in the restaurant for choices off the full menu. If you look around, it seems everyone goes for the burgers. Dewey's Gorgonzola Burger, Moe's Ultimate, or the Garden Isle Vegetarian Burgers are popular choices. Plus, they offer a great selection of large salads like the Waioli Salad (with grilled veggies, goat cheese, and mango dressing) or the tropical flavored Hanalei Waldorf. At night, you can still get sandwiches and burgers, but they also have a nice selection of dinner plates. To start, the artichoke dip or artichoke toast are fantastic; or the smoked Hawaiian seafood sampler will satisfy your protein fix. Dinners vary from mac-nut fried chicken to fish-and-chips; from the udon stir-fry to Gorgonzola chicken pasta. If you get here early enough, they have early-bird and happy-hour specials. But no matter when you come, if you order right, you can still have a decent meal for under 10 bucks; around 20 if you want a plate of seafood. Earlier in the evening bring the little ones, because they have a big kids' menu and coloring books for them to play with. But later, this place heats up with loud live music nightly, and drinks poured until late.

Hanalei Wake Up Café

808-826-5551.
5-5140 Kuhio Hwy., Hanalei.
Open: Daily.
Price: Inexpensive.
Cuisine: Hawaiian/American.
Serving: B.
Credit Cards: Cash only.
Handicapped Access: Yes.

Though the breakfast options on the north shore are slim, don't lose hope. I visit this little surf shack every day while in Hanalei. Not only does the laid-back vibe with pictures of surfers lining the walls, the small lanai, and the unpretentious atmosphere make you feel at home, but the food does, too. This is simple, completely unfancy breakfast fare like omelets, breakfast quesadilla, Over the Falls French Toast (decadently decorated with custard, fruit, and whipped cream), and the insanely good mac-nut cinnamon roll. I have never had a bad meal here. Service is so fast, you can usually get in and out in less than an hour—they know you need to eat and hit the waves.

Kalypso's

808-826-9700.
5-5156 Kuhio Hwy., Hanalei.
Open: Daily.
Price: Inexpensive–expensive.
Cuisine: American/Hawaiian.
Serving: L, D.
Credit Cards: AE, DC, MC, V.
Handicapped Access: Yes.

This is a fun place to hit up in the evening for some bar-and-grill fare and tropical drinks. Decorated like an island getaway, with colorful artwork, a funky bar with bamboo accents, and big TVs, Kalypso's makes you feel like you are on *vacation*. It is a bummer that even though people talk this place up, I don't usually love the food. It used to be Zelo's, a popular bar and grill, but recently it was remodeled and turned into a more upscale version with the same bar food—as well as higher prices and an often robotic staff. However, they prepare seafood well. So if you are hungry, the seafood chowder, Waldorf salad, fish-and-chips, or tacos are good choices. They offer wraps at lunch, but the last time I was here, the tortilla was microwaved and the insides were too heavy to fit inside. For dinner, the menu gets a bit larger, with a few more chicken, fish, and meat dishes. All in all, you should depend on Kalypso's for decent-sized portions, tropical drinks, and evening fun.

Neide's Salsa and Samba

808-826-1851.
5-5161 Kuhio Hwy., Hanalei.
Open: Daily.
Price: Inexpensive—moderate.
Cuisine: Mexican/Brazilian.
Serving: L, D.
Credit Cards: MC, V.
Handicapped Access: Yes.

Outdoor dining, with views of the birds singing in the trees, gives this Mexican and Brazilian spot a remote feeling even though it is in the heart of Hanalei. This restaurant has quickly become a local favorite, serving up heaping bowls of free chips and salsa to go with your beer while you wait for Neide to prepare your meal. Everything comes out fresh, and that means it can take a little while to get your food. Specialties go two ways—Mexican or Brazilian. I always go Brazilian, but that doesn't mean the Mexican food isn't worth trying: heaping portions of fish tacos, carne asada, enchiladas, huevos rancheros, or Mexican-style fresh-caught seafood plates (make sure to ask the market price before ordering, as prices can be high). But I find the Brazilian fare is what to get. The muquecas (fish in a coconut and red palm oil broth) are often better than some you'll find in northeastern Brazil (where the dish originates). The panquecas are a great choice for vegetarians. Brazilian beef dishes spill over the already big, colorful plates. You won't find food like this elsewhere on the island.

Polynesia Café

808-826-1999.
5-5190 Kuhio Hwy., Hanalei.
808-822-1945.
1639 Kuhio Hwy., Kapa'a.
Open: Daily.
Price: Moderate—expensive.
Cuisine: American/Hawaiian.
Serving: B, L, D.
Credit Cards: AE, MC, V.
Handicapped Access: Yes.

When the first location of the Polynesia Café opened on the north shore in 2001, serving up "Gourmet food on paper plates," no one was quite sure what to make of it. Soon, locals and tourists found out that the food was actually pretty tasty, despite the hefty price tag. Now the Polynesia Café has opened another location in downtown Kapa'a and serves up consistently great food in a colorful environment. Both locations offer an open-air dining experience, with artwork by local artist Avi Kiriaty lining the walls and island motif tables and chairs available for purchase. In both spots, there are outdoor picnic tables (the Kapa'a location offers views of the beach across the street). Aside from the funky vibe, people actually come here for the food. Look for a large selection of Hawaiian, American, and international-style food with creative twists that make both meat eaters and vegetarians happy (almost everything can be made into a vegetarian version). Some unique breakfast offerings are the blue crab loco moco (which is more like an eggs Benedict), kalua pork loco moco, huevos rancheros, blintzes, and gingerbread pancakes, for about $10 each. Lunch gets a bit greasier with a vast selection of salads (like the 'ahi or fajita), sandwiches (favorites include the fajita-seared tofu sandwich or the burger), and some Mexican dishes (yep, here you can find heaping enchiladas, nachos, and quesadillas). Dinner gets a bit pricier, but is still creative. Try the delicious 'ahi katsu sashimi, kalua pork lumpia, crab and scallop potato cakes, pineapple jam pork, liliko'i scallops, Thai curry boats, and Kaua'i jungle chicken. The Kapa'a location is actually one of my favorite places to get a tropical drink and a pupu after the beach. If you want to drink at the Hanalei location, make sure to bring your own.

✪ Postcards Café

808-826-1191.
5-5075A Kuhio Hwy., Hanalei.
Open: Daily.
Price: Moderate–expensive.
Cuisine: Gourmet organic
seafood/vegetarian.
Serving: D.
Credit Cards: AE, D, MC, V.
Handicapped Access: Yes.
Reservations recommended.

In 1996, when Postcards Café opened in this 140-year-old plantation-style cottage, north shore food lovers didn't know how lucky they'd just become. Serving up some of the most consistently delicious and creative gourmet seafood and natural foods around, this torchlit dinner spot never fails to make diners happy—and bring back a string of local regulars. You can sit either on the romantic candlelit lanai or inside the house, where pictures of Hanalei history line the walls. To start, check out their selection of organic wine—or try out the hibiscus cooler, banana shake, a smoothie, or the Hanalei Rush (fresh vegetable juice). When ordering, remember that they pride themselves on serving only organic vegetables (which they grow themselves) and locally purchased food. No meat, poultry, or chemicals are served up here. To go along with this slow-food mentality, also bear in mind that often service, though friendly, can be slow. So ask for bread if it is busy and order accordingly. Appetizers span the globe with Thai summer rolls, amazing taro fritters, seared 'ahi, crab quesadilla, porcini-crusted scallops, and seafood rockets (which are basically lumpia); since everything is tasty, you might try the pupu platter. Every night they also offer a vegan soup and organic salads. The small entrée menu offers seafood in one of three ways (my favorite is the peppered-pineapple chutney), wasabi-crusted 'ahi, a vegetarian southwestern dish called the Sombrero, plus a decent kids' menu. Make sure to save room for the vegan desserts (which don't taste vegan). The big hunk of carrot cake keeps you satisfied long after you leave this homey spot.

Sushi Blues

808-826-9701.
www.sushiandblues.com.
Ching Young Village, 5-5190 Kuhio Hwy.,
Hanalei.
Open: Daily.
Price: Expensive.
Cuisine: Japanese.
Serving: D.
Credit Cards: MC, V.
Handicapped Access: Yes.

Perched on the second floor of the Ching Young Center with views of the mountains and Bali Hai, this open-air sushi spot attracts people from all over the island. With music blaring and murals lining the walls, I always feel like I am entering a rock-and-roll club instead of a civilized sushi spot. They serve up massive sushi rolls with creative combinations like the Waimea Roll (garlic tuna) and Grasshopper Roll (BBQ eel, avocado, and macadamia nuts). Plus they offer a variety of traditional sushi favorites in the form of hand rolls, nigiri, and sashimi. If you aren't into raw fish, they also serve big salads (though most come with seafood), a seafood stir-fry or pasta, or the locally caught fish prepared grilled in a sake cream sauce, wok charred in an orange BBQ glaze, or sesame crusted in a passion fruit/coconut *buerre blanc*. Nonseafood items include the grilled kiwi teriyaki chicken or sweet-and-sour baby back ribs. Vegetarians have slim pickings here. However, the main draw is actually the nightlife. With 10 different martinis, 20 tropical drink options, and a decent selection of international beer, wine, and sake, locals come here to get their drink on and enjoy the nightly live jazz.

Kilauea

✪ Kilauea Fish Market

808-828-6244.
4270 Kilauea Lighthouse Rd., Kilauea.
Open: Mon.–Sat.

Price: Inexpensive–moderate.
Cuisine: Organic Hawaiian.
Serving: L, D (until 8 PM only).
Credit Cards: MC, V.
Handicapped Access: Yes.

Don't let the name fool you. This is not a mere fish market. These folks serve some of the freshest chow around. Yes, this happens to be one of the best places to purchase fresh-caught local seafood, but you can also sit down at the plastic tables, set in the back of a strip mall with views of an open field, and grub on the best food deal on the north shore. My favorite item is the *'ahi* or tofu wrap, bulging with rice, vegetables, cabbage, and organic greens. The surprisingly large menu offers salads, burritos, fish tacos, healthy gourmet plate lunches (with hormone-free meat), and organic

The hidden Kilauea Fish Market is worth a stop.

rice bowls. Plus you'll find a variety of deli items, including free-range filet mignon, wild Alaskan salmon, sesame 'ahi poke, real wasabi root, organic greens, and tropical salads. For dessert, check out their gluten-free brownies, macaroons, or tapioca. Understand that this is not a fancy affair. In fact, it is one of the cheapest places to eat on the north shore, which is why you'll always find the locals lining up at lunch.

Lighthouse Bistro
808-828-0480.
www.lighthousebistro.com.
2484 Keneke St., Kilauea.
Open: Daily.
Price: Inexpensive—very expensive.
Cuisine: Pacific/European fusion.
Serving: L (Mon.–Sat. only), D.
Credit Cards: MC, V.
Handicapped Access: Yes.
Reservations recommended.

When you enter the Lighthouse Bistro, you'll think you've walked into someone's plantation house. Tables are carefully spaced along the big open windows; there are high ceilings, bright colorful artwork on the walls, a small bar, and a nice lanai. Four nights a week, a local musician strums the guitar. Coming here always makes me feel like I have stumbled into a secret locals' spot. And even better, the food is good. Lunch is a simple affair of sandwiches and burgers, wraps and burritos (all inexpensive). But dinner is when the creativity of this small restaurant thrives (and the prices rise dramatically). Tropical drinks are served in martini glasses to match the theme of the particular beverage you order. Appetizers (though expensive) fuse tastes from the Philippines, Italy, and Hawai'i, with fish rockets and artichoke piccata being the stars. There are a couple of salad options each night and a soup of the day (which is usually tasty and unique). If you are looking for an inexpensive meal (or

something for the kids), the all-you-can-eat pasta bar with four sauce choices for less than $20 always leaves me content (especially because their mac-nut pesto is so good). If you are looking for hearty entrées, you can get fish served three ways (blackened with papaya salsa, grilled with lemon *buerre blanc*, or ginger-crusted with soy wasabi), and steak three ways (blackened, delmonico, or grilled). Other entrée options are the shrimp Parmesan, the Lighthouse Napoleon (a hearty stack of vegetables), or the coconut-crusted pork loin. Entrées tend to be on the big side, so if you order right, two people can eat for 40 bucks.

Princeville

Bali Hai
808-826-6522.
Hanalei Bay Resort, 5380 Honoiki Rd., Princeville.
Open: Wed.–Sun.
Price: Moderate—very expensive.
Cuisine: Gourmet Hawaiian.
Serving: B, D.
Credit Cards: MC, V.
Handicapped Access: Yes.
Reservations recommended.
Special Features: Bali Hai restaurant can be rented for special events.

Around town the joke about this restaurant is that the birds often get to your table before the waiters. But with this view of Hanalei Bay, who cares? Even if you don't want to fork over the exorbitant amount of money you'll have to pay for food, stop here for a drink, a picture, something. And the food? Well, it is actually pretty good—one of the only true Hawaiian-style gourmet restaurants around. They like to brag that they use locally grown organic vegetables and herbs. I actually like to come here for breakfast, when they serve up a mean Portuguese sausage, *poi* pancakes, chicken apple sausage (one of the only places on

Diners at high-end Princeville-area restaurants will enjoy the sun setting over Bali Hai and the Hanalei Bay.

Kaua'i to find this breakfast favorite), tropical fruit with mint yogurt, mac-nut waffles, and traditional egg dishes with *nori*. Dinner, as you might imagine (this restaurant is consistently voted "Best View" in local magazines and newspapers) is expensive. Pupus range from Asian cold tofu to the *ahi poke* tower, with a few salad offerings. Entrées are heavy on meat and seafood. The specialties are the steak *Olowalu*, the lobster pasta medley, a sweet Singapore curry, and the fresh seafood catch served four ways (mac-nut crusted, peppered with pineapple and mango chutney, pan-seared, or topped with portobello, crab, and Boursin cheese). If all you can swing is a nightcap, this is a perfect spot for some chocolate and Kona coffee. Just make sure to visit this restaurant, because this is that place where people propose, couples celebrate anniversaries, and romantics wish they could write poetry to accurately capture the view. But bring a sweater because often if the wind is kicking, it can get chilly inside this open-air restaurant.

Café Hanalei

808-826-2760.
www.princevillehotelhawaii.com.
Princeville Hotel, 5520 Ka Haku Rd.,
Princeville.
Open: Daily.
Price: Moderate—very expensive.
Cuisine: Gourmet Pacific Rim.
Serving: B, L, D, SB.
Credit Cards: AE, D, DC, JCB, MC, V.
Handicapped Access: Yes.
Reservations recommended.

Just below the chandeliers of the palatial Princeville Hotel sits Café Hanalei. Don't let the *café* part of the name fool you: This high-end restaurant, with sweeping views of Hanalei Bay, serves some of the most decadent dishes on the north shore at steep prices. This is the spot to get a seat on the terrace and splurge. Breakfast centers on eggs and griddle goods with sweet toppings: taro pancakes with bananas, for instance, or vanilla Belgian waffle. My favorite is the pricey Japanese breakfast with salmon and eggs, miso soup, tofu, and vegetables. On Sunday they serve a buffet packed with traditional brunch goodies like blintzes, deli meats and seafood, pancakes, and eggs. Lunch features lighter fare like salads (Hawaiian-style chicken or a Caesar), an 'ahi trio, sushi rolls, the 'ahi sandwich, or a bento box. In general portions are pretty small, so if you are hungry (and don't want to fork over almost 20 bucks for a salad), you might want to try somewhere else for lunch. Dinner is where the Café Hanalei shines. Yes, it is still expensive, but the romantic setting might be just what you want to feel; princely (or princess-like). Appetizers rely heavily on seafood with blue crab cakes, diver scallops, and varieties of 'ahi. Entrées offer options for almost everyone—the tofu tower, organic chicken breast with a pad Thai salad, Angus tenderloin with miso-glazed prawns, or catch-of-the-day. If you are planning to go big, I recommend the three-course dinner with an appetizer, entrée, dessert, and French press coffee for over $50 a person.

CJ's Steak and Seafood
808-826-6211.
Princeville Shopping Center, 5-4280 Kuhio Hwy., Princeville.
Open: Daily.
Price: Expensive—very expensive.
Cuisine: Steak and seafood.
Serving: L (Mon.–Fri.), D.
Credit Cards: AE, D, DC, JCB, MC, V.
Handicapped Access: Yes.
Reservations recommended.

For steak and seafood lovers who want a laid-back atmosphere, CJ's has been serving chops to the north shore area for over 25 years. Located in a big building in the Princeville Shopping Center, the vibe might remind you of the mainland chain restaurants, but the food has a distinctly Hawaiian twist. The sign outside the restaurant says, COME HUNGRY, and that is exactly what you should do. Though the fare isn't cheap, the servings are quite hefty. Pupus aren't much to speak of, and since each entrée comes with a visit to the salad bar, vegetables and fruit, rolls and rice, you don't need to worry about going hungry. Standard fare includes the catch-of-the-day served three ways (broiled, sautéed, or Cajun), shrimp (sautéed, in a macadamia coconut batter, or teriyaki), or a variety of steak cuts (prime rib, top sirloin, tenderloin, and more). Vegetarians definitely should eat elsewhere. This is a good option for people staying in Princeville, families, and people craving bovine protein.

La Cascata
808-826-2761.
www.princevillehotelhawaii.com.
Princeville Hotel, 5520 Ka Haku Rd., Princeville.
Open: Daily.
Price: Expensive—very expensive.
Cuisine: Mediterranean—Pacific Rim fusion.
Serving: D.
Credit Cards: AE, D, DC, JCB, MC, V.
Handicapped Access: Yes.
Reservations recommended.

People who stay at the Princeville Hotel expect regal treatment, and so guests at their restaurants get to slip on that crown for their short reign as royalty, too. La Cascata knows how to offer this service. From the moment guests cascade down the steps and enter the dining area (which the restaurant shares with Café Hanalei), views of the expansive Hanalei Bay open up. If dining above the parade of fish, surfers,

A wall of windows at the Princeville Resort's La Cascata.

and mere common folk on the Hanalei beaches isn't enough, then the food is sure to offer that little special feeling. Basically, La Cascata is an Italian restaurant using Hawaiian ingredients. For pupus you'll notice rigatoni with hamakua mushrooms, or seafood ravioli with local shrimp and diver scallops. Dishes like linguine pomodoro with Koloa asparagus, an organic chicken breast with Hawaiian sweet potatoes, or the black-pepper-crusted duck breast with a sweet potato mash make up some of the entrée selections. The chef will often make additions to the menu depending on what is in season. If you really want the royal dining experience, try the three-course menu with an appetizer, entrée, dessert, and coffee drink.

Paradise Bar and Grill

808-826-1775.
Princeville Shopping Center, Princeville.
Open: Daily.
Price: Inexpensive–expensive.
Cuisine: American/Hawaiian.
Serving: L, D.
Credit Cards: D, MC, V.
Handicapped Access: Yes.

If you are tired of cooking, want a fun place to take the kids, or are looking for a reasonably inexpensive lunch in Princeville,

Paradise Bar and Grill might be just the ticket. This is probably the cheapest place to eat in Princeville. Offering up a sports bar vibe, with a young energetic wait staff, loud music playing, plastic tablecloths, and a giant surfboard table at the bar, this is an easy place to relax with a beer and some bar food, watching sports on the big-screen TVs in the late afternoon. The thatched roof and local artwork make this little hole-in-the-wall seem like a find, but locals know it as a good place to get cheap burgers, salads, and fried food priced at under 20 bucks. You can also sit on the lanai, if you want a view of the strip mall.

FOOD PURVEYORS (BY NEIGHBORHOOD)

Separated from the mainland United States by 3,000 miles, Hawai'i has had to become agriculturally self-sufficient. And because of the distance between islands, locals actually have a semi-sustainable agricultural practice. You will find a wealth of locally grown vegetables and fruit sold at farmer's (or Sunshine) markets, at roadside stands, and even in some restaurants. Also, because food is so pricey here, many supermarkets and bakeries offer heaping plate lunches for only a couple of dollars. The following are some of the unique places and products to make your trip to Kaua'i taste better . . . without obliterating your wallet. Since chain stores are predictable and easy to spot, there is no need to mention them here. Instead, I have chosen to focus on unique Kaua'i food purveyors, where you might find local delicacies such as *poi* or *haupia* or maybe. hiding in a roadside stand, the best banana bread you've ever tasted.

Bakeries

Hawaiians love their baked goods. And even though you'll find sweets everywhere, there are a few shining stars that are serving up delicious bread and pastries. We'll start on the east shore, where **Country Moon Rising** (808-822-0345; 4-1345 Kuhio Hwy., Kapa'a) opened up shop in a little garage-like space in downtown Kapa'a. This is the spot to get organic bread and pastries, but get here early, because they sell out fast. Most local organic restaurants serve their bread, and when the aroma of their goods baking dances through downtown Kapa'a, you'll know why. Another bakery to explore is **Lotus Root** (808-823-6658, 4-1384 Kuhio Hwy., Kapa'a), the little sibling of Blossoming Lotus, which serves organic, vegan (and some raw) pastries, sandwiches, salads, and smoothies.

Up on the north shore, **Kilauea Bakery and Pau Hana Pizza** (808-828-2020, Kong Lung Center, Kilauea) offers some of the best pizza, sandwiches, and pastries on the island. You might also check out **Mango Mama's** and **Banana Joe's** (see Coffeehouses, below, for both).

Caterers

Many restaurants cater private parties, so you might want to ask around at spots you particularly like (or ones listed in the restaurant section that sound especially good). Below are private catering companies and a few restaurants that also specialize in creating meals. If you are staying at the Sheraton, Hyatt, or Princeville, ask the concierge about their private beachfront dining options.

Blossoming Lotus (808-823-6658). Gourmet organic vegan cuisine.

Casablanca (808-742-2929). Mediterranean cuisine.

Gaylord's Restaurant (808-245-9592). Continental American/Hawaiian.

Heavenly Creations Gourmet Cuisine (808-828-1700; www.heavenlycreations .org). Gourmet healthy food for receptions, buffets, and romantic beachside dinners.

Buy local produce or get a frosty at Banana Joe's.

Kaua'i Cuisine (808-635-3722; www.kauaicuisine.com). Dinner menus honor the diversity of the island. Specializing in locally bought produce, they will create a menu rich in fusion flavors. **Windward Market** (808-822-9332; 4-1543 Kuhio Hwy., Kapa'a). These professional chefs serve up gourmet local goods with an emphasis on comfort food.

COFFEEHOUSES, CAFÉS, AND BREAKFAST SPOTS

Even though mainland coffee shops charge big bucks for Kona coffee, it can be hard to find a good place to enjoy it in Kaua'i. The local-coffeehouse vibe has struggled here since the arrival of national chain coffee shops. Listed are some coffeehouses and cafés that are surviving. Just. I have also included some small spots to get a decent breakfast or lunch with your coffee.

EAST SHORE

Java Kai
808-823-6887.
4-1384 Kuhio Hwy., Kapa'a.

The first of this locally owned chain is a popular choice for folks who want not only the coffeehouse vibe of artwork, pastries, and the smell of fresh-burned beans, but also free wireless access. This little spot in downtown Kapa'a feels like it could be on the mainland. Specializing in local fair-trade brews made fresh when you order, espresso drinks, pastries, and some small breakfast and lunch offerings, this little café draws a loyal following.

✪ Small Town Coffee
808-821-1604.
www.smalltowncoffee.com.
4-1495 Kuhio Hwy., Kapa'a.

This is by far the best coffee house on Kaua'i. It's nestled in a little blue house right on the river in Kapaʻa, with views of the ocean and river from all three patios. The owners understand that a coffeehouse is a gathering place, a communal space. And they have the best coffee. Using Barefoot Coffee Roaster's beans, they serve espresso drinks, flavored coffees, and pastries. Co-owner Anni Caporuscio won the 2006 Hawaiʻi Barista Challenge and has a slew of regulars driving over 40 miles a day for one of her lattes. Given its free wireless access and a great ambience, you might immediately understand why this place is often packed. Unfortunately, parking is difficult. At press time, the owners were battling with the city council to get a crosswalk built so people could park and legally cross the street.

SOUTH SHORE

Kalaheo Café and Coffee Co
808-332-5858.
www.kalaheo.com.
2-2560 Kaumualiʻi Hwy., Kalaheo.
Open: Daily.
Serving: B, L, D (Wed.–Sat.).

For the past decade and a half, this has been the only place to get a decent caffeine fix on the south shore. This spacious café is often packed with locals and tourists indulging in fresh-baked pastries as well as traditional breakfasts of egg sandwiches, pancakes, French toast, and fruit for a reasonable price. For lunch they serve hearty pastrami, Cajun tofu, and tuna fish sandwiches (to name a few), or a wealth of Kalaheo green salads. Dinners are a mishmash of home-style American fare (burgers, macaroni and cheese), Mexican entrées (enchiladas, nachos), and local plates (seafood or meat with rice).

Tutu's Café
808-332-0555.
2-2436 Kaumualiʻi Hwy., Kalaheo.

Open: Tues.–Sun.

A welcome addition to the south shore breakfast and lunch scene, this little hole-in-the-wall in Kalaheo serves up affordable food with a homey flair. Tutu (which means "grandma" in Hawaiian) opened this little spot, just past Papalina off Kaumualiʻi Highway, in late 2005. She cooks. Her grandson sometimes works the register. Her family is a constant presence. Aside from the plastic chairs, you might feel like you are at her house. Breakfast is quite simple, with scrambles, omelets, and pancakes, while lunch consists of "local grindz" for you to eat in or take out.

WEST SHORE

Grinds
808-335-6027.
4469 Waialo Rd., Hanapepe.

Small Town Coffee serves the best lattes on the island.

This old diner, reminiscent of a Dairy Queen, serves up breakfast all day—omelets, *loco moco*, or griddle fare—for a good price. They bake their own bread daily and have a wealth of pastries. For lunch and dinner, they offer organic salads, pizzas, sandwiches, and plate lunches with your choice of meat. Though the food is not the best, nor the coffee the most interesting, locals love the laid-back atmosphere of this place.

Aloha-n-Paradise

808-338-1522.
9905 Waimea Rd., Waimea Town.

This little espresso bar and art gallery is a mellow spot to stop on your way to or from Waimea Canyon. Here you can learn about local artists (and maybe purchase something to take home). Plus, they offer Internet access.

NORTH SHORE

Banana Joe's

808-828-1092.
Located on the mountain side of Kuhio Hwy., just north of the Kilauea turnoff.

This funky little shack serves up some of the tastiest frosties, smoothies, and pastries on the north shore. You can purchase locally grown fruits and vegetables, coffee, and small eats, but the big draw here is the banana frosty.

Java Kai

808-826-6717.
5-5183 Kuhio Hwy., Hanalei.

The Hanalei location of this local chain is found inside a little house in the center of town. People hang out all day on the small lanai; by the end of your stay, you'll probably be recognized by the locals. Often this

Sweets, smoothies, and coffee in downtown Hanalei.

little coffeehouse reminds me that Hanalei truly is a small town. It seems that everyone in town pops in to say hi. The owners go out of their way to advertise organic, fair-trade brews, smoothies, and food (but I do have to complain that they don't offer an organic milk option). Often there is free wireless (as long as the signal is working). At press time, the owners were looking to serve lunch here as well.

Mango Mama's Café
808-828-1020.
At the Hookui Rd. turnoff along H 56.

You can't miss this hot-pink shack with black-and-white zebra-striped signs on the beach side of the road just past Kilauea. They specialize in organic coffee, smoothies, and juices. Plus the pastries, nuts, and produce are always fresh. In addition to the juice drinks, they also serve bagel sandwiches, organic granola, veggie burgers, tuna, and turkey sandwiches. Since there aren't really any breakfast spots in Kilauea, this is a good place to stop before heading out on an adventure. Bear in mind that they do not have a restroom.

Na Pali Art Gallery and Coffee Shop
808-826-1844.
Hanalei Colony Resort, Haena.

This little coffee shop/art gallery mainly serves the Hanalei Colony guests and the few passersby heading to and from Ke'e Beach. With not many hearty options (smoothies, bagels, and pastries), the main draw here is coffee and espresso drinks. There are only a few tables scattered in the parking lot, because inside is an art gallery/gift shop. They do have wireless here (though I have often found that it doesn't work well).

Spinners Coffee
Princeville Shopping Center.

Not wanting the Princeville folks to get left out of the espresso craze, Spinners Coffee opened a kiosk in the Princeville Shopping Center. Here you can get espresso drinks (made with Peet's Coffee), pastries, smoothies, and a few breakfast and lunch options.

DESSERTS

In addition to **Lappert's** numerous locations (808-822-0744; Coconut Marketplace, Wailua. 808-742-1272; 5242 Koloa Rd., Koloa. 808-335-6121; across from Wong's in Hanapepe. 808-826-7393; Princeville Center, Princeville) and the shave ice spots listed in the sidebar, locating a place to satisfy your sweet tooth is easy as pie.

If you are on the east shore, **Beezer's Ice Cream** (808-822-4411; 1380 Kuhio Hwy., Kapa'a) is an old-school soda-pop shop that specializes in huge servings of ice cream, pies, and cakes. **Zack's Frozen Yogurt** (Coconut Plaza Marketplace, Wailua) is another option to give you a brain freeze. Or if it's baked goods you want, head over to the **Hanalima Baking Co** (808-246-8816, 4495 Puhi Rd., Lihu'e).

On the rest of the island, the best places to satisfy your sweet tooth are at one of the shops listed in Coffeehouses. On the north shore, my favorite is **Banana Joe's**, but friends swear by the pastries at **Java Kai** or **Mango Mama's**.

FARMER'S (SUNSHINE) MARKETS

Created to encourage local farmers to share their bounty, the Sunshine Markets of Kaua'i sell only locally grown produce. You will find other farmer's markets along the roadside, but these listed are officially organized by the county, ensuring that the

Shave Ice Locations

This Hawaiian tradition dating back to missionary times isn't your typical snow cone. There is an art to shaving the ice in such a way that it almost melts in your mouth. True, this Hawaiian treat is nothing more than ice with sugary syrup poured over the top, but good places know how to do it and even add a little extra to the experience. I recommend trying a local fruit shave ice (*liliko'i*, pineapple, coconut, mango) with ice cream or—my favorite—with red *azuki* beans at the bottom. It sounds strange, but tastes great. Below are some places that specialize in shave ice.

EAST SHORE
Halo Halo Shave Ice: 808-245-5094; Hamura Saimin, 2956 Kress St., Lihu'e.

SOUTH SHORE
Da Opu Kaa: This truck parks across from the Beach House Beach in Poipu daily.

WEST SHORE
✪ **Jo-Jo's Clubhouse:** 9734 Kaumuali'i Hwy., Waimea. Ask any locals: They will tell you that this is the best shave ice on the island. Worth waiting in line, worth poor service, even worth the headache you will get from too much sugar. Open 10:30–5:30 every day and serving 60 flavors.

NORTH SHORE
Shave Ice Paradise: 808-826-6659; 5-5161 Kuhio Hwy., Hanalei.
Wishing Well Shave Ice: You will see this truck on the side of road in Hanalei.

Locals swear Jojo's makes the best shave ice on the island.

Stock up on fruit at a Sunshine Market.

fruit and vegetables you buy are grown here. Markets begin with a chant; then the masses are let in. Get there early, because the good produce sells out quickly and most of the markets only last for about an hour. Make sure to try fruit that you have never seen before. Kaua'i produces some of the best star fruit, guava, and lichee I have ever tasted.

Also, if you are shopping for organic fruit and vegetables, be cautious. I have found that often growers will tell me an avocado or banana is organic, but later I'll hear from another grower that the salesperson lied just to sell his or her goods. A friend's mantra is if the seller smells, the fruit is organic. Lately I have gone by that.

Here is the Sunshine Market schedule:

Monday	noon	Koloa (Knudsen) Park, Koloa
Monday	3 PM	Kukui Grove Shopping Center, Lihu'e
Tuesday	3 PM	Wailua Homesteads Park, Wailua
Tuesday	3:30 PM	Kalaheo Neighborhood Center, Kalaheo
Wednesday	3 PM	Kapa'a New Town Park, Kapa'a
Thursday	3:30 PM	Hanapepe Town Park, Hanapepe
Thursday	4:30 PM	Kilauea Neighborhood Center, Kilauea
Friday	3 PM	Vidinha Stadium, Lihu'e
Saturday	9 AM	Kekeha Neighborhood Center, Kekaha
Saturday	9:30 AM	Hanalei Neighborhood Center, Hanalei

GOURMET AND NATURAL FOOD MARKETS

Since the arrival of Wal-Mart and Costco on Kaua'i, local markets have felt dramatic losses to their businesses. And because it's so easy to spot the mega-markets scattered around the island, I have mainly listed food stores that specialize in natural or gourmet food.

On the east shore, there are a bunch of markets set up to serve all types of food lovers. Not only will you find the big markets stretched along Kuhio Highway through Lihu'e, Wailua, and Kapa'a, but you'll spot many smaller stores worth a peek, too. My favorite place to get organic food, take-out sandwiches, and salads is **Papaya's Natural Foods** (808-823-0190; Kaua'i Village Shopping Center, 4-831 Kuhio Hwy., Wailua). Even though it is one of the most expensive places to shop, you can find organic dairy products, international food, and fresh produce grown on the island.

The new **Windward Market** (808-822-9332; 4-1543 Kuhio Hwy., Kapa'a), opened by three ex-chefs from Postcards Café, Coconuts Restaurant, and the late Aromas Restaurant, serves gourmet food lovers on Kaua'i. They sell locally caught seafood as well as hormone-free meats and chicken, foie gras, specialty cheeses, hamakua mushrooms, and venison. In addition, they have a vast selection of plate lunches, soups, salads, and sandwiches to go.

On the south shore, **Koloa Natural Foods** (808-742-8910; 5356 Koloa Rd.) has a small array of natural and organic products at very high prices. They also have iffy hours. I can't tell you how many times I came here when they were supposed to be open and found a sign on the door saying they'd be back.

Though it doesn't offer any organic or gourmet products to speak of, I can't write about markets without mentioning the legendary **Sueoka's Store** (808-742-1611; 5392 Koloa Rd., Koloa), which offers a huge selection of food at reasonable prices (by Hawaiian standards). They also have souvenirs and local food to try.

Over on the west shore, aside from a couple mini marts and big markets, the 75-year-old **Ishihara Market** (808-338-1751; 9894 Kaumuali'i Hwy., Waimea) has almost everything you need to stock up a kitchen (save gourmet or natural food products). Plus they serve a huge selection of food to go.

If you want natural foods on the north shore, you are in luck. **Papaya's Natural Foods** (808-826-0089, Hanalei Center, Hanalei) has a large location in the center of town. And in Kilauea, **Healthy Hut Natural Foods** (808-828-6626, Kiahuna Plantation Center, Kilauea) offers a good selection of local natural foods and some favorites from the mainland.

For fish, meat, and organic greens, head over to the **Kilauea Fish Market** (808-828-6244; 4270 Kilauea Lighthouse Rd., Kilauea). The **Hanalei Dolphin Fish Market** (808-826-6113; 5-5016 Kuhio Hwy., Hanalei) sells fresh local fish and pre-prepared sushi, teriyaki shrimp and beef, and salads.

PLATE LUNCH/LOCAL FOOD

Hawaiian food is a cultural fusion. With ingredients from Japan, Polynesia, China, the Philippines, and Portugal, not to mention the infamous Spam and *poi*, it is nearly impossible to classify a plate lunch. Basically what you can expect is some hearty artery-clogging food that often tastes better than anything you pay big bucks for at the Grand Hyatt.

When ordering a plate lunch, generally you can expect a couple pieces of meat or fish, two scoops of white rice, and macaroni salad. Other additions like *poke*, *poi*, seaweed salad, or Spam are good side additions, in case your plate lunch won't fill you up. This is the cheapest way to eat on the island. Most local food spots either don't have seating, or have a small area. What they lack in ambience, they make up for in flavor—both cultural and sensory. Having a plate lunch on Kaua'i is a must. And below are some of the best places to try it out.

The best (and cheapest) place to get take-out local food on the east shore is **Pono Market** (4-1300 Kuhio Hwy., Kapa'a). With a nice selection of *poke*, salads, seafood, and meat plate lunches, plus typical market goods, this makes the perfect stop to stock up your refrigerator. This is also where to buy leis.

If you are in Lihu'e, **Ara's Sakana-ya Fish House** (808-245-1707; Hanamaulu Plaza, Kuhio Hwy. and Hanamaulu Rd.) serves up big plate lunches and takeout, including a generous selection of *poke*. The menu changes daily, depending on what is fresh.

For a more traditional sit-down dining experience in Lihu'e, the **Oki Diner** (808-245-5899, 3125 Kuhio Hwy.) offers plate lunches until 3 AM. Or the famous **Tip Top Café/Sushi Katsu** (808-245-2333, 3173 Akahi St., Lihu'e) serves Hawaiian-style breakfast and lunch, and Japanese dinners (every day but Mon.) in a giant cafeteria filled with big gray booths. This is the place to try out some local favorites like oxtail stew, saimin, or plate lunches at good prices. Finally, if you really want an inexpensive plate lunch to clog those arteries, the **Lihu'e Bowling Alley** (808-245-5263; 4303 Rice St., Lihu'e) has a pretty darn good one.

In Koloa, attached to Sueoka's Market, **Sueoka's Snack Shop** (808-742-1112; 5392 Koloa Rd.) offers hefty plate lunches for cheap prices. But for the best local food and plate lunches on the island, make sure to stop at the literally hole-in-the-wall **Koloa Fish Market** (808-742-6199; 5482 Koloa Rd., Koloa). They serve up the best *poke* I have ever tasted, fantastic seaweed and macaroni salads, and massive plate

lunches. The menu changes daily (depending on what comes in fresh), and there is usually a line out the door. Also, there are only a couple of chairs on the lanai, so get takeout and head home or to the beach.

QUICK EATS AND SNACKS

Kaua'i locals spend so much time outdoors that often they choose to eat faster meals or get takeout. So there is a wealth of these little joints to choose from. Since chains are easy to spot, I have chosen to include only local and unique options.

The east shore is your best bet for fast food. The most popular (and best) take-out sandwiches on the island are at the **Deli and Bread Connection** (808-245-7115; Kukui Grove Center, 2600 Kaumuali'i Hwy., Lihu'e). Open all day, every day, they have an excellent selection of huge sandwiches, fresh-baked breads, and sweets. Some island-style favorites are the lobsta roll, *kalua* pork, or traditional turkey, beef, and veggie sandwiches.

For take-out health food, try **Papaya's Natural Foods** (Kaua'i Village Shopping Center: 808-823-0190; 4-831 Kuhio Hwy.; or 808-826-0089; Hanalei Center, Hanalei). They serve mostly organic food, with a decent selection of salads and sandwiches, which you can enjoy on one of the outdoor picnic tables dotting the grass. If it is seriously healthy fare you are after, **Lotus Root** (808-823-6658, 4-1384 Kuhio Hwy., Kapa'a) is Blossoming Lotus's little sister, and serves smoothies, sandwiches, and salads.

The Coconut Marketplace (4-484 Kuhio Hwy., Wailua) has a slew of quick-stop restaurants, perfect for those of you wanting a bite while shopping or before a film. **Old Manila Bakery and Café** serves up American and Filipino-style pastries for breakfast and lunch. If you want some sweet barbecue, try **Harley Ribs-n-Chicken** (808-822-2505). **Aloha Kaua'i Pizza** (808-

822-4511) calls itself the best pizza on Kaua'i. Though that might be bold of them, the Artichoke Eddie pizza is worth a test run.

The best fast-food joint in Poipu is **Puka Dogs** (808-635-6354; Poipu Shopping Village, 2360 Kiahuna Plantation). With only a choice of veggie dog or Polish sausage, you decide if you want mild, spicy (which is spiced, but not hot), or killer garlic sauce; then choose which tropical fruit relish you like (mango, coconut, papaya . . .). Finally, your dog is grilled until the skin is a little crunchy. They squirt a ton of sauce on your wiener and stuff it into an oversized bun. Try the fresh-squeezed lemonade (but watch out: They use an obscene amount of sugar), or bring your own drink. **Brennecke's Deli** (808-742-1582; Poipu Beach Park, 2100 Hoone Rd., Poipu) is a good place to get a cheap club sandwich during your day at the beach.

After a journey around Koke'e, try out **Koke'e Lodge** (808-335-6061; 3600 Koke'e Rd.) next to the gift shop and museum. They serve eggs, pancakes, or French toast for breakfast. Lunch offers salads, chili and corn bread, sandwiches, beer, and cold refreshments with a view of the roosters running around the park.

If it is tacos you're after, you're in luck because the popular after-surf craze has arrived. On the east shore, **Monico's Taqueria** (808-822-4300: Kinipopo Shopping Village, 4-356D Kuhio Hwy., Kapa'a) recently started dishing up authentic Mexican delights. Their tacos actually taste like they come from San Diego, or maybe even Cabo. Open for lunch and dinner, but closed Tuesdays, this hidden strip mall restaurant is often busy, so if you want your food to go, call ahead. On the north shore, **Tropical Taco** (808-827-8226; 5-5088 Kuhio Hwy., Hanalei) serves up giant (and cheap) burritos. Though a better option for Mexican fare is **Neide's** (see the North Shore Restaurants section). In

Haena, the ever-popular **Red Hot Mamas** (808-826-7266, 5-6607 Kuhio Hwy., Haena) is a mere crack-in-the-wall in the Last Stop Shopping Center. They serve organic burritos, tacos, and Mexican fast food, using hormone-free chicken, grass-fed beef, and organic vegetables.

Dying for a quick burger? No worries—burger madness has hit Kaua'i with a vengeance. The best on the island (which you'll know by the wait) is **Duane's Ono Charburgers** (808-822-9181; 4-4350 Kuhio Hwy., Anahola), which I mention in detail in the above Restaurant section. If you can get over **Bubba's Burgers** (808-823-0069; 4-1384 Kuhio Hwy., Kapa'a. 808-826-7839; 5-5183 Kuhio Hwy., Hanalei) slogan—*We cheat tourists, drunks, and attorneys*—you'll find this a convenient choice, though definitely not the biggest or tastiest burger. In Poipu, **Poipu Tropical Burgers** (808-742-1808; Poipu Shopping Village, 2360 Kiahuna Plantation) is about your only option for a giant burger (or even an early-morning breakfast). The impressively large menu serves up half-pound burgers at reasonable prices for the high-rent neighborhood.

And if you crave pizza and can't make it to Brick Oven, try **Pizzetta** (808-742-8881; 5408 Koloa Rd., Poipu; 808-823-8882; 1387 Kuhio Hwy., Kapa'a), which serves huge pizzas, salads, and Italian fare. The Koloa location has been threatening to open a deli for the past year, and though the case is on display, no deli food has arrived. I always like the pizza at the Kapa'a location better. **Pacific Pizza and Deli** (808-338-1020; 9852 Kaumuali'i Hwy.) in Waimea is an easy option on your way back from Koke'e. The north shore's option is the delicious and popular **Kilauea Bakery and Pau Hana Pizza** (808-828-2020; Kong Lung Center, Kilauea), where you get large slices of pizza with fresh vegetables, sandwiches, and sweets for decent prices.

Laze the day away in Hanalei.

7

RECREATION

Mea Ho'onanea

When you live on an island with perfect weather most of the year, what better way to spend your time than outdoors? Visitors find that what Kaua'i may be lacking in nightlife, it makes up for in the daytime hours. There is more to do than you will even have time for. Kaua'i's beaches consistently gets props for being the world's best. Hiking is a treat, with the mountains, beach trails, and the infamous Kalalau Trail (which people training to trek Mount Everest traverse). Bird-watchers will find rare birds unseen anywhere else on the planet. Surfers, windsurfers, and water sport enthusiasts will be overjoyed. Walkers, runners, cyclists, helicopter junkies, campers, and everyone in between find plenty to do rain or shine. And if that isn't enough, finding time to relax with a good book is a must. Below are ways to fill up your days and ensure you will want to return to this bountiful island.

Above Ke'e Beach in Haena.

BEACHES

Technicolor reefs abundant with sea life, white sand, and water so clear you can see your toes—the beaches of Kaua'i are its number one attraction. Though all are open to the public, the land leading up to some beaches is privately owned, so I have chosen to only include those that are safe and legal for you to get to. Beaches are described by neighborhood, traveling clockwise from the northernmost point of the east shore around the island.

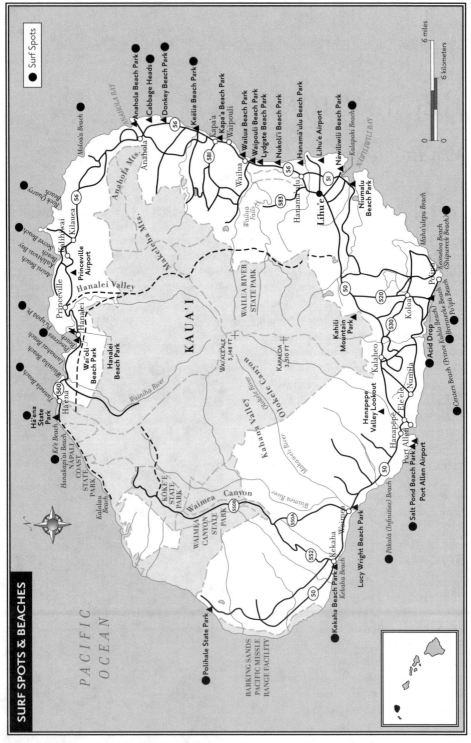

SURF SPOTS & BEACHES

Surf Spots

PACIFIC OCEAN

ANAHOLA BAY

Moloaa Beach
Anahola Beach Park
Cabbage Heads
Donkey Beach Park
Kealia Beach Park
Kapa'a
Kapa'a Beach Park
Waipouli
Wailua Beach Park
Waipouli Beach Park
Lydgate Beach Park
Nukoli'i Beach Park
Hanamā'ulu Beach Park
Lihu'e Airport
Nāwiliwili Beach Park
Numalu Beach Park
Kalapaki Beach
NĀWILIWILI BAY

Rock Quarry Beach
Secret Beach

Anini Beach
Kalihiwai Bay
Kalihiwai Beach
Kilauea
Kalihiwai

Princeville
Princeville Airport

Hanalei Valley

Anahola Mts.

Makaleha Mts.

Anahola

Wailua
Wailua Falls
Hanamā'ulu

Lihu'e

WAILUA RIVER STATE PARK

KAUA'I

WAI'ALE'ALE
5,148 FT

KAPALOA
3,310 FT

Kahili Mountain Park

Hanalei
Tunnels Beach
Lumahai Beach
Wainiha Beach
Wai'oli Beach Park
Hanalei Beach Park

Wainiha River

Hā'ena
Hā'ena State Park
Kē'ē Beach
Hanakāpī'ai Beach

NĀPALI COAST STATE PARK

Kalalau Beach

KŌKE'E STATE PARK

WAIMEA CANYON STATE PARK

Waimea Canyon

Olokele Canyon

Kahana Valley

Olokele River

Makaweli River

Waimea River

BARKING SANDS PACIFIC MISSILE RANGE FACILITY

Polihale State Park

Kekaha Beach Park
Kekaha Beach

Lucy Wright Beach Park

Waimea

Kekaha

Pakala (Infinities) Beach

Salt Pond Beach Park
Port Allen
Port Allen Airport

Hanapepe
Hanapepe Valley Lookout

'Ele'ele

Kalaheo

Numila

Koloa

Acid Drop

Centers Beach (Prince Kuhio Beach)
Brennecke Beach
Po'ipu Beach

Keoneloa Beach
(Shipwreck Beach)

Maha'ulepu Beach

Pō'ipū

51
50
520
530
56
581
583
56
560
50
550A
550B
552

6 miles
6 kilometers

CP132 01 Kaua'i Surf Spots & Beaches

Officially, nudity is not permitted on Kaua'i, though you might notice some folks baring all, especially on the north shore. In the past, some beaches have been known to attract a crowd wanting to erase those tan lines. Still, nudity is never legal on any Kaua'i beaches, and it's not worth an embarrassing ticket.

EAST SHORE

East shore beaches tend to be more crowded and polluted than those elsewhere. However, there are still a few gems to check out.

✪ **Moloa'a Beach** (between Kuhio Hwy. Mile Markers 16 and 17, turn onto the first Ko'olau Rd.; follow it to Moloa'a Rd., then drive to the end). Though this is not a swimming beach, it is one of the most picturesque spots on Kaua'i (which is probably why they filmed the beginning of *Gilligan's Island* here). This very secluded crescent-shaped beach with a bit of lagoon on the northern tip is a place to get away from the crowds. There are no services.

Anahola Beach Park (north of Kapa'a on Kuhio Hwy., turn onto Kukuihale Rd.). This big

Beach Safety

Though the clear-blue water surrounded by lush palms and ironwoods looks inviting, the Pacific Ocean can be very dangerous and unpredictable. Kaua'i has one of the highest drowning rates in the United States. So it is important to take precautions when playing in the water.

Waves in Kaua'i are powerful—so strong that in the past, ships couldn't sail to the island. On days when the sea is rough (*in general* the north shore is moodiest in winter, while the south shore is turbulent in summer), don't go in the water.

Other concerns are rip currents and undertows. Even on calm days, they can be invisible. A rip current occurs when strong waves block beach water from draining back into the sea. The water gathers, searching for a weak spot to travel back out to the ocean, creating a narrow passage. When there is no weak spot, the water pushes back to sea under the waves, which is called an undertow. Trying to swim against a rip is impossible; save your strength and remain calm. Go with the flow until it releases you (and it will). Then swim parallel to the shore until you no longer feel the power of the current.

Other safety tips that you should follow:

- Always swim where a lifeguard is present.
- Never swim alone.
- Never turn your back on the ocean.
- Remember, waves come in sets.
- Always follow posted signs. When jellyfish and sharks are hanging around, lifeguards post signs and often close beaches.
- Look for locals. If you don't see locals swimming at a particular beach, there is usually a reason: It might be too dangerous.
- Stay out of murky water and river mouths.
- If you are tired, don't swim.
- Beaches change conditions. One day I was swimming at Ke'e Beach in a lovely calm ; the next day the rips were so strong, no one could swim there.
- For safety videos, visit www.kauaiexplorer.com.
- If the seas aren't calm, stay out of the water. The motto is: *If in doubt, don't go out!*

Swing the day away on the remote Moloa'a Beach.

Picking Up Shells

Those of you who haven't seen the *Brady Bunch in Hawaii* special might not know the curse of the shells. On the record, it is illegal to take any shells from a Hawai'i beach. But even deeper, folklore shows that if you remove shells from beaches, you will be cursed. Since there are few precious shells left, which are important to the biodiversity of the land, please do not take them with you. If you really want a Hawaiian shell, buy one from a shop.

The history of this curse goes back to the days of Pele, the fire goddess. Ancient Hawaiians believed that to take lava rock from the island would anger the fiery goddess, who would then place a curse on the wrongdoer. Hawaiians still take this bit of folklore very seriously. In fact, when I was a kid, I remember watching a show about people who had taken shells and lava rock from the beach and actually gotten in a car accident that day. Neither I nor anyone else I know has ever tempted the ancient curse.

beach is protected by an offshore reef, which snorkelers and experienced surfers adore. Fisherman and families come here at sunset for bonfires. There are a lot of squatters living here, so don't leave your valuables unattended.

Kealia Beach Park (just off Kuhio Hwy., past Mile Marker 10). A long stretch of white sand beach with a lifeguard station, BBQ grills, and pavilions. Kealia often is crowded with local surfers and families. However, this is *not* a good swimming beach: Currents and waves get really strong.

Kaua'i beaches offer the perfect atmosphere for a siesta.

Kapa'a Beach Park (in the center of downtown Kapa'a). This grassy field leading up to the ocean is often the site of festivals. It can get crowded with locals, and the water isn't the cleanest.

✪**Lydgate Beach Park** (on the south side of the Wailua River, off H 56). A lava rock barrier creates a natural swimming and snorkeling area, perfect for *keikis*. With a lifeguard on duty, showers, toilets, picnic areas, a gigantic play structure for the kids (see Family Fun), BBQs, and pavilions, this is the perfect place to spend a day.

Kalapaki Beach (at Kaua'i Marriott Resort, where Rice St. becomes H 51). Though the water can be polluted because of its location on Nawiliwili Harbor, locals love this beach. Since most of the year the waves are gentle, this is an excellent swimming, boogie boarding, and windsurfing spot. Be cautious in winter, as there are pretty decent swells.

SOUTH SHORE

Poipu-area beaches get crowded. The sun shines almost year-round. And since there are so many safe locations for kids and inexperienced swimmers, people flock here from all over the island.

✪ **Maha'ulepu Beach** (pass the Hyatt, drive down the 2-mile unpaved (and very bumpy) Poipu Rd., turn right onto Maha'ulepu Rd., and continue until it ends). The land leading up to Maha'ulepu Beach is privately owned, yet this beach is a sacred site for Hawaiians, so people are allowed to visit—but only during the day (the gates are locked between 7 PM and 7 AM). Please show respect for this land, as the owners can choose to close it to the public anytime, which would be a shame because this is one of the most beautiful beaches on the south shore. There is a dune trail to get to this expansive white sand beach with turquoise water. Though there is a swimming spot with an enclosed lagoon, be careful—the currents get very strong, and there are no lifeguards. Not recommended for inexperienced swimmers.

A common sight in Kaua'i, a giant turtle takes a break from the sea.

Keaneloa Bay "Shipwrecks" Beach (at the eastern end of the Grand Hyatt Resort, take Poipu Rd. to Ainako Rd. in Poipu). Though this isn't a swimming beach, it is a decent sandy spot to hang out in the shadows of the Grand Hyatt (and use their services). Body boarders and boogie boarders favor the eastern end. Locals jump off the giant sandstone cliff, but it is pretty dangerous, so use extreme caution. Tourists have been gravely injured here.

Brennecke's Beach (Pe'e Rd., at the east

edge of Poipu Beach). A popular surf and boogie board location, though the waves can be rough, especially in winter. Since the beach is so small, surfboards are not allowed near the shore.

✪ **Poipu Beach Park** (where Hoʻowili Rd. meets Peʻe Rd.). Voted one of America's top beaches by numerous travel magazines, this is one of Kauaʻi's best-developed beach parks. At this expansive area, which also includes the beach at the Sheraton, visitors join ranks with the monk seals and whales, dolphins and turtles that frequent the beach. You'll find an enclosed lagoon for children to snorkel, access to the open sea for surfers and body boarders, a lifeguard, a playground, a grassy area for barbecues, picnic tables, showers and toilets. Recently, archaeologists found the remains of an ancient sporting site for war games near the sea; they are working toward making this a *heiau* site.

Prince Kuhio Beach (across from Prince Kuhio Park on Lawaʻi Rd.). A decent snorkel and dive spot, with an awkward entrance into the water: You have to walk over a variety of sharp coral. In summer, there is a decent surf swell.

Beach House Beach (next to the Beach House restaurant on Lawaʻi Rd.). I have heard this beach called many names (Lawaʻi Beach, *Keiki* Beach, Baby Beach), but since it is next to its restaurant namesake, the *Beach House* moniker seems to have stuck. The rocky bottom makes this an uncomfortable swimming beach, but sunbathers and families love the sandy area (when the tide hasn't swallowed the sand). Surfers populate the water during winter swells.

WEST SHORE

Locals favor west shore beaches. They tend to be less visited by tourists. Here long expanses of sand lead to turbulent seas. Currents get very strong, so (as with all Kauaʻi beaches) use extreme caution. If you don't see locals going in the water, don't go in. These beaches have the best sunset views on the island.

Monk Seal Etiquette

Chances are you will see a Hawaiian monk seal at a local beach. Though they are endangered species, because Kauaʻi is the only Hawaiian island to ban Jet Skis and other loud watercraft, visits from these majestic animals are frequent. To ensure their protection, please help make the beach a place they will want to return to by following these simple guidelines.

- Stay 100 feet away and inland from a monk seal in the water, on the sand, or on the rocks. Often lifeguards will rope off the area around them; do not enter the roped-off area.
- Do not come between a mother and her pup. Monk seals can become aggressive.
- Seals come out of the water to rest, so please remain quiet in their presence.
- Don't feed the seals.
- Do not use a flash when taking pictures.
- Keep children away from these animals, as they can be aggressive.

Fines for harassing monk seals are steep (at least $25,000 and jail time). If you observe any monk seal disturbances, please call the state monk seal hotline: 808-983-5715.

The hard-to-get-to Polihale Beach offers 15 miles of white sand strolling.

✪ **Salt Pond Beach Park** (in Hanapepe past the 17-mile marker off Lele Rd.). Families gather here to swim and barbecue. The beach has all services: a lifeguard, showers, bathrooms, and picnic areas. Monk seals hang out on the sand. The water is fairly calm for swimming because of the natural rock ridges protecting the eastern waters. On the western side, surfers and windsurfers practice. Along the road you might notice actual salt ponds that are still harvested to make sea salt.

Lucy Wright Beach Park (across from the Waimea River in the northern park of Waimea Town). This beach is where Captain Cook first stepped on Hawaiian soil. Yet residents named it for Lucy Wright, a popular community member who died in 1931. Since the river empties into the ocean, the water is a bit murky. On weekends, people picnic at this 5-acre beach park, kids play on the playground, sporting events take place on the grassy field, and plenty of people hit the waves. Swimming and surfing are only good when the water is clear. The sand can get hot since it is a mixture of lava rock and sediment from the river.

Kekaha Beach (at the west end of Kekaha off H 50). This long stretch of sun-bleached sand is actually connected to Polihale—if you are feeling motivated, you can walk the 15 miles of uninterrupted coastline. This is where locals come to the beach for a picnic or to swim (when the sea is calm), snorkel, and surf. Since there are hazardous waves, use caution when entering the water.

✪**Polihale State Park** (off H 50, turn left onto the dirt road 200 yards past the Missile Facility). As you drive the 4 bumpy miles on the potholed road, keep in mind that Polihale Beach is one of Kaua'i's finest. White sand stretches for 15 miles, butting up to the edge of the Na Pali Coast; there are also rolling sand dunes, favored by locals in trucks and dune

Salt Pond Beach.

The Na Pali Coast from Ke'e Beach. Photo taken by Oliver Reyes

buggies, and clear blue seas. You can camp here with a permit, but the last time I was here, the bathroom and water pump were not working, so bring everything you need with you; it's about half an hour to the nearest services. Experienced surfers ride waves here, but the current is very strong and not recommended for beginners or even body boarders. However, if the sand gets too hot, Queen's Pond, a reef-protected swimming area, is a nice place to get wet. This is the perfect spot to bring a picnic and watch the sunset. Note that driving out to Polihale Beach means that you are breaking your rental car contract. If you really want to come here, make sure to rent a 4x4. The one time I drove out here in a regular car, we almost cracked the axle. It is a tough journey, no doubt.

NORTH SHORE
Everyone loves to visit the famous north shore. With Bali Hai's spectacular jagged peaks spilling into reef-speckled waters, a plethora of sea life, and great surf, beaches here often get crowded. Unfortunately, rain often inhibits beach days, especially in winter, but when the sun shines expect crowded waters all day long.

✪ **Ke'e Beach** (head north on H 56 until it ends). Here you will find one of the most beautiful spots in all of Kaua'i. This white sand lagoon, protected by a rocky reef and tucked into a mountainous nook, is great for snorkeling. You must be a decent swimmer, because the current is extremely strong in winter. Even if you don't get more than your feet wet, come here: This is the only beach that offers a glimpse of those sought-after views of the Na Pali Coast. For you photographers, the morning light rocks. The parking lot gets busy, so come early. There are a couple of toilets here, and in 2008 the state added lifeguard services.

Haena Beach Park (at mile marker 9 on Kuhio Hwy.). This campsite/surf beach has a lifeguard, showers and toilets, grills, and pavilions; it's a great place for a picnic. However, because of the challenging currents and active sea life (sharks are often spotted here), this is not a recommended swimming beach. This is where Bethany Hamilton, the famous teenage surfer, lost an arm to a shark.

Makua "Tunnels" Beach (just past Mile Marker 8 on Kuhio Hwy.). This snorkel/dive spot and surf beach is hard to

This 'Anini Beach shower has views.

In the afternoon, Hanalei Pier draws hundreds of people learning to surf.

find. The best way is to park at Haena and walk along the beach half a mile back toward Hanalei. This is one of the best sunset-viewing beaches around. There are no services here.

Lumiha'i Beach (a little turnoff just past Mile Marker 5 off H 56; or continue, then turn right into a dirt parking lot near Mile Marker 6). This dramatic beach, dotted with lava rocks and treacherous currents, is too dangerous to swim in. Often people come here to sunbathe, take sunset walks, or wade in the green river spilling into the turquoise ocean. There are no services.

✪ **Hanalei Beach Park** (take Aku Rd. north from Hanalei and turn right onto Weke Rd.). This crescent of beach in Hanalei Bay is hugged by mountains and filled with surfers. There are three main areas along the bay. The westernmost is the surf beach Pine Trees. Next is the Pavilion, which has lifeguard services, toilets, picnic tables, and grills. Though the surf can get big, this is where people swim. And finally, Black Pot (near the pier) is where kids learn to surf; on sunny days, the water is crowded with swimmers. A grassy area with services and pavilions sits on the east side of Black Pot Beach.

Pu'u Poa "Princeville" Beach (take Ka Haku Rd. to the end; there is a little path near Princeville Hotel to get down to beach). With the hulking Princeville Resort to your rear and the reef-dotted Pacific and Bali Hai in the forefront, this is a great location to sit on the sand and watch surfers. Though big waves make it a little difficult to swim here, experienced snorkelers will find much to delight in.

Pali Ke Kua "Hideaway" Beach (near the end of Ka Haku Rd.; park near the Pali Ke Kua

The Hawaiian state bird—the nene.

This island, at the Kilauea Bird Sanctuary, is populated by rare seabirds.

condo complex, then walk down the paved path near building 1). This steep trail leads to one of the best snorkel spots on the north shore. Often fishermen come here, so watch out for lines and hooks.

✪ **'Anini Beach.** (Coming from the east shore off Kuhio Hwy., turn onto the second Kalihiwai Road—it's the first Kalihiwai Road if you're traveling from the north. Then turn onto Anini Rd. and drive till you see the big grassy area.) One of the best (and safest) north shore beaches, popular with locals and tourists. The lengthy reef that spans the entire beach is a great spot for swimming, windsurfing, and snorkeling. With picnic areas, restrooms, and showers, you'll find a way to spend the entire day lounging beneath an ironwood tree and wading in the knee-deep clear water that seems to stretch out into eternity.

Kalihiwai Bay Beach (coming from the east shore on Kuhio Hwy., turn onto the first Kalihiwai Rd.). This long sandy bay is a calm summer swimming spot. In winter, surfers take over, and swimming conditions become too harsh. There are no services here.

BIRD-WATCHING

Birders rejoice when they arrive on Kaua'i—home to some of the rarest birds on the planet, many of them endangered. Land has been set aside to accommodate the permanent homes and migration patterns of these yearly visitors. Ironically, it may be too late. Birds in Kaua'i are becoming extinct at an alarming rate. Forty percent of birds on the US endangered species list are Hawaiian.

However, in winter, you might still glimpse indigenous endangered birds in the forested uplands of Kokeʻe, including the ʻelepaio, ʻakekeʻe, ʻakikiki (a gray honeycreeper), ʻapapane, Hawaiian owl, ʻanianiau, ʻiʻiwi, and the elusive nukupuʻu. Year-round, since the State Department of Land and Natural Resources has increased the amount of wetland habitat, shorebirds are abundant and fairly easy to spot. The birds you are most likely to notice, though, are mainland introductions—including some you may recognize from home. A great publication to pick up is *The Birds of Kauaʻi* by Jim Denny.

EAST SHORE

In Wailua, wetland birds lounge in the **Wailua Reservoir** and at **Smith's Tropical Paradise** (which also has an impressive collection of peacocks). The **Kauaʻi Lagoons** (near Nawiliwili) is a guaranteed place to observe the nene, the Hawaiian state bird.

WEST SHORE

The most exciting place to go bird-watching is **Kokeʻe State Park**—namely, the **Pihea Trail in the Alakaʻi Swamp** (see Hiking for a detailed map). Though it is often cold and rainy up here, it is worth the trip. The construction of the wooden boardwalk has made the trek a bit easier, but it's still muddy. Make sure to rinse off your shoes *before* walking into the forest, as seeds lodged in the creases can drop into the land and introduce a new invasive species of plant. Here you will see a wealth of endangered birds, which should not be disturbed under any circumstances.

After heavy rains the **Hanapepe Salt Pond** is a good place to spot wetland birds like the ʻakekeke. At the **Kawaiele Bird Sanctuary** (past Kekaha and before the Pacific Missile Range Facility), you'll likely spot the aeʻo, ʻalae keʻo keʻo, ʻaukuʻu (a night heron), Hawaiian ducks, and the ʻulili.

NORTH SHORE

Shorebirds migrate through Kauaʻi annually, creating a spectacle for bird lovers. The most dramatic (and educational) place to see shearwaters, red-footed boobies, great frigates, and Laysan albatross is the **Kilauea Point National Wildlife Reserve** (808-828-0168). Open daily 10–4; visitors pay $3 for close-up views of these beautiful animals. Volunteers lead hikes and show videos of the mating habits of albatross, while explaining what those specks of white, mating on the cliffs and the island, are. Recently, they have partnered with the Pacific Missile Range Facility to relocate albatross eggs from their base (where birds were dying off due to missile testing) to the KPNWR.

To see wetland birds in this notoriously wet region, head to the taro fields and ponds in the **Hanalei National Wildlife Reserve** (at the west end of the Hanalei Bridge, on ʻOhiki Rd.), which was created in 1972 to protect its large population of ducks, Hawaiian coot, stilt, and gallinule.

BOATING, CHARTERS, AND CRUISES

You can only drive or hike so far. Sometimes the only way to see the dramatic Na Pali Coast cliffs is by getting out on a boat. Known not merely for the striking views, boating adventures offer visitors a way to experience the wealth of sea life inhabiting the waters off Kauaʻi. Whether it is a diving or snorkeling adventure, a gentle river cruise, a sunset cruise, or a rafting tour of the Na Pali Coast, Kauaʻi outfitters deliver.

Note that the ocean is very choppy, especially in winter. Often your tour will get canceled or rescheduled. This is for your safety. You might want to schedule your trip when you first arrive, so that if it does get canceled, you can still reschedule. If you are visiting in winter, note that some outfitters go out in choppy weather; it is advisable to take precautions against seasickness—a very common happening on tours. Because of the tumultuous seas, many companies do not allow young children or pregnant women.

Since outfitters often have numerous types of trips, I have included companies in this section that offer a variety of services, including snorkeling, diving, sunset cruises, and fishing—often on the same journey. If a company specializes in a particular arena (such as diving), it will be listed only under Diving.

Rates vary depending on the type and length of your trip. But you can expect to pay $120–170 per person for a four- to five-hour journey. Most outfitters are closed on Sunday and major holidays.

Commercial Trips and Rentals

Blue Dolphin Charters (808-335-5553; www.kauaiboats.com; P.O. Box 869, 'Ele'ele). They offer catamaran tours to the Na Pali Coast and occasionally to Ni'ihau, with snorkeling, scuba diving, food and beverages, and a slide off the back of the boat. They also take couples out on sunset cruises.

Captain Andy's Sailing Adventures (808-335-6833 or 800-535-0830; www.napali.com; Port Allen Marina Center, 4353 Waialo Rd., Suite 1A-2A, 'Ele'ele). Sunset and snorkel tours on sailboats, and raft expeditions to the Na Pali Coast are Captain Andy's specialties. On these trips, you can indulge in beer and wine, though in winter I'd avoid the alcohol.

Captain Sundown Catamaran Kuuipo, (808-826-5585; www.captainsundown.com; P.O. Box 697, Hanalei). Crew members take pride in being the only catamaran tour departing from Hanalei. They offer fishing, snorkeling, sunset cruises, and plenty of story from the Hawaiian native captains. They are closed Sunday.

Holo Holo Charters (808-335-0815; www.holoholocharters.com; 4353 Waialo Rd., Suite 5A, 'Ele'ele). These guys take guests out on the 61-foot catamaran to the Na Pali Coast and Ni'ihau (they are the only outfitter to "officially" do this). They have a shaded cabin, food and beverages, snorkel gear, and instruction. Plus, their sunset cruises are perfect for couples.

Kaua'i Sea Tours (808-335-5309; www.kauaiseatours.com; Port Allen Marina Center, 4353 Waialo Rd., Unit 2B, 'Ele'ele). Quality catamaran and raft snorkel tours to the Na Pali Coast.

Bonfires

It is legal to have bonfires on the beach at night. But the law says you must be using the flame for cooking. Unfortunately, marshmallows don't count. A while ago a friend was having a bonfire and the police came. She pulled out a bag of marshmallows and was told they were not acceptable. From that point forward, we all make sure to have a hot dog or burger close by. And if you do choose to have a bonfire, please make sure to clean up afterward.

Liko Kaua'i Cruises (808-338-0333; www.liko-kauai.com; 9875 Waimea Rd., Waimea). This outfit is owned by native Hawaiians and delivers snorkel cruises to the Na Pali Coast—often traveling farther along the coast than any other west shore tour company. They are one of the only companies to allow pregnant women and young children on their cruises. They take Sunday off.

Napali Riders (808-338-9955; www.napaliriders.com; P.O. Box 1082, Kalaheo). This is one of the cheapest ways to see the Na Pali Coastline. Guests go out on this outfitter's rigid hull rafts (with no shade) for snorkeling, whale-watching, or sea cave tours. They serve snacks. During winter, these rafts can be extremely uncomfortable.

Smiths Fern Grotto Riverboat Tour (808-821-6892; www.smithskauai.com; 174 Wailua Rd., Kapa'a). The tours start at 9 AM. Boats leave throughout the day (depending on the season; call for schedules). This is a great (and cheap—$18 per person) way to explore the sacred Wailua River, hear traditional Hawaiian music, learn the hula, and take a short walk in a nature reserve. Tours last 80 minutes. Bring mosquito repellent.

CAMPING

Local Hawaiians have a long tradition of sleeping outdoors. The ancients used to hike to the top of Wai'ale'ale to honor the gods; the lepers lived in the Kalalau Valley; and now myriad families use the ocean or birdsong to lull them to dreamland. Campsites are open year-round, though those on the north shore and in Koke'e get a ton of wind and rain in winter.

For all campsites, you need a permit. You will be fined for not having one. Good news, though: Camping is cheap. County permits cost $3 per person per day, while state permits are $5–10 per night, per site. At county beach parks (listed below), permits are good for up to seven days per campground. Contact the **Division of Parks and Recreation** (808-241-4463; www.kauai.gov; 444 Rice St., Pi'ikoi Building, Suite 350, Lihu'e 96766) in advance.

For state parks (listed below), contact the **Department of Land and Natural Resources Division of State Parks** (808-274-3444; www.hawaii.gov/dlnr; 3060 'Eiwa St., Room 306, Lihu'e 96766). Here, camping is limited to five consecutive nights per site.

To camp in specified forest reserve areas in the Waimea and Koke'e regions, contact the **Division of Forestry and Wildlife** (808-274-3433; www.hawaii.gov/dlnr; 3060 'Eiwa St., Room 306, Lihu'e 96766). Camping is limited to three to four nights total within a 30-day period. When booking, pick up the *Recreational Map of Western Kaua'i*. These sites are accessible only by a four-wheel drive vehicle or hiking in.

EAST SHORE

Anahola Beach Park (north of Kapa'a on Kuhio Hwy., turn onto Kukuihale Rd.). A somewhat remote and spacious stretch of beach shaded by ironwoods, this camping spot is popular with squatters. Never leave your valuables unattended. Campers need a county permit.

Kalapaki Beach (at Kauai Marriott Resort, where Rice St. becomes H 51). Showers, toilets, picnic tables, lifeguards, and grills on a grassy area on the ocean make this a local favorite. Campers need a county permit.

Lydgate Beach Park (on the south side of the Wailua River off H 56). Recently built handicapped-accessible campsites here are lifted off the ground. It's located on the beach in Lydgate Park, in a grove of palms with BBQ pits nearby, and showers and bathrooms. Campers need a state park permit.

Kalapaki Beach.

SOUTH SHORE

Poipu Beach Park (where Ho'owili Rd. meets Pe'e Rd.). This crowded tourist beach offers showers, toilets, grills, picnic tables, and lifeguards; it's across the street from a market and restaurant. Campers need a county permit.

WEST SHORE

Koke'e State Park (at the end of H 550). Tent campers with a state park permit can set up shop across the meadow from the museum, where you'll find picnic tables and toilets. If you get a permit from the State Division of Forestry and Wildlife, you can camp in more rustic areas deeper into the park. Also, if you want the feeling of camping without actually sleeping outdoors, at press time the **Koke'e Lodge** (808-335-6061; Box 819 Kokee State Park, Mile Marker 15, Waimea; www.thelodgeatkokee.net) still rented a couple of *very rustic* cabins inside the park for under $100 a night. However, a high-end resort has been slated to begin development here anytime, ending the reign of these shacks. Cabins include refrigerators, wood-burning stoves, hot showers, basic kitchen utensils, linens, towels, blankets, and pillows. Maximum length of stay is five nights, and some cabins can sleep up to seven.

Lucy Wright Beach Park (across from the Waimea River, in Waimea). With a county permit, you can camp at this popular locals' beach park. Picnic tables, toilets, showers, and a playground make this spot great for kids—though the beach can get loud and the water is polluted.

Polihale State Park (off H 50, turn left onto the dirt road 200 yards past the Missile Facility). One of the most remote and beautiful spots to camp on the west shore: 15 miles of uninterrupted white sand beach with toilets, showers, pavilions to get out of the sun, and grills. There are no services nearby, and it gets very hot and dry here, so bring lots of water and food. With a state park permit, you can tent or RV camp. The campsite is at the top of the left dune before you get to the far northern end.

Salt Pond Beach County Park (in Hanapepe past the 17-mile marker off Lele Rd.). One of the best beaches to spend the night. Often monk seals camp here, too. With amenities like showers, toilets, a lifeguard and BBQ pavilions, and the close proximity to Hanapepe, this is a popular local spot. You need a county permit to camp here.

NORTH SHORE

'Anini Beach (coming from the east shore off Kuhio Hwy., turn onto the second Kalihiwai Rd., then veer left onto Anini Rd.). With a county permit, you can camp under ironwoods, gazing out onto the expanse of the Pacific. There are showers, picnic tables, toilets, and grills, plus a grassy area to laze the day away.

Haena Beach Park (at Mile Marker 9 on Kuhio Hwy.). You can camp here only with a county permit. With a lifeguard on duty, picnic tables and BBQs, bathrooms and showers, this oceanfront beach park is in demand. Winters get very rainy. Close to a general store, a taco shop, and plenty of swimming and hiking, this is a safe and civilized place to sleep.

Hanalei Beach Park (take Aku Rd. north from Hanalei and turn right onto Weke Rd.). Campers with a county permit enjoy the area near the pavilion. This popular spot offers showers, toilets, grills, picnic tables, and a lifeguard, in the center of Hanalei Town, with stellar views of Bali Hai.

✪ **Kalalau Beach.** (The only way in or out is to hike the difficult 11-mile Kalalau Trail.) Campers need a state park permit to even pass the 2-mile marker of the trail. There are no services at this beach, and the water (especially in winter) can be ruthless. Bring all your food and drinking water with you. And please remember to pack out all supplies.

YMCA Camp Naue (808-246-9090 or 808-826-6419; P.O. Box 1786, Lihu'e 96766). Four miles past Hanalei, between Mile Markers 7 and 8 on the beach side, are a group of ocean-front buildings. Though they mainly cater to large groups, single travelers are welcome in the bunkhouse on a first-come, first-served basis. There are four coed rooms for up to 12 people. Beds cost $12 a night, and if you are really interested, call in advance—especially in summer when this area fills up. They provide hot showers and toilets, but no bedding; cooking facilities are available only to groups. For $10 a person, guests are allowed to tent camp near the ocean, plus use of the BBQ pavilions and bathrooms.

CANOEING AND KAYAKING

Kayaking and canoeing can be a mellow way to explore some the Kaua'i's richest ecosystems. Meandering along lush rivers, meeting only birds and the occasional bovine, is a delightful way to spend a few hours. Many outfitters rent kayaks and canoes by the hour, or take people out on river tours. The best rivers to explore are the Wailua and the Hanalei. If you are considering an ocean kayak adventure, please go on a tour. Even if you are a very experienced kayaker, the waves are extremely dangerous. Below are companies that rent and/or take people on tours.

Tours and Rentals

Ali'i Kayaks (808-241-7700; www.aliikayaks.com; 3501 Rice St., Suite 107B, Lihu'e). This locally owned kayak tour company offers guided tours down the Wailua River with a picnic at Secret Falls.

Kamokila Hawaiian Village (6060 Kuamoo Rd., Wailua). This family-owned company rents kayaks to meander down the Wailua River while also offering tours of a classic Hawaiian village.

Kayak Hanalei (808-826-1881; www.kayakhanalei.com; P.O. Box 90, Hanalei). Tour guides are native Hawaiians who specialize in small kayak expeditions into the Hanalei National Wildlife Refuge.

Kayak Kaua'i (808-826-9844; www.kayakkauai.com; P.O. Box 508, Hanalei). They offer ocean tours to the Na Pali Coast.

Outfitters Kaua'i (808-742-9667; www.outfitterskauai.com; 2827A Poipu Rd., Poipu). Guided sea tours to the Na Pali Coast in summer.

CYCLING

Kaua'i appears a cyclist's dream—long windy roads leading through mountainous terrain, seemingly endless stretches of ocean views along the main roads, trees offering much-needed shade, and the occasional rain to cool you off. However, the idea of bike paths (or

Kayakers explore the Hanalei River.

even sidewalks in some parts) hasn't arrived on the island, and roads are a little too crowded for the novice biker to feel safe (locals often drive pretty fast). There are plenty of places to ride; just make sure to follow safety precautions and watch your back . . . literally.

The newest addition to the Kaua'i bike scene is the **Coastal Bike and Pedestrian Trail**. Starting at Lydgate Park, this trail is anticipated to stretch north along the coast for 16 miles. Currently it is about 4 miles long.

Guided Tours and Rentals:

Outfitters Kaua'i (808-742-7421; www.outfitterskauai.com; 2827A Poipu Rd., Poipu). This outfit takes you to the top of Waimea Canyon, serving muffins and coffee along the way, then straps you into helmets and bikes and sends you the 12 miles downhill. There are morning and afternoon tours. The average cost is $100 per adult. They also rent bikes.

Kaua'i Cycle and Tour (808-821-2115; www.bikehawaii.com/kauaicycle; 4-934 Kuhio Hwy., Kapaa). These folks rent bikes and take people on daylong mountain bike adventures.

DIVING, SCUBA, AND SNORKELING

Some of the best views you'll see in Kaua'i are beneath the sea. With one of the longest reefs in the world (you can see the north shore reef from space), the mellow Ni'ihau reefs, and a couple of dive spots (**Koloa Landing**, **Makua "Tunnels" Beach**) that you can access from land, the plentiful marine life and underwater beauty keep divers entertained for days.

Below are companies that specialize in dive trips and rent dive and snorkel gear. I have included other companies in Boating that, during tours, allow guests to snorkel and dive from the boat. Under Beaches, I have listed places where you can walk out and snorkel from land.

Rentals, Trips, and Dive Certification

Bubbles Below Scuba Charters (808-332-7333; www.bubblesbelowkauai.com; P.O. Box 157, 'Ele'ele). This outfit offers dive trips to the south and west shores off Kaua'i as well as taking you to explore the Lehua Crater near Ni'ihau (summer only). They recommend that you dive with them once before going out to Ni'ihau, since the trip is rough. Once a week, they also take divers out to the Na Pali Coast Mana Crack (a sunken barrier reef).

Dive Kaua'i Scuba Center (808-822-0452; www.divekauai.com; 4-1038 Kuhio Hwy., Kapa'a). This crew offers first-time dive trips as well as certifications. They also rent Nitrox tanks. They take divers to the south and west shores in summer and, when weather permits, the remainder of the year. During summer, you can also charter boats to go on dive trips to the Ni'ihau coast.

Fathom Five Divers & Ocean Quest Watersports (808-742-6991; www.fathomfive.com; 3450 Poipu Rd., Poipu). For over 25 years, they have taken divers to south and north shore locations in their six-person boats. Their philosophy is to take you where you want to dive, rather than tell you where to go—this includes shore dives.

Mana Divers (808-335-0881; www.manadivers.com; 4310 Waialo Rd., Bay 3, 'Ele'ele). This west shore company does training, takes families to sea, and charters boats to remote locations like Ni'ihau. They also have eco-informed guided dives.

Seasport Divers (808-742-9303; www.seasportdivers.com; 2827 Poipu Rd., Poipu. 808-823-9222; 4-976 Kuhio Hwy., Kapa'a). This outfit offers free pool lessons before taking you out on the sea. They also take divers to Ni'ihau two days per week in summer. In general, they offer two south shore dive trips per day. They also have a one-hour photo lab on site to take pictures of you on your dive.

Snorkel Bob's (808-742-2206; wwwsnorkelbob.com; 3236 Poipu Rd., Koloa; or 808-823-9433; 4-734 Kuhio Hwy., Kapa'a). This Hawaii chain of stores rents snorkel gear and can direct you to the best seasonal snorkeling spots. Snorkel Bob's also arranges kayak tours.

FAMILY FUN

Kaua'i is a children's paradise, with plenty of activities to keep the little ones engaged (and to exhaust them by nightfall). Most places that are great for adults are also meant for children (beaches, boat trips, hiking, and so on). Below are some special places devoted to children.

Fun Factory (808-822-3660; 4771 Kuhio Hwy., Kapa'a). This arcade is open 10 AM–10 PM and until midnight on Friday and Saturday.

Kaua'i Marriott's Kalapaki Kids Club (808-245-5050; Kaua'i Marriott, 3610 Rice St., Lihu'e). They take kids from 5 through 12 on treasure hunts, obstacle course races, swimming, and to learn about island activities like hula. Rates vary (depending on length of stay and whether or not you want them to feed your child) from $25 to $45 per day.

***Keiki* Aloha Club** (808-742-1661; Sheraton Kaua'i, 2564 Ho'onani Rd., Poipu). The folks at the Sheraton teach 3- through 12-year-olds hula, history, kite flying, 'ukulele, ancient fishing techniques, and sand castle building. Rates are $35–70 depending on whether it is a full day or half day, and if you want lunch included.

Lydgate Park and Kamalani Playground (in Wailua, on the south side of the Wailua River, off H 56). By far this is the best place on the island for the *keikis*. Moms and dads will enjoy lounging by the water, while the little ones swim in a lava-rock-enclosed ocean pool or explore the Kamalani Playground. A communitywide project created Kamalani Park. Children drew what their ideal beach park would look like, and from their suggestions, a giant wooden play structure and wheelchair-accessible beach-viewing bridge/slide came to fruition. Over two weekends, thousands of people volunteered to build the playground, some doing the labor, others offering child care, food, what have you. Now the community leaders keep the park up, having cleanup days and refurbishing run-down aspects. For more information on Lydgate Beach Park, see Beaches.

Poipu Beach Park (where Ho'owili Rd. meets Pe'e Rd.). This family-friendly beach has an enclosed swimming area for the little ones as well as a play structure right on the beach.

FISHING

From the beginning of time, fishing was the primary source of sustenance for Kaua'i people. Now that fishing is big business (as well as a sport), visitors will find plenty of places to reel them in. From most beaches, you'll see locals fishing from the coast. If you don't

The keikis *will never be bored in Kaua'i.*

want to take a boat, some of the companies listed below also rent equipment and will show you where the best places to land fish are. If you want to get out onto the ocean, these companies have private and shared charters. In Boating, I have also listed when tour companies allow guests to fish.

Charters and Rentals

Anini Fishing Charters and Tours (808-828-1285; www.kauaifishing.com).

Captain Don's Sport Fishing (808-639-3012; www.captaindonsfishing.com; P.O. Box 1452, Hanalei).

Deep Sea Fishing Kaua'i (808-634-8589; www.deepseafishingkauai.com; 6022 Kolopua St., Kapa'a).

Kai Bear Sportfishing Charters (808-652-4556; www.kaibear.com; 4067 Ho'olako Place, Lihu'e).

True Blue Charters (808-246-6333; P.O. Box 1722, Lihu'e).

GOLF

Golfers come from all over the world to participate in the PGA Grand Slam of Golf every year. And with so many world-class courses, all with spectacular beach and mountain views, you'll find it difficult to choose where to play. Note that specific challenges to your golf game might include common Bermuda grasses, which make up the majority of putting surfaces; those moody winds can also affect your game. Each course has a PGA professional on duty to answer any questions you may have.

As with most worthwhile activities on Kauaʻi, green fees are not cheap. However, almost all courses have discounted twilight rates. Prices change, often without notice, so check with your concierge or the course for details.

EAST SHORE

Kauaʻi Lagoons Golf Course (808-241-6000 or 800-634-6400; 3351 Hoʻolaulea Way, Lihuʻe). This resort course has recently been renovated. Designed by Jack Nicklaus, this spot gives golfers ocean views at every turn. The Kiele's (meaning "gardenia") cliff-side holes are 18 holes, par 72. Kiele fees: $175; $125 twilight. The pro on duty is Scott Ashworth.

Puakea Golf Course (808-245-8756 or 866-773-5554; 4150 Nohou St., Lihuʻe). Kauai's newest course is a wide expanse of green nestled between the ocean and Mount Hauʻpu. Built in 2003 by architect Robin Nelson, he integrated natural Grove Farm streams and deep ravines into the course. Eighteen holes, par 72. Fees: $59–99, plus rental and cart fees. The pro on duty is Patrick Hunt.

Wailua Golf Course (808-241-6666; 3-5350 Kuhio Hwy., Lihuʻe). This is one of Kauaʻi's best public courses, with very reasonable rates. It was built in the 1930s; in the '60s, architect Toyo Shirai added another 9 holes to make this an 18-hole course, par 72. Right on the ocean, and close to the airport, this course can bring a challenging wind. Fees: $32–44 (half-price twilight hours), plus rentals and cart.

SOUTH SHORE

Kiahuna Golf Club (808-742-9595; 2545 Kiahuna Plantation Dr., Poipu). Recently renovated, this course has a range of tees from junior to expert, many with views of the ocean and Mount Kahili. Robert Trent Jones Jr. designed it, blending flowering trees with rock gardens and remnants from an ancient Hawaiian village. Eighteen holes, par 70. Fees: $95; twilight $75. The pro on duty is Matt Torry.

Kukuiolono Golf Course (808-332-9151; 854 Puu Rd., Kalaheo). Built in 1929 and donated to the state by Walter McBryde, this course is one of the best-kept secrets on the island. With low rates, stellar views of lush Japanese Gardens (which is where King Kamehameha's son Walter is buried), the ocean, and lava rock gardens, this golf experience is a must. But since it is first-come, first-served, get here early. Fees: $7, plus rental and cart fees.

Poipu Bay Golf Course (808-742-8711; 2250 Ainako St., Koloa). This course, designed by Robert Trent Jones Jr., isn't home to the PGA Grand Slam of Golf for nothing. Situated on 210 acres of rolling oceanfront greens, with an array of tropical plants and ancient Hawaiian sites along the course, it is no wonder the greats play here. Maybe they also like the citrus-scented towels to keep you cool, the in-cart navigation, or the on-course beverage cart. The wind and the 84 bunkers add many challenges to this 18-hole course, par 72. Fees: $125–200 ($75 twilight), plus cart and rental fees. Hyatt guests get considerable discounts. Note that if you go at twilight, you might not get a whole round in.

NORTH SHORE

The courses at Princeville at Hanalei (808-826-5070 or 800-826-1105; Prince Course: 5-3900 Kuhio Hwy., Princeville; Makai Course: 4080 Lei O Papa Rd., Princeville). Planted between the expansive sea and 4,421-foot-high Mount Namolokama, these two courses are rated number one in the state by *Golf Digest*. Ancient streams, waterfalls, tropical flora, and lava tubes have been embedded into the courses by architect Robert Trent Jones Jr. The Makai Course is actually three nine-hole tracks, par 108. And one of the most challenging courses in Hawai'i, the Prince Course, has 18 holes, par 72, with 7,309 yards to explore. Fees: $120–175 (after 3:30, $50), plus rental and cart fees.

HELICOPTER TOURS

One of the most impressive ways to glimpse the whole of Kaua'i is by helicopter tour. This is how the movie companies find locations to shoot those tropical scenes. It is also the highlight of many travelers' visits, because you get to see views that you can't get to otherwise: waterfalls cascading down Mount Wai'ale'ale, the Na Pali Coast, and Manawaiopuna Falls (the waterfall in *Jurassic Park*).

Note that the weather in Kaua'i changes by the hour. Often helicopter tours will get canceled due to bad conditions. This is a good thing. If a pilot cancels your flight, it is for your safety. However, since rain brings rainbows and waterfalls, a bit of rain is okay, so don't get freaked out. To avoid having a canceled trip for your entire journey, book your tour early in your vacation, so you have time to reschedule.

When selecting a tour company, don't be afraid to ask questions regarding the price versus the length of the tour. On average you can guarantee that for an hour tour, you'll pay over $200. Also make sure to ask about the aircraft, your particular pilot's experience and flight record, the aircraft itself, and the company's safety record. For helicopter tours over Ni'ihau, see chapter 9.

Tour Companies

Air Kaua'i (808-246-4666; www.airkauai.com). Owner and pilot, Charles DiPiazza has been flying these A-Star air-conditioned helicopter tours since the early 1980s. Tours take six people (and your pilot) over spectacular views of the classic helicopter-tour hot spots. Aircraft offer floor-to-ceiling windows that do not open (so pictures might not be the best) and skylights for those two people stuck in the middle of the backseat. As of press time, this outfit has an excellent safety record.

Blue Hawaiian Helicopters (808-245-5800; www.bluehawaiian.com). The only company to fly the pricey (and comfortable) Eco-Star helicopters, Blue Hawaiian is a good option for people who need lots of room. Even though there are six passengers, the seats are spacious. The 180-degree views are unobstructed and almost equally good for everyone. The high technology of these aircraft puts them among the safest in the business. And the priciest. Tours range between 50 and 55 minutes, and with Internet deals you can get a tour for around $200. They also make DVDs to record your entire flight.

Kaua'i's elusive interior.

Island Helicopters (808-245-8588; www.islandhelicopters.com). Curt and Bonnie Lofstedt have run this company since 1980. They are concerned with the ecological impact of tourism on Kaua'i, so the tours are set up to give you a better understanding of the ecology of the island. They are also involved in the movie industry, often renting out their A-Star helicopters for movie shoots. Aircrafts have six seats and are air-conditioned. Tours are 55 to 60 minutes and generally take the same route as the other companies.

Jack Harter Helicopters (808-245-3774; www.helicopters-kauai.com). Owners Jack and Bev Harper have owned and operated the longest-running helicopter tours on Kaua'i. They have six-passenger A-Stars with air-conditioning, along with four-passenger open-window Hughes helicopters. Note that if you sit in the backseat of the open-window helicopter, bring a jacket—it gets cold. They offer 60- and 90-minute tours and pride themselves in employing pilots who know a vast amount about Kaua'i.

Safari Helicopters (808-246-0136; www.safarihelicopters.com). Owned by Preston and Grace Myers, this company flies air-conditioned A-Stars on both the Big Island and Kaua'i. They pride themselves on having a unique "Safari Skylight"—a picture window nestled vertically above for good views of waterfalls. Their onboard DVD system records your 55-minute trip.

Will Squires Helicopter Tours (808-245-8881; www.helicopters-hawaii.com). This 20-year-old family-owned business has an excellent safety record. They use A-Star helicopters, which means the six of you will get to know one another quite well during your 55- to 60-minute tour. At least the aircraft is air-conditioned. Many movie scouts travel with Will to search for locations.

HIKING

Hikers have some of the most rugged and spectacular parts of Kaua'i to themselves. Whether you are looking for mellow beach strolls, bird-watching walks, strenuous mountain treks, or access to waterfalls, you'll find a wealth of hikes that cater to your desires.

Because of safety concerns, I have only included hiking trails that are kept up by the state or county offices. For all trails, take note of the weather. If it rained the night before or might rain that day, be wary of going out (especially on the Kalalau Trail). You should

Hikers stumble upon bamboo groves in the Kaua'i highlands.

Though it looks inviting, Kipu Falls is a dangerous place to swim.

A Note About Kipu Falls

I am not trying to be secretive about these falls. I just can't tell you how to get here. It is easy enough to find out about, if you do your research. But when I talked to locals about this book the one thing everyone asked me was not to list Kipu Falls. Why? Locals feel territorial about this waterfall. And rightly so. This secret swimming hole/waterfall has popped up on the tourist radar and has locals reeling.

If you want to come here, sign on with a zip line adventure tour (**Outfitters Kaua'i**: 808-742-9667; www.outfitterkauai.com), or ask around. But know that hiking in officially breaks the law. You must cross private property to get to the falls. Furthermore, locals, who know the waterfall intimately, swing into the water below on a rope swing. Tourists, misjudging the height and depth of the water, have been seriously injured here; one person even died. Ultimately it is for your safety that I recommend you swim in the many other places listed in this book.

also plan on starting a hike early (before 8 AM) to beat crowds and heat. Bring plenty of water and food, mosquito repellent, and hats for shade.

For detailed information about hiking trails, pick up the excellent book *Kaua'i Trailblazer* by Jerry and Janine Sprout. You can also write to the **Hawaii Geographic Society** (P.O. Box 1698, Honolulu 96806) for their information packet and map. Another great resource is the **Sierra Club, Kaua'i Group** (www.hi.sierraclub.org/Kauai); they not only have great hike information but also lead a variety of guided weekly hikes. The **State Division of Forestry** (P.O. Box 1671, Lihu'e, Kaua'i 96766) publishes a good map.

If you hope to travel farther than 2 miles into the Na Pali Coast on the Kalalau Trail, you need a permit, which you can get from the **DLNR State Parks office** (808-274-3444; www.hawaii.gov/dlnr; 3060 'Eiwa St., Room 306, Lihu'e 96766).

State Parks and Popular Hikes

EAST SHORE

Keahua Arboretum (in Wailua, on H 580, drive 7 miles past H 56 and park before the spillway). The tropical highlands of this young arboretum offer many popular hikes, with a variety of views and difficulty levels. The **Kuilau Ridge** is a 2.1-mile forest walk with lush monkeypod trees and view of Sleeping Giant. The **Moalepe Trail** weaves across steep ridges, offering views of the Kapa'a coastline. And finally, the big daddy, the **Powerline Trail** is a 13-mile maintenance road traveling from the east shore to the north shore, now used mostly by hunters and rescue vehicles.

Nounou Mountain Forest Reserve has three well-worn trails. The **Sleeping Giant West Trail** (in Wailua, take H 580; turn right onto H 581; drive 2 miles and park at telephone pole number 11) is the most direct way to the top of the mountain, with plenty of shade. The **Nounou Mountain East Trail** (in Kapa'a, 1 mile up Haleilio Rd., the trailhead is near a water pump station) is a steep, but rewarding 1.75-mile trek to ocean vistas. The **Kuamo'o Trail** (in Wailua, up H 580, past Opaeka'a Falls, park on the right, across the highway from Melia Street) is less of a workout, meandering along a stream with plenty of mountain views.

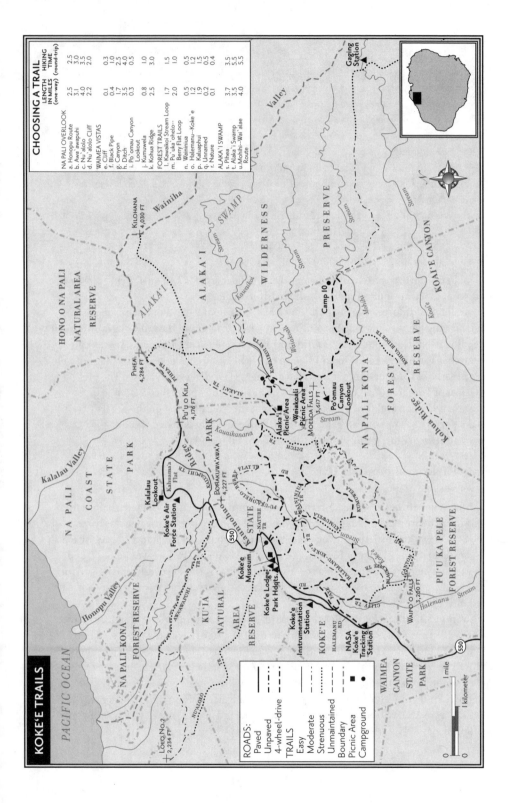

KOKE'E TRAILS

CHOOSING A TRAIL

	LENGTH IN MILES (one-way)	HIKING TIME (round-trip)
NA PALI OVERLOOK		
a. Honopu Route	2.5	2.5
b. Awa awapuhi	3.1	3.0
c. Nu alolo	4.0	3.5
d. Nu alolo Cliff	2.2	2.0
WAIMEA VISTAS		
e. Cliff	0.1	0.3
f. Black Pipe	0.4	1.0
g. Canyon	1.7	2.5
h. Ditch	3.5	4.0
i. Po'omau Canyon Lookout	0.3	0.5
j. Kumuwela	0.8	1.0
k. Kohua Ridge	2.5	3.0
FOREST TRAILS		
l. Kawaikoi Stream Loop	1.7	1.5
m. Pu'uka 'ohelo–Berry Flat Loop	2.0	1.0
n. Wainiha	0.5	0.5
o. Halemanu–Koke'e	1.2	1.2
p. Kaluaphui	1.9	1.5
q. Unnamed	0.2	0.5
r. Nature	0.1	0.4
ALAKA'I SWAMP		
s. Pihea	3.7	3.5
t. Alaka'i Swamp	3.5	5.5
u. Mohihi–Wai alae Route	4.0	5.5

ROADS:
- Paved
- Unpaved
- 4-wheel-drive

TRAILS
- Easy
- Moderate
- Strenuous
- Unmaintained
- Boundary
- ■ Picnic Area
- ● Campground

PACIFIC OCEAN

HONO O NA PALI NATURAL AREA RESERVE

ALAKA'I SWAMP

WILDERNESS PRESERVE

Wainiha

KILOHANA 4,030 FT

Kalalau Valley

NA PALI COAST STATE PARK

NA PALI-KONA FOREST RESERVE

Honopu Valley

PIHEA 4,284 FT

PU'U KILA 4,176 FT

Kalalau Lookout

Koke'e Air Force Station

Kahuama'a Flat

PU'UKA PANIA 4,227 FT

Koke'e Museum

Koke'e Lodge Park Hdqts.

Koke'e Instrumentation Station

NASA Koke'e Tracking Station

KOKE'E STATE PARK

KU'IA NATURAL AREA RESERVE

LOLO No.2 2,234 FT

Camp 10

Po'omau Canyon Lookout

Weiakolli Picnic Area

MOEKA FALLS 3,617 FT

Alaka'i Picnic Area

NA PALI-KONA FOREST RESERVE

Kohua Ridge

KOAI'E CANYON

Gaging Station

WAIPO'O FALLS 3,200 FT

PU'U KA PELE FOREST RESERVE

WAIMEA CANYON STATE PARK

HALEMANU RD.

550

550

0   1 mile
0   1 kilometer

WEST SHORE

Koke'e State Park and Waimea Canyon
At the end of H 550.

Unless you live in Kaua'i for years, you will never access all the hiking opportunities in Koke'e. Located 4,000 feet above sea level, the climate and flora change dramatically throughout the park. You can find everything from Kaua'i native plants to a redwood grove, plus a wealth of endangered bird species (see Bird-Watching). For specific hiking directions, visit the Koke'e Information Center and Museum.

The most unusual hike in Kaua'i is the **Pihea Trail**. A boardwalk created through the **Alaka'i Swamp** allows visitors an easier trek through this extremely wet region, which is home to most of the remaining native Kaua'i birds and trees. However, even with the wooden walkway, thigh-high deep mud is not uncommon here. Wear sturdy shoes and clothes you don't mind getting dirty. Understand that this bridge helps and hurts, by displacing native fragile plants, but protecting the ground from invasive seeds and feet. So be sure to clean the bottoms of your shoes *before* heading out onto the trail.

If you are interested in hiking in Waimea Canyon, the **Iliau Nature Loop**, **Kukui Trail**, or **Halemanu Trails** offer

You'll see healthy ferns like these growing all over the island.

hikes at a variety of difficulties. Most have views of waterfalls, streams, the canyon, native trees, and birds. Other types of trails here include Na Pali overlooks and rain forest trails. Since it gets cool and rainy up here and mosquitoes can be aggravating, bring jackets, rain gear, and bug spray.

Na Pali Coast State Park
At the end of H 56 on the north shore to the end of H 50 on the west shore. You can access trails from the Kalalau overlook in Koke'e, or from Ke'e Beach in Haena.

This 6,175-acre natural wonder is best seen by foot. Spiked verdant cliffs spill into the untouched Pacific. Streams, waterfalls, coffee and mango trees, and unequivocal views make this a hiker's paradise (and probably the best hiking spot in all Hawai'i). The most popular (and my favorite) is the **Kalalau Trail**, an 11-mile steep trek along the Na Pali cliffs with stops at rocky beaches, waterfalls, and spectacular view spots. This trail is not advisable soon after or during rain, when it is extremely slippery and steep. Please use caution when deciding to hike here. Make sure to start before 8 AM, to beat the crowds and the heat.

Though it's not safe to hike to in winter, Queens Bath attracts locals and adventurous travelers in summer.

Photo taken by Edward Broitman

Beach Hikes and Strolls

Most of the beaches listed under Beaches are great places for a stroll—especially Hanalei Bay, Kekaha Beach, and Ke'e Beach. Below are trails leading to beaches (and some beach walks) you probably don't want to miss out on.

EAST SHORE

Coastal Bike and Pedestrian Trail (in Wailua, off H 56). This much-awaited trail is slated to be 16 miles of paved beach walking from Lydgate Park stretching north.

SOUTH SHORE

Maha'ulepu Beach (pass the Grand Hyatt Resort, drive down the 2-mile unpaved and very bumpy Poipu Rd., turn right onto Maha'ulepu Rd., and continue until it ends). This beach stretches luxuriously from Shipwrecks Beach to the Ha'upa Ridge. See Beaches for more information.

WEST SHORE

Polihale State Park (off H 50, turn left onto the dirt road 200 yards past the Missile Facility; drive 4 bumpy miles to the beach). Fifteen miles of white sand beach strolling, which, as you can imagine, is a romantic sunset spot.

NORTH SHORE

Kauapea "Secret" Beach (west of Kilauea, turn onto Kalahiwai Rd.; turn right the first dirt road). A 15-minute steep trek down (and then what feels like miles back up a vertical mountain) a slippery path to a beautiful beach, where seas can be very choppy. I don't recommend you come here in winter or soon after rain. Local people are very territorial about this beach, probably because it's not a secret spot for birthday-suited hippies anymore.

Queen's Bath (in Princeville, take Ka Haku Rd. and turn right onto Punahele Rd.; look for a dirt parking lot on your right, where the trail begins). Heading down here should not be attempted in winter or when it is wet (a friend fractured a disk in his back hiking down here in the rain). The trail winds past a waterfall and offers framed ocean vistas before depositing you at the lava rock ocean pools. *Do not attempt to swim here in winter.* This can be a very difficult hike—often the county closes this trail because it is so dangerous. Check with the visitors bureau before attempting the trek. There are much better places to swim on the north shore.

Sealodge Beach (in Princeville, take Ka Haku Rd. to Kamehameha Rd.; the trail to the beach starts at the Sealodge Condo complex). Yet another hidden beach gem that is tricky to get to. In winter it is not worth the trek, because the trail is slippery and you can't swim here. But if the conditions are right (and you feel comfortable maneuvering a steep and rugged path), you'll have access to a relatively mellow section of the largest reef in Hawai'i. This is not the kind of trek you'd take your grandparents on.

HORSEBACK RIDING

If you want a unique way to see more the beaches or interior of Kaua'i, saddle up with one of the island's cowboys. Since the arrival of livestock and horses in the early 1800s, Hawaiians have become adept ranchers. The *paniolos* (cowboys) participate in rodeos throughout the state, and if you are lucky you'll be in town to observe a Hawaiian-style rodeo (check local papers for listings). The stables listed below offer guided horseback riding tours.

CJM Country Stables (808-742-6096; www.cjmstables.com; P.O. Box 1346, Koloa). You can arrange trail rides to beaches in the Poipu area.

Princeville Ranch Stables (808-826-6777; www.princevilleranch.com; P.O. Box 888, Hanalei). Riders head to waterfalls, to beaches, and on *paniolo* cattle drives; also private guided tours of the Hanalei area. You can arrange a trip every day but Sunday.

Silver Falls Ranch (808-828-6718; www.silverfallsranch.com; P.O. Box 692, Kilauea). These guys offer trail rides along mountains, streams, and waterfalls, as well as to exotic palm and fern gardens. Private guided tours of the Kilauea area are available, but they primarily take people out on group rides.

RUNNING

Though no specific services or runs are set up for striders, with a little diligence you will find some beautiful places to strengthen those legs and lungs around Kaua'i. Since there are rarely sidewalks and Kaua'i roads are narrow, the best places to run are on the beaches and trails. For specific details, see Beaches and Hiking.

SPAS

After a day of swimming or hiking, visitors to Kaua'i often can think of nothing more relaxing than a spa treatment. With a wealth of options from ylang ylang body polishes and volcanic clay facials to traditional *lomi lomi* massage treatments on the beach, spagoers tend to walk around with that blissful massage face well into the evening. As with most island activities, expect to pay more than you might on the mainland.

Alexander Spa and Salon (808-246-4918; www.alexanderspa.com; Kaua'i Marriott, 3610 Rice St., Suite 9A, Lihu'e). This salon offers full-service body treatments.

Anara Spa (808-240-6440; www.anaraspa.com; in the Grand Hyatt, 1571 Poipu Rd., Koloa). The queen of Kaua'i spas. With a recent renovation and expansion to include lava rock showers, a giant lap pool, an outdoor aerobic area, plus an array of spa treatments (including some for kids, like mini manicures, temporary tattoos, cornrows, and spray-on hair color). They also offer public wellness classes all day long.

Angeline's Mu'olaulani (808-822-3235; www.auntyangelines.com; P.O. Box 576, Anahola). With over 20 years of experience healing sore muscles out of her bungalow, Angeline serves up a unique massage. This is not a day spa, but rather an experience. The special treatment includes a salt scrub, a steam, and a four-handed *lomi lomi* massage.

Hanalei Day Spa (808-826-6621; www.hanaleidayspa.com; at the Hanalei Colony Resort, 5-7130 Kuhio Hwy., Haena; closed Sun.). Beach, garden-front, or indoor body treatments, private yoga treatments, baby massage classes, and meditation instruction, in addition to more traditional services can all be found at this small hut on the north shore.

Hartfelt Massage and Day Spa (808-338-2240; www.hartfeltmassage.com; Waimea Plantation Cottages, 9400 Kaumualii Hwy., Unit 40, Waimea). A variety of treatments including craniosacral massage, acupuncture, Raindrop Therapy, and Ginger or Kelp Wraps will take the kinks out of any traveler's neck.

Puu Day Spa and Salon (808-822-6669; www.hawaiianrainforest.com; Resortquest Kaua'i Beach at Maka'iwa 650 Aleka Loop, Kapa'a). This is a small salon and spa offering a range of services, including oceanfront and couples massage, and hot stone treatments.

Spa by the Sea (808-822-2171; www.spabytheseakauai.com; 4-1558 Kuhio Hwy., Kapa'a, 96746). This small spa serves up traditional treatments with an ocean view.

Waipouli Beach Resort and Spa (808-823-1488; www.waipoulibeachresort.com; 4-820 Kuhio Hwy., Suite 3, Kapa'a). Here you can find the first Aveda Spa on the island. These folks use only natural products. Some of their specialties are the Waipouli Flower Milk Bath Soak, Elemental Nature Massage, and Sun Relief Lavender Wrap.

SURFING

Nothing is more synonymous with Hawai'i than surfing. And Kaua'i has some of the best spots in the world. As in all water activities, the ocean here—though it looks beautiful—can be menacing and cruel. I have tried to indicate when surf spots are safe for beginners. But always check the local surf report and ask around before heading out. Never underestimate the power of the ocean. Summer generally heaves large waves to the south side, while in winter, huge, powerful swells pound the north and west shores. These waves can be extremely dangerous and unpredictable.

A surfer enjoys a rare winter swell on the east shore.

Lazy surfboards enjoy the Hanalei sun.

When there is a west wind, north shore waves get blown out (this only happens about 60 days of the year). During this rare west wind, head to the east shore. The rest of the year, you can depend on the trade winds to give consistent surf conditions. In all of the listed locations, be cautious of rocks, rips, urchins, sharks, and territorial locals. Surf spots are listed below by region, in alphabetical order.

Rentals and Lessons

Nukumoi Surf Shop (808-742-8019; 2080 Hoone Rd., Poipu. Or 808-338-1617; 9640 Kaumuali'i Hwy., Waimea). With two stores, one across from Brennecke's Beach in Poipu and the other in Waimea, this surf shop has a huge selection of boards and surf gear for rent and for sale. They give lessons as well.

Progressive Expressions (808-742-6041; 5420 Koloa Rd., Koloa). Now owned by the Hanalei Surf Company, the first surf shop on the south shore still carries a sense of history and authenticity in its surfboard shaping and designs. They sell and rent boards, gear, and clothing.

Tamba Surf Co. (808-823-6942; 4-1543 Kuhio Hwy., Kapa'a). You'll see loads of locals wearing the Tamba Surf logo. For good reason: This little surf shop on the east shore has been one of the *it* spots for surfers since it opened.

Where to Surf

EAST SHORE

Anahola Bay. (Ten minutes north of Kapa'a. On Kuhio Hwy., turn onto Kukuihale Rd.; the break is at the north end of the beach near the Hawaiian Homes land.) This long, wide sand-bottomed break is only for very experienced surfers (read: kamikazes and pros). Since the rights and lefts can get up to 300 meters long on a good day, locals get territorial over this spot. Requires *kona* winds from the south, winter north swells, or trade winds from the east.

Cabbage Heads (the second break to the right of Anahola Pier, north of Kapa'a). This low-tide right is a good spot for all levels of surfers. The hollow short wave can reach up to 6 feet on a big day and breaks on coral.

Kalapaki Beach (off Rice St., in front of the Kaua'i Marriott). A standard fun wave with few sharp rocks (though they can pop up between the flatter rocks, so use caution), this is an all-levels spot. It's a good place for beginners in summer, but the pollution from the harbor makes it less stellar.

Kealia (the first beach you see from the road after passing through Kapa'a). This popular local spot is for experienced surfers looking for a fast, powerful right and left point break. Trade winds blow this spot out. Northeast and *kona* days are great.

SOUTH SHORE

Acid Drop (in Poipu, off Lawa'i Beach Rd., on the far right side of Prince Kuhio Beach). Coral reef breaks with a rocky bottom, lefts, and rights make this spot popular for experienced locals. The waves are hollow, fast, and powerful, and generally go for 100 meters.

PK's (Prince Kuhio's) (in Poipu, across from Lawa'i Beach Resort and directly adjacent to the Beach House Restaurant). A good spot for all surfers, this fun, short right and left break is popular with locals and tourists. Watch the rocky bottom and rips. You want southeast swells and northeast winds.

Poipu Beach Park (park in the Sheraton parking lot and cross the grassy field to the beach). This standard, consistent, and hollow left breaks in mid-high-tide over reef and rocks. Recommended only for experienced surfers. The beach is very crowded with swimmers, body boarders, and families.

Shipwrecks (Hyatt Beach) (off Poipu Rd., go to the Hyatt and park there). This right and left reef break offers a consistent, hollow ride up to 300 meters on a good day. Waves can get big—up to 16 feet. Few people surf here, and most are locals. This is only for experienced surfers.

West Shore

Pakala "Infinities." (Take H 56 west from Hanapepe. Stop about 100 yards west of Mile Marker 21. Beach access is on the south side of the road near the sticker-covered guardrail. Pass through the gate and walk about five minutes on the dirt path. The break is on your left.) Expert surfers found Pakala and nicknamed it Infinities because the ride seems to last forever. This world-class left reef-breaking wave is for all levels. You can get up to a 500-meter ride. Little annoyances are the rocky bottom and territorial locals. Breaks on south swells with northeast trade winds.

North Shore

Bobo's Haena. (North shore, near Ke'e Beach, at the end of Haena Rd. Park at Ke'e Beach and head north.) In the 1960s and '70s, the land here was a nudist colony called Taylor Camp. Now the left reef breaks offer epic rides for pros and kamikazes. The rocks can be very sharp.

Cannons (near Ke'e Beach, next to Tunnels). These hollow, fast, and very powerful waves are for experienced surfers only. The water gets polluted here. And this spot tends to be crowded, especially when this left wave reaches over 10 feet. Trade winds can blow this spot out in winter.

Hanalei Bay (in Hanalei, head north on Aku Rd.). One of the most picturesque surf spots in the world. These world-class waves are for experienced surfers only. Hollow and powerful, crowded with locals and sharks, it's an unfriendly place for beginners. Other spots in the bay are **Kings** and **Queens Reef** (tow-in spots), **Hideaways** (an intermediate right coral break), **Pine Trees** (this left breaks with a solid north swell, with east to south winds), and the **Bowl** (a crowded easy wave that gets massive in winter swells).

Horners. (Take Kuhio Hwy. north to Hanalei. Cross the Wailua River Bridge. Continue north on the highway for 200 yards to a parking lot with a large tree on your right. Park here and surf in front.) This right and left beach break is excellent for all levels, though it gets crowded on weekends. This spot is best in winter north swells.

Kalihiwai Point (in Kilauea, at the end of Kalihiwai Rd.). This epic right point break, also called The Y, is hollow, fast, powerful, and fun, but recommended only for experienced surfers. Breaks in all tides. The spot needs glassy mornings or south to southeast winds.

Care to practice your sun salutations on the beach? Try a yoga class.

This is a locally favored spot, so use proper etiquette. And note that this is also a popular spot with nudists.

Kilauea Bay Beach (rock quarry) (In a small cove at the end of the Kilauea River). You'll find right and left beach breaks at this forgiving spot, which is good for all levels because of its sandy bottom and calm seas. The water is often murky, and sharks like to hang around here. Note that Kaua'i's homeless often camp at Kilauea Beach.

Pu'u Poa (Park in the Princeville Hotel lot and look for the trail). This epic right point break sometimes gives riders up to a 500-meter ride. That is why only experienced surfers should test out this fast and powerful wave that gets huge in winter.

Makua "Tunnels" Beach (In Hanalei, cross the bridge and head toward Ke'e Beach). The paddle out is rough. Experienced surfers love this world-class consistent wave. Hollow and powerful with strong rips, a rocky bottom, and huge waves in winter, this spot is not favored by many, so it can be relatively uncrowded.

Waikoko's (Directly across from the Hanalei Bay surf area, on the west side of the bay. Park on the side of the main highway, then walk about five minutes to the break). Another world-class break for experienced surfers only. It's fast and powerful, with ledges that can carry surfers for up to a 300-meter ride. This fickle right and left reef break needs solid winter swells.

TENNIS

With warm weather and the scent of *pikake* in the air, tennis players fill the Kaua'i courts year-round. Most courts are located in high-end hotels and condos, but there are a few public access spots.

EAST SHORE
Kaua'i Lagoons Golf and Tennis Club (808-241-6000; 3351 Ho'olaulea Way, Lihu'e). Rents eight courts during the daylight hours.

SOUTH SHORE
Anne Knudsen "Koloa" Park (on H 520, just before you enter Koloa). You'll find free courts open to the public.

Hyatt Regency Tennis Garden (808-249-6391; 1571 Poipu Rd., Poipu). The resort rents courts for $20 an hour.

Kiahuna Swim and Tennis Club (808-742-9533; 2290 Poipu Rd., Poipu). The club rents courts, in a garden setting, for $10 an hour, per person. Afterward there is a large pool and restaurant to cool off in.

Poipu Kai Tennis Club (808-742-8706; 1941 Poipu Rd., Poipu). You can rent rackets and courts at reasonable prices in a relaxed setting.

NORTH SHORE
Hanalei Bay Resort Tennis Club (808-836-6522; Hanalei Bay Resort, 5380 Honoiki Rd., Hanalei). Rent equipment and courts ($6 per hour) with spectacular views.

Princeville Racquet Club (808-826-1230; 4180 Lei O Papa Rd.). This fancy spot charges $18 for a 90-minute court rental.

WINDSURFING AND KITEBOARDING

See also Beaches and Surfing.

Conditions for windsurfing can be perfect here on Kaua'i. Still, pay close attention to weather and wind reports, because a mellow spot can suddenly be blown out or turn dangerous. The best windsurfing spots are '**Anini Beach**, **Poipu Beach Park**, and **Kalapaki Beach**. If you are advanced, check out **Makua "Tunnels" Beach**, **Haena**, **Maha'ulepu**, and **Salt Pond Beach Park**.

Kiteboarding is the latest water sport craze to hit beaches worldwide. Parents note that the kids will probably want to learn how to kiteboard more than surf. The best spots to try are **Baby Beach**, **Maha'ulepu**, '**Anini**, and **Hanalei Bay**.

Rentals and Lessons

Aloha Surf and Kiteboarding Lessons (808-639-8614; 4524 Lae Rd., Kalaheo). These guys rent boards and offer lessons at four times during the day. Call for details.

Kaua'i Kite with Keith Cabe (808-635-4341). Keith offers kiteboarding lessons; call to arrange a time and date.

Windsurf Kaua'i (808-828-6838). Celeste gives group lessons and rents boards. Call for details.

YOGA AND PILATES

Whether you want to meditate during a rainy afternoon or prefer morning sun salutations on the sand, there are plenty of yoga classes to go around. Be sure to call and check current times and prices; for beach yoga classes, make sure they are happening that day.

Beachfront Yoga @ Waimea Plantation Cottages (808-338-2240; 9400 Kaumuali'i Hwy., Waimea). Offers classes three days a week.

Bikram Yoga Kaua'i (808-822-5053).

Ocean Front Yoga (808-639-9294; www.aloha-yoga.com). Joy teaches oceanfront classes on a grassy area in Poipu to all levels. Call for details.

Yoga Hanalei (808-826-YOGA; 5-5161E Kuhio Hwy., Hanalei). Classes daily 6 AM–7:30 PM to all levels and any style of practice. Call for the schedule.

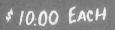

$ 10.00 Each

Fresh
Tropical
Flowers

10 AM
SUN-THURS.

8

SHOPPING

Makanas

Inevitably, when that rainy time of day occurs, stores on Kaua'i are there to welcome you (and your money). Since the majority of items on the island are shipped in from elsewhere, you might be astounded by the prices. I have tried to list items created on Kaua'i. Unfortunately, most clothing, shoes, and even art that was once made on the island is now commonly crafted throughout the South Pacific and Asia. Listed below are your best options for local finds.

In general, you can expect stores to be open 10 AM–6 PM. Though don't forget that's Hawaiian Time, so tag an *ish* on the end of those numbers.

ANTIQUES

EAST SHORE

Bambulei Antiques (808-823-8641; 4-369 D Kuhio Hwy., Kapa'a). Located in two adjoining plantation houses, this antiques shop is cluttered with Hawaiiana, vintage and new clothes, plus some funky finds like records, books, and even furniture.

Hoomana Thrift Shop (808-821-2818, 4531 Kuamoo Rd., Kapa'a). On the road to Opaeka'a Falls, this giant thrift shop has a fantastic selection of Hawaiian clothing, music, DVD, books, and furniture. Goods are really cheap, which makes it okay that they accept only cash. They only open the shop in the mornings, every day but Sunday.

WEST SHORE

Collectibles and Fine Junque (808-338-9855; 9821 Kaumuali'i Hwy., Waimea). This is a fun place to sift through Hawaiiana antiques and collectibles on the way back from Koke'e. Located in a small antique shack, this spot offers a giant selection of everything from jewelry to Japanese buoys.

This antiques store in Waimea has goods as old as the historic building it's housed in.

Kauaʻi Fine Arts (808-335-3778; 3905 Hanapepe Rd., Hanapepe). Specializing in antique maps and prints, this little house in Hanapepe is crowded with fun memorabilia from days gone by.

NORTH SHORE

Yellowfish Trading Co. (808-826-1227; Hanalei Center, Hanalei). This is the best high-end antiques shop on the island. Located in the back of the Hanalei Center, with goods spilling out of the door, this little find offers a vast array of collectible Hawaiian furniture, clothing, and trinkets, plus some thoughtful one-of-a-kind gift ideas.

BOOKS

In the few bookshops on Kauaʻi, you'll be able to locate pretty much anything you might want to read while lazing away on your lanai. Aside from the spots listed below, you can also find books about Kauaʻi flora and fauna, history, geology, plus fun kids' books at the gift shops listed a little farther on in this chapter.

EAST SHORE

Borders Books and Music (808-246-0862; 4304 Nawiliwili Rd., Lihuʻe). This giant house of books has the best selection of new titles on the island. Plus they have an air-conditioned café and a giant Kauaʻi section.

Tin Can Mailman Fine Books and Curiosities (808-822-3009; 4-356 Kuhio Hwy., Kapaʻa). This is my favorite place to disappear during a rainy spell. It's stacked with used and rare books on everything from romance to Hawaiian history, literary fiction to kids' titles, plus a nice selection of antique maps and tapa cloth; I never seem to be able to leave here empty handed. They buy books. And the folks at the Mailman take the day off on Sunday.

WEST SHORE

Talk Story Books (808-335-6469; 3567 Hanapepe Rd., Hanapepe). Open on weekdays and Friday evenings, this bookshop/café sells new and used titles in an open space in downtown Hanapepe. During the art walk, this is one of my favorite places to have a coffee and people-watch.

NORTH SHORE

Hanalei Book Store (808-826-2568; 4489 Aku Rd., Hanalei). This little spot, located behind the Hanalei Wake Up Café, has a small but decent selection of new and used titles and gifts. They also buy books.

CLOTHING

Kauaʻi is a T-shirt, board shorts, and flip-flops kind of place. It is not uncommon to see people walking around in just swimsuits, so you probably won't find the greatest selection of Jimmy Choos here. Instead you'll want to keep your eyes peeled for island wear. To some that means the aforementioned casual attire of most Hawaiians; to others it means that Hawaiian shirt you've been eyeing forever, a cute summer dress, or sandals. Since there aren't many clothing stores exclusively for men, check out Surf Shops. There you'll find a generous selection of stores specializing in the aforementioned Hawai'i style, plus an array of accessories.

One word of advice: if you happen to buy the same aloha shirt as your spouse, avoid wearing it to a lu'au. I have seen plenty of people get made fun of this way.

EAST SHORE

Island Hemp and Cotton (808-821-0225; 4-1373 Kuhio Hwy., Kapa'a). Just as the name infers, this store in downtown Kapa'a sells comfortable (and quite stylish) hemp and cotton clothes for men and women.

Jungle Girl Clothes (808-823-9351; 4-855 Kuhio Hwy., Kapa'a; and 808-742-9649; Old Koloa Town, 5424 Koloa Rd.). Located in the back of a parking lot in Kapa'a (and in downtown Koloa), this funky spot offers island attire for the *wahines*. They also sell Indonesian imports and gift items. They close on Sundays.

Kilohana Clothing Co. (808-246-6911; 3-2087 Kaumuali'i Hwy., Lihu'e). Worth a quick peek while you're at the Kilohana Plantation, this clothing store sells tropical casual wear, including aloha shirts for the *keikis*.

Marta's Boat (808-822-3926; 770 Kuhio Hwy., Kapa'a). This funky spot sells high-end women's and kids' clothing, plus jewelry and gifts. Though it is pricey, you'll find some name-brand kids' clothes that you can't get anywhere else on the island, plus a bunch of local Hawaiian brands. They close on Sunday.

Naturally Birkenstocks (808-822-3627; 4-1467 Kuhio Hwy., Kapa'a). With a generous selection of sandals (by more than just the good folks at Birkenstock), you'll likely find those higher-end sandals you've been searching for at this store on the northern side of Kapa'a.

The Root (808-823-1277; 4-1435 Kuhio Hwy., Kapa'a). For higher prices (since everything is imported from the mainland), The Root offers an array of surfer girl and island attire, including popular name brands like Roxy. They sell a nice selection of shoes and accessories. They also have a location in downtown Hanalei.

SOUTH SHORE

Crazy Shirts (808-742-7161; 5356 Koloa Rd., Koloa; and in Poipu Shopping Village). Okay, so you really have to have one of those ever-so-popular Crazy Shirts. Well, you're in luck, because there happens to be a store in downtown Koloa *and* in the Poipu Shopping Village. If you've never seen one of these shops, and you are a fan of sometimes-witty T-shirts, it's worth a jaunt inside.

Pohaku T's (808-742-7500; 3430 Poipu Rd., Koloa). This souvenir shop is definitely worth a visit, since *everything* is made by Kaua'i residents. Here you'll find a vast selection of T-shirts and gift items unique to the island. Plus, you'll support local artisans and the folks trying to raise awareness of the cultural legacy of this region.

Reyn Spooner (808-742-7279; Grand Hyatt Resort, Poipu). Designer Reyn McCullough is the pioneer of aloha shirts made of breathable rayon, with beautiful designs. Most businessmen wear his designs, and he has now forayed into the women's market as well. If you are looking for a lovely Hawaiian souvenir (and are willing to pay for it), this is the place to go.

Sandal Tree (808-742-2009; Grand Hyatt Resort, Poipu). Sandal Tree sells a wide range of designer and high-end sandals to those of you who might need another pair. They offer a wealth of leather options.

West Shore

Red Dirt Shirt (808-335-5670; 4350 Waialo Rd., 'Ele'ele). With two other locations in Lihu'e and Kapa'a (but you'll find the best deals at the location listed above), this might be one of the most popular Kaua'i souvenirs. Yes, a T-shirt. The folklore has it that after Hurricane 'Iniki a windstorm blew red dirt into Robert Hedin's screen-printing T-shirt business, covering his whole stock with that colorful dirt that soon you'll be trying to get out of your clothes. After discussing this with a friend, he decided to take a gamble . . . and a multimillion-dollar business was formed. Just a little hint: When new, make sure to wash your shirt separately. And don't wear it in the rain.

North Shore

Bikini Room (808-826-9711; 4489 Aku Rd., Hanalei). Relocating from San Clemente, California, owner Gisele Gardner thought Kaua'i could use an all-bikini shop. So she opened up one that offers a wide selection of Brazilian bikinis, plus European and *keiki* styles.

Cake (808-828-6412; 2474 Keneke St., Kilauea). If you're looking for designer clothes,

At one of the surf clothing shops on the island, you can become a surfer (or at least look like one).

Cake is the place to explore. Located in the Kong Lung Center, this little boutique specializes in dresses, shirts, and pants for those who aren't content with the shorts-and-bikini uniform of Kaua'i.

Hot Rocket Clothing (808-826-7776; Ching Young Village Center, Hanalei). This funky local spot sells everything from kitsch souvenirs to aloha shirts made by the Hawaiian legend, Reyn Spooner.

Tropical Tantrum (808-826-6944; Hanalei Center, Hanalei). This Hawaiian chain creates designs from original fabrics and then ships them out to Indonesia to be made into colorful island-style clothing for *wahines*.

ESPECIALLY FOR KIDS

Don't be put off to learn that there aren't many stores especially for kids on Kaua'i. It seems that every gift store, museum shop, and even mainstream clothing store also has a decent selection for the *keikis*. Below are a few special places worth a peek.

Though the little ones might want to play on the sand all day, they will also delight in the north shore kids' stores.

Kokonut Kids (808-826-0353; 5-5190 Kuhio Hwy., Hanalei). If you are looking for locally crafted kids' clothing, gifts, and toys, this is the place to stop. With a nice selection of clothes for babies to kids, it's tough to walk out of here without picking up a little something.

Magic Dragon Toy and Art Supply (808-826-9114; Princeville Shopping Center, Princeville). This magical toy store will take you back in time to when you were a kid. With a slew of unique toys and gifts, you'll likely find something to amuse the little ones in your life.

Rainbow Ducks (808-826-4741; Hanalei Center, Hanalei). Rainbow Ducks specializes in toys and clothing for the wee ones. Plus it is connected to the women's clothing and gift store next door, so you'll find funky outfits for the whole crew here.

FURNITURE

Are you in love with the koa wood tables and chairs in your condo? Is that rattan sofa in your hotel room way more comfortable than you ever imagined one could be? Are you suddenly talking about redecorating your house with island-style furniture? Well, there are some places on Kaua'i set up to help make your island-style living reverie come alive.

Coconut Style (808-828-6899; Kong Lung Center, Kilauea). This small shop sells not only hand-painted clothing and fabrics designed by the owner, but also some of the most beautiful pieces of furniture on the island. Though not a giant selection, this is the spot to find high-end goods made of expensive wood.

Otsuka's (808-822-7766; 1624 Kuhio Hwy., Kapa'a). It seems everyone who moves to Kaua'i ends up decorating the house with Otsuka's island-style designs. The largest furniture and accessory store on the island offers furnishings for the home, office, and outdoors by brand-name companies, and local ones, too.

Two Frogs Hugging (808-246-8777; 3215 Kuhio Hwy., Lihu'e). The first things you notice about this furniture store are the frogs hugging and the giant chair outside the building. Once you get inside, you'll find teak indoor and outdoor furniture, sofas, cabinetry, Asian antiques, and accessories that will add spice to your rooms back home.

GALLERIES

One of my favorite rainy-day activities is to go gallery-hopping. Mainly because local art here is a unique combination of brilliant color schemes, tributes to modern and ancient cultures, plus there is an array of tapa cloth, sculptures, glass, and international artwork.

EAST SHORE

Aloha Images (808-821-1382; 4504 Kukui St., Kapa'a). Located in the center of Old Kapa'a town, this gallery features affordable paintings by over 20 local artists. Often there will be local painters creating in the store.

Davidson Arts (808-821-8022; 4-1322 Kuhio Hwy., Kapa'a). This local art gallery, featuring koa furniture, sculpture, and paintings by John and Hayley Davidson (plus a few exhibits by local friends), is a good place to learn about the current Kaua'i art trends.

Earth and Sea Gallery (808-821-2831; 4504 Kukui St., Kapa'a). With an array of coconut-carved gifts (mostly made in Indonesia, but designed by the gallery owner), lamps, and other gift ideas, here you might find that unique gift for that tough-to-shop-for family member.

✪**Kaua'i Recycling for the Arts** (808-632-0555; Kaua'i Resource Center, 3460 Ahukini Rd., Lihu'e). This studio art space not only offers workshops and classes to people interesting in creating art from recycled glass and other products, but also has a beautiful gallery filled with jewels, functional art pieces, and architectural pieces. When you get a look at this fantastic collection, you'll be amazed that anyone ever thought the materials junk.

Kela's Glass Gallery (808-822-4527; 4-1354 Kuhio Hwy., Kapa'a). It is tough to pass by this little glass gallery without peeking inside at the fluidity of these colorful glass sculptures. They sell vases, paperweights, blown glass, fish sculptures, bowls, platters, and much more. And they ship to the mainland.

Kilohana Galleries (808-245-9352; 3-2087 Kauamuali'i Hwy., Lihu'e). Located throughout the historic Kilohana Plantation. There are a number of galleries to explore. The most impressive (and unique) collection of local clay products can be found in **Clayworks at**

Kilohana Plantation offers shops, restaurants, train rides, a lu'au, and historical tours.

Kilohana. You can find a number of paintings, sculptures, and gifts in their **Hawaiian Collection Room**, **Artisan's Room**, and the **Makana Gallery**. The building itself is a work of antique art worth exploring.

South Shore

Christian Riso Fine Art and Framing (808-742-2555; 5400 Koloa Rd., Koloa). This small gallery in Koloa features paintings, etchings, photos, and fine woodcarvings that promote local talent and themes.

James Hoyle Gallery (808-742-1010; 5420 Koloa d., Koloa). James Hoyle is a master with paint. Inspired by impressionist painters, he moved to Kaua'i and began capturing beautiful naturalist scenes with his own unique twist. Note that he sells these pieces at big prices.

West Shore

The majority of Kaua'i's galleries are located in the small art town of Hanapepe. On Friday evening, the galleries stay open for the weekly community Friday Night Art event. On these nights, galleries serve wine and cheese; you can also meet local artists and hear live music. Since I have included a bunch of information about the participating galleries in chapter 4, for specific information about these galleries, please refer there. Note that galleries change often; check local listings for new openings in the Hanapepe area.

Aloha-n-Paradise (808-338-1522; 9905 Waimea Rd., Waimea). This gallery/café in Old Waimea Town showcases the talents of Kaua'i resident artists. With a variety of painting styles (though mostly they re-create island life), originals and reproductions, crafts, and collectibles, Aloha-n-Paradise makes a nice pit stop after a long hike or beach day. They also have Internet access.

Native Hawaiian Arts and Crafts

Though the definition of *native* is often debated, one thing is for sure—native arts and crafts are becoming rare phenomena. Since everything functional was once constructed by hand, even the smallest items like spoons or bowls are considered works of art. Unfortunately, the lost arts of the native Kauaʻi people are tough to find (check out the Kauaʻi Museum for the best collection). Below are some unique items to look out for and a few that are actually available for purchase.

WOODCARVINGS

As with most native island societies in the South Pacific, canoes and woodcarvings represent the apex of high art for past cultures. To craft the ancient-style canoes, which could carry up to 200 people, plants, trees, seedlings, food, animals, and more, master builders crafted these out of koa or other waterproof hardwoods using little more than their hands. You won't see any of these remaining on the island, but there are some examples of family-sized ones at the Kauaʻi Museum. If you want to purchase a woodcarving, you can find *poi* pounders, bowls, and furniture at local galleries. One of the best places to explore this ancient art is the **Kamaʻaina Koa Wood Gallery** (808-335-5483; 3848 Hanapepe Rd., Hanapepe).

FEATHERWORK

A lost art—and a sad reality about the progress of the island—is featherwork. Using the red and yellow feathers of native birds, the ancient royal *aliʻi* fashioned headpieces to show their power. Now most of the native birds used to make these headpieces are extinct, and featherwork is a thing of the past.

LEIS

In a similar genre, the use of flowers as jewelry is the greatest symbol of Hawaiʻi. Lei making is an art that will probably never die, both because flowers are plentiful, and because native and tourist cultures keep the market alive for these unique necklaces. Typically the tourist leis are simple affairs of plumeria or tuberose strung through the middle. The true art of lei making comes with those leis you might glimpse on a local graduate, in a wedding party, at a birthday or special occasion, or on local political figures. Traditionally Hawaiians give leis for special occasions and to royal guests (which is why the big hotels often greet you with them). Once you get a glimpse of traditional leis, you will see the true artistry blossom (excuse the pun). For special events, men usually wear *maile* leis, which are ferns or ti leaves braided together in a rich heavy pattern. For weddings, women often wear *pikake* (or jasmine) leis; if you happen to see a local wearing a *pikake* lei, note that the more strands of flowers she dons, the more royal she appears.

Kauaʻi (as with all Hawaiian islands) has its own local lei, the *mokihana*—which are not flowers but small purple fruit (though on a lei they turn green) that smells slightly like anise and can be really scratchy to wear.

When giving leis, it is customary for the giver to kiss you on both cheeks. Legend says never to give pregnant women leis, as it metaphorically strangles the baby.

Another type of lei is crafted from Niʻihau shells (see chapter 9). These are actually considered fine jewelry and are quite rare. Since they are made of delicate shells from the coast around the elusive isle, these are actual leis that you can take home. You can locate these handmade necklaces at high-end jewelry stores. Make sure to ask if the necklace has a certificate of authenticity—which can only be awarded if the shells are from Ni'ihau.

CLOTH ART: TAPA AND QUILTS

Tapa cloth is a beautiful representation of what natives could do with a bit of fig tree bark. Though the original indigenous way of constructing this cloth is lost (and most cloth available to purchase on Kaua'i comes from elsewhere), you can still find places on the island that sell tapa cloth—including from a woman who makes tapa-covered journals at the Grand Hyatt Hotel craft kiosks.

Another kind of cloth art you'll find is the quilt. Brought by the missionaries and then perfected by Hawaiians, quilt designs range from pillow covers to giant wall hangings and are usually decorated in bright colorful fruits, flowers, and geometrical patterns. You can find these at specialty stores around the island for big prices.

Locals offer aloha to the keikis, *too.*

NORTH SHORE

Banana Patch Studio (808-335-5944; Kong Lung Center, Kilauea; or 3865 Hanapepe Rd., Hanapepe). This chain of galleries sells locally made ceramic tiles, pottery, paintings, and sculpture. Plus they offer an array of gifts, such as children's books, photos, wooden utensils, and tiki goods.

Hanalei Moonflowers (808-652-9296; 5-5080 Kuhio Hwy., Hanalei). This small gallery features the colorful and fluid paintings of local artist Jenifer H. Prince. Though her work can be seen in a number of local galleries, this is her studio and chances are, when you visit, you'll get to meet this interesting artist, who paints brilliantly colored Kauaʻi scenes and landscapes.

Kim McDonald Gallery (800-588-3448; Hanalei Dolphin Center, Hanalei). You'll see Kim McDonald's oil paintings all over the island—on menus, on walls, in hotels, and more. If you like the vibrant colors of the South Pacific, you can go check out her originals near the Hanalei Dolphin restaurant. If you can't bear the high price of her paintings, you can find her work on place mats, coasters, and more.

Lotus Gallery (808-828-9898 or 808-742-8649; 2484 Keneke St., Kilauea; or in the Beach House Restaurant, 5022 Lawaʻi Rd., Koloa). The two locations of this high-end gallery sell jewelry and fine art produced by the owners Tsajon and Kamalia. Plus, they specialize in Asian art made of minerals and antique jewels. The Beach House location has a large selection of Tahitian pearls and golden South Sea pearls as well.

GIFT SHOPS

Differentiating between gift shops and galleries is a bit tough. Below are outfits that do sell local artwork, but since they also carry a wealth of other items, I chose to include them here. There are many more gifts shops on the island, including some major chains (where you can get cheap coffee and Hawaiiana gifts). Below are unique stops that focus primarily on local gifts you can't find elsewhere.

EAST SHORE

Earth Beads (808-822-0766; 1392A Kukui St., Kapaʻa). Not only do the folks at this little store sell beads from all over the globe, but they also offer a lovely array of jewelry, bags, and other gift items. They mainly specialize in goods from the East.

Flowers and Joys (808-822-1569; 4-1302 Kuhio Hwy., Kapaʻa). This is one of the premier flower shops on the island. However, they also sell gift baskets, blown glass, and plants. They ship to the mainland.

Growing Greens Nursery (808-822-3831; 6660B Kawaihau Rd., Kapaʻa). These growers specialize in tropical plants and have been perfecting their craft for almost 15 years. Among their special treats are what's called fun gardens—tropical plants grown in lava rock. They also ship plants to the mainland.

Hilo Hattie (808-245-3404; 3252 Kuhio Hwy., Lihuʻe). So you arrive in Kauaʻi and start wondering where all the tourists got those Hawaiian shirts—well, look no farther. Though it may be the tourist mecca of the island, Hilo Hattie's has a huge selection of aloha wear, gifts, food, and much more. Plus they have hotel pickup service and offer shoppers a shell lei, juice, and plenty of help upon arrival.

Kapaia Stitchery (808-245-2281; 3-3351 Kuhio Hwy., Lihu'e). Julie Yukimura (along with a number of local *kapuna*) stitches and sells quilts, shirts, and other items at this shop near the Wilcox hospital. Sewers can also buy top-quality fabrics. And if you want to design your own aloha shirt, they take special orders.

Kaua'i Museum (808-246-2470; 4428 Rice St., Lihu'e). This is one of the best shops on the island. With this vast selection of Hawaiiana books, crafts, jewelry, and gift items, you might spend more time in the shop than in the actual museum.

Kaua'i Products Fair (808-246-0988; in the northern part of Kapa'a, on the mountain side of Kuhio Hwy.). Selling locally made crafts Thursday through Sunday 9–5, this craft fair is the largest on the island. Local artisans hawk hippie clothes, traditional cloth, pottery, and jewelry.

Kaua'i Products Store (808-246-6753; Kukui Grove Shopping Center, Lihu'e). While most gift shops specialize in goods that *look* like they were made on the island, this store really delivers. With a nice selection of arts and crafts, quilts, food, jewelry, and more—all locally made—this is the place to support local artists without dipping into your eating budget.

Pono Market (808-822-4581; 4-1300 Kuhio Hwy., Kapa'a). Unless you have a great portable fridge to take their amazing *poke* home with you, the only gift items to get here are leis. This little shop in the center of Old Town Kapa'a has a good selection of leis for decent prices.

Wilcox Memorial Hospital (808-245-1143; 3420 Kuhio Hwy., Lihu'e). Okay, so heading over to the hospital to shop seems like a drag. It's all for a good cause, and they actually have great gifts. All proceeds go to supporting the hospital.

SOUTH SHORE

Grand Hyatt Hotel Craft Kiosks (808-742-1234; 1571 Poipu Rd., Poipu). These kiosks rotate often, so I can't write specifically about any one vendor, but I always seem to find that perfect Hawaiian gift here, from tapa-cloth journals to recycled glass jewelry. Not necessarily worth a special trip to shop, but if you happen to be on the property, check out the local artists selling their goods.

Hawaiian Quilt Collection (808-742-1818; Grand Hyatt Hotel, 1571 Poipu Rd., Poipu). Because of the high prices, this place may seem like more of a gallery than a gift shop, but if you are serious about bringing home a quilt, stop in here to see some of the magnificent handmade local works.

Kaua'i Coffee Company (808-335-5497; 1 Numila Rd., Kalaheo). This is the largest coffee grower in Hawai'i, and their gift shop promises to tempt even non-coffee-drinkers inside its aromatic walls. They offer free coffee samples while you shop for not only the roasted beans, but also a wealth of locally made products including soaps, dolls, ceramics, books, and more.

NTBG McBryde and Allerton Gift Shop (808-742-2433; 4425 Lawa'i Rd., Koloa). This is another one of my favorite places to buy unique gifts with lots of aloha spirit. You'll find a nice selection of books on plants, geology, and Kaua'i history, plus a lovely selection of jewelry, local crafts and bath products, pottery, and even some plants.

Enjoy the view and a free cup of coffee while you shop at the Kaua'i Coffee Company.

WEST SHORE

Aunty Liliko'i's Passion Fruit Products (808-338-1296; 9875 Waimea Rd., Waimea). Since 1990, Aunty has been creating a plethora of condiments, jellies, spreads, and body care items using the famous Hawaiian passion fruit as a base. Some unique local items to taste are the *liliko'i* syrup or mustard, and the passion teriyaki.

Kaua'i Granola (808-338-0121; 9633 Kaumuali'i Hwy., Waimea). Owners and granola lovers Cheryl and Joy recently opened a granola store in Waimea. Their varietals include pina colada, Hawaiian zest, *liliko'i*, espresso, and guava crunch granola.

Kaua'i Kookie (800-361-1126; 1-3529 Kaumuali'i Hwy., Hanapepe). These bakers have been serving up Kaua'i cookies and unique condiments since 1965. If you're in the Hanapepe area, pop into their factory outlet to see what's cookin'. They also ship to the mainland.

Koke'e Natural History Museum Gift Shop (808-335-9975; Koke'e State Park, Waimea). After learning about the rich geological history of the island, you might want a relic. This fun gift shop sells books, minerals, and locally made crafts. You'll also find great hiking maps and posters.

Waimea Plantation Cottages Gift Shop (808-338-1625; 9400 Kaumuali'i Hwy., Waimea). This newly expanded gift shop (though still quite small) sells locally crafted art, including dolls, books, jewelry, and clothing. Ask about the owner's doll line: little teddy bears dressed Hawaiian-style.

West Kaua'i Craft Fair (on the ocean side of Kaumuali'i Hwy., Waimea Town; Thurs.–Sun.). This smallish fair brings the local artists out to mingle with the community. Often you'll find live music, hula shows, local food, and a small collection of artists representing the diverse talent of the island.

Wrangler's Steakhouse Gift Shop (808-338-1218; 9852 Kaumuali'i Hwy., Waimea). Shopping at a steak house might seem unreal, but this local institution (owned and run by the Faye family of Waimea Plantation Cottages) has some of the best local crafts and books around. Their quilts, dolls, and toys are uniquely crafted and decently priced.

NORTH SHORE

Island Soap and Candle Works (808-828-1955; 2474 Keneke St., Kilauea; or 808-742-1945; 5428 Koloa Rd., Koloa). With two locations of this fun shop (and also a healthy expansion onto the other Hawaiian islands and online), your senses will be overstimulated by the rich aromas just walking past. The folks at this shop hand-pour tropical soaps, lotions, oils, and candles.

Kong Lung Company (808-828-1802; 2490 Keneke St., Kilauea). They like to say they are the "Gumps of the cane fields," which is a nice sentiment—but you can rejoice that they do not sell $200 spoons. Instead, located within this plantation-style building (listed on the National Register of Historic Places), you'll find arts and crafts, antiques, bath products, fashion, and gifts with an Asian flair.

Na 'Aina Kai Botanical Gardens Gift Shop (808-828-0525; 4101 Wailapa Rd., Kilauea). Even those of you who aren't into floral gifts or botanical gardens will find interesting arts and crafts, photos, books, hats, and more at this healthy gift shop. Often you'll locate unique handmade gifts that can't be found elsewhere on Kaua'i.

Sand People (808-826-1008 or 808-742-2888; 5-5161 Kuhio Hwy., Hanalei; or 2360 Kiahuna Plantation, Poipu). This two-store chain, though not specializing in locally made products, offers some of the most beautiful and sophisticated gifts on the island. From unique frames to bath products and everything in between, I always find myself wanting to buy something—though their prices are pretty steep.

JEWELRY

Shells, beach glass, pearls, and the occasional metal are the elements you can expect in Kaua'i jewelry stores. Unique types of island jewelry are Ni'ihau shell leis and Hawaiian lauhala-patterned jewels.

A jewelry store clerk and his dog hang loose.

EAST SHORE

Goldsmiths Kaua'i (808-822-4653; 4-356 Kuhio Hwy., Kapa'a). Local designers Mark Meador and Dana Romsdal use a method called lost-wax casting to create most of their one-of-a-kind designs. They add exotic pearls, diamonds, and colored stones, including garnets and sapphires. All designs are created and crafted right on the island.

Grande's Gems (808-245-3445; Kilohana Plantation, 3-2087 Kaumuali'i Hwy., Lihu'e; they also have stores in Coconut Marketplace and the Marriott Resort). Hawaiian jewelry designer Denny Wong creates pieces that use black pearls, opal, and tanzanite.

Jacques Amo Jewelry (808-822-9977; 4-1340 Kuhio Hwy., Kapa'a). Jacques Amo designs one-of-a-kind handmade jewelry. Born in Tahiti, Jacques creates the entire piece from precious materials, including black pearls. If you don't see something you like, he can collaborate with you to create your own keepsake from Kaua'i.

Jim Saylor Jewelry (808-822-3591; 1318 Kuhio Hwy., Kapa'a; also located in the Princeville Resort). For the past 25 years, this Kapa'a-based jeweler has been creating high-quality jewelry designs. He casts black pearls, diamonds, and other precious gemstones in unique settings.

Robert's (808-246-4653; 2976 Kress St., Lihu'e; or 808-335-5412; 3837 Hanapepe Rd., Hanapepe). This store has served the Garden Island since 1946 and repeatedly wins awards as the best jewelers on the island. Specializing in Hawaiian heirloom jewelry, black pearls, and jade, their prices are often reasonable and their staff seem more interested in educating you about the specific pieces than making that sale.

SOUTH SHORE

Na Hoku (808-742-7025, 808-742-1863; Poipu Shopping Center and Grand Hyatt Hotel). This is the jewelry store you go to for those uniquely Hawaiian-style pieces—a golden flip-flop with diamonds pendant, a palm tree charm, or a bird-of-paradise necklace—all made of high-end (and very expensive) jewels.

Sheldon Gate Jewelry Designs (808-742-6591; 5330 Koloa Rd., Koloa). Gemologist Sheldon Gate created this one-of-a-kind store. He uses heirloom gems as the centerpieces of unique creations made from scratch. Pieces range from the daringly simple to the extravagant.

Xan Designer Jewelry (808-742-7600; 2360 Kiahuna Plantation, Poipu). This gallery in the Poipu Shopping Center sells rare jewelry accenting the abundant gems on display. Prices are high, but you won't find designs like this in many other spots on the island.

NORTH SHORE

Black Pearl (808-826-9992; 5-5016 Kuhio Hwy., Hanalei; or 808-742-5055; 2360 Kiahuna Plantation, Poipu). As you probably guessed by its name, this three-store chain (there's another one in Aspen) specializes in the romantic pearls of the Pacific, often selling rare finds at big prices.

MALLS

Often malls (or strip malls) are the center of social gatherings, hula shows, art exhibits, or even local political events. It might not feel quaint to be wandering through the giant malls of Lihu'e, but when you are, know that you are having a typical Kaua'i day. At press time, development was in the works to create a new shopping center in the Koloa area as well as to revamp the Princeville Shopping Center.

Aloha Center (808-245-6996; 3371 Wilcox Rd., Lihu'e). Set up for cruise ship and Superferry passengers, this double-story craft kiosk sells local souvenirs for tourists. You might find a few interesting works of art or crafts made by local artists. Occasionally there is live music here, too.

Ching Young Village Shopping Center (808-826-7222; 5-190 Kuhio Hwy., Hanalei). What used to be a general store over 100 years ago now has blossomed into one of the largest outdoor shopping centers on the north shore. Look for locally made gift items as well as clothing stores, surf shops, restaurants, and even some funky north shore finds.

Coconut Marketplace (808-822-3641; 4-484 Kuhio Hwy., Wailua). This lovely outdoor shopping center offers everything for the shopper: a vast selection of gift shops, clothing stores, galleries, jewelry shops, a movie theater, ice cream, and tons of food options in the heart of the Coconut Coast. There are also late-night bars with live entertainment and a weekly hula show on Wednesday evening.

Harbor Mall (808-245-6255; 3501 Rice St., Lihu'e). Down by Kalapaki Beach, this retail area, with plenty of restaurants and other services, mainly serves cruise ship passengers and the folks staying out at the Marriott. Here you'll find gift shops selling much of the same gear you can find elsewhere.

Kukui Grove Shopping Center (808-245-7784; 3-2600 Kaumuali'i Hwy., Lihu'e). The biggest mall on Kaua'i is home to many of the chain stores you'd find at home (Macy's, Sears, Borders, Longs), plus over 55 shops and restaurants, a movie theater, a Starbucks, and tons more. This is where the locals hang. Every Friday they offer live music and hula shows.

Poipu Shopping Village (808-742-2831; 2360 Kiahuna Plantation, Poipu). Tastefully landscaped with high-end restaurants, some unique shops, and a bunch of funky colored birds, this outdoor shopping center is sure to be a center of activity if you are in the Poipu area. There are free hula shows throughout the week, so check local listings.

Princeville Shopping Center (808-826-9497; Kuhio Hwy., Princeville). Though there aren't many shopping choices in this sprawling center (you'll mostly find real estate offices), at press time the owners were looking to sell. There are big hopes for this plaza (which the condo renters in Princeville will surely enjoy). But for now, you're stuck with a few necessities (gas station, coffee, restaurants, and groceries), and a couple of gift stores.

MUSIC

Want to try out a 'ukulele? Or find a locally made guitar? Or maybe you're interested in the sounds of Hawai'i? Though your options are slim, here are a few places you might want to explore.

Bounty Music (808-823-8000; 4-991 Kuhio Hwy., Kapa'a). This small store sells new and used 'ukuleles, guitars, jewelry boxes, and more. One of their signature items is a koa wood 'ukulele. They also give lessons for those of you who have never tried your fingers at the traditional Hawaiian stringed instrument.

Paradise Music (kiosks located at Coconut Marketplace and Princeville Shopping Center). Here you'll find Hawaiian music. They make great recommendations and help support local Kaua'i musicians whenever possible.

Scotty's Music (808-332-0090; 2-2436 Kaumuali'i Hwy., Kalaheo). Scotty's sells 'ukuleles, guitars, and keyboards at reasonable prices. They also sponsor local shows and events, so pop in if you want the scoop on local music happenings.

Tropic Isle Music Company (808-245-8700; Anchor Cove Shopping Center, 3416 Rice St., Lihu'e). Here is the spot to find that Hawaiian song you've heard all over the island that you can't locate anywhere else. You can listen to many of the CDs before purchase. They also have a nice selection of koa 'ukuleles, hula gear, Hawaiian books, and videos.

SURF SHOPS

Most people on Kaua'i peruse surf shops not only for boards and gear, but for clothing, too. For the most part, you can expect surf shops to carry an extensive line of men's, women's, and kids' clothing, plus all the gear you'll need to battle those waves. These are usually among the cheapest places to find sandals, too.

EAST SHORE

Tamba Surf (808-823-6942; 4-1543 Kuhio Hwy., Kapa'a). After a couple of days on the island, you'll probably notice all the surfers wearing Tamba board shorts. This locally owned surf shop caters to serious surfers.

The Wave Surf Co. (808-821-1199; 1267 Ulu St., Kapa'a). This east shore shop offers rentals, instruction, and plenty of gear. They sell surf and boogie boards, snorkel equipment, and beach clothing (mostly for women).

SOUTH SHORE

Nukumoi Surf Shop (808-742-8019; 2080 Hoone Rd., Poipu; and 808-338-1617; 9640 Kaumuali'i Hwy., Waimea). With two stores, one across from Brennecke's Beach in Poipu and the other in Waimea, this locally owned surf shop sells clothes for men, women, and *groms*, plus they have a huge selection of boards and surf gear. They also rent boards and give lessons.

Progressive Expressions (808-742-6041; 5420 Koloa Rd., Koloa). Now owned by the Hanalei Surf Company, the first surf shop on the south shore still carries a sense of history and authenticity in its surfboard shaping and designs. They sell boards, gear, and clothing as well as offering rentals and lessons.

NORTH SHORE

Hanalei Surf Company (808-826-9000; 5-5161 Kuhio Hwy., Hanalei). This outfit has been a staple on the north shore for years. They sell everything for the surfer (plus gear for a fun day on the sand), including hip beach clothes; you might find it hard to resist a little purchase.

Hanalei Surf Company Backdoor (808-826-1900; 5-5190 Kuhio Hwy., Hanalei). Located in the Ching Young Shopping Village, the younger sibling of the Hanalei Surf Company offers a large selection of boards, brand-name clothing, juniors' clothing, kite surfing and skateboarding equipment, and aloha wear.

You can buy or rent surfboards at one of the many surf shops on the island.

Kai Kane Surf Shop (808-826-5594; 5-5088 Kuhio Hwy., Hanalei). Mostly hawking a variety of men and women's clothing and hats, this large store also sells and rents surf gear.

9

Ni'ihau

Kapu: The Forbidden Isle

Nothing creates intrigue like hearing a place is off limits. Ni'ihau, the tabletop plateau 17 miles from Kaua'i that can sometimes be seen in the distance from the west shore in Koke'e, is just that—an elusive and forbidden land.

How did one Hawaiian island get away with alienating itself while the others swarm with tourists? Well, Ni'ihau is privately owned by the Gay and Robinson family. Now, don't start imagining some rich dudes holed up on an island forcing native Hawaiians to herd sheep while beautiful women cater to their daily needs. Rather, this island has a history of deceit, hope, and despair: one that generations talk story about to this day.

History

In ancient times, it was believed that Ni'ihau was the afterbirth of Kaua'i. And it was here that Captain Cook brought enough trouble to complicate life in the whole chain of islands. Leaving goats and syphilis on what he termed Yam Island, Cook changed both the ecological face of the island and the health of its people. After the goats ate the native plants and the people became ill, these 70 square miles became an arid dry land, physically, metaphorically, and now literally (there is no alcohol allowed on the isle).

In 1864, the native Hawaiians, descendants of those who survived the syphilis epidemic, were not pleased when, in an effort to keep the affluent Scottish widow, Eliza Sinclair and her family in Hawai'i, King Kamehameha sold Ni'ihau to them for $10,000. Unfortunately for her (but luckily for us), the king had first attempted to sell her the marshy (and undeveloped) Waikiki, but she turned it down to have what then seemed like an abundant remote island to herself. However, that year had brought Ni'ihau unusual rains. When the Sinclairs realized that they had actually bought a desert-like island with poor soil and angry inhabitants, they had to reevaluate.

Eliza Sinclair brought sheep to Ni'ihau, started the still-working sheep ranch, and hired the indigenous people to work there. To give back to their employees, the Sinclairs (who joined with the Robinson family through marriage) decided to keep Ni'ihau a private island and not allow any visitors. Then the family moved to Kaua'i and started up in the sugar business (the Gay and Robinson Sugar plantation is the only one still working on Kaua'i—see chapter four for tour information). Ni'ihau is private to this day.

Life and Culture Now

Today over 200 people live in the shadow of Ni'ihau's highest point—the 1,281-foot Pani'au, which is made of limestone and sand dunes. Here, interestingly, in the shadow of the

Though 17-miles from Kaua'i, Ni'ihau holds the allure of another universe.

Ni'ihau Shell Leis

Though the people of Ni'ihau live simply, their craftwork sells for as much as the island cost Eliza Sinclair. This intricate process has been practiced and passed down though the generations.

When, after the harsh storms of winter, tiny shells only found in the reef surrounding Ni'ihau wash up to shore, nearly the entire community comes out to collect the *kamoa*, *momi*, *laiki*, and *kahelelani*. Shells are carefully judged by purity of color, shape, fullness, and unity, with only a small percentage kept for necklaces. No two necklaces or leis are alike. They take hours to create and can be single or multistrand pieces connected by a series of intricate hand-tied knots. In general, they are rare. They tend to be passed down through families as heirlooms. However, if you are interested in purchasing these one-of-a-kind pieces, they are sold at high-end jewelry stores on Kaua'i (see chapter 8).

rainiest place in the world, sits the driest place in Hawai'i—it often rains less than an inch a year. Yet there are three lakes (including the biggest in the Hawaiian chain). Unfortunately, they tend to dry up and turn into red mudflats each year.

The majority of the population lives in the community of Pu'uwai. This is the only island where Hawaiian is the primary language (though children learn English in grade school). Rumor has it this is the only place where some full-blooded Hawaiians still exist. A notable irony since the people who own the island are non-Hawaiian. There is no electricity (but people use power generators for their televisions and refrigerators); no cable TV, phone service, indoor plumbing, wireless, or paved roads. However, the schoolhouse recently became solar powered (a first in the islands). For work, the residents farm and create shell necklaces and craftwork that sells for big bucks on Kaua'i (see the sidebar). Unfortunately, the economy is suffering from droughts, hurricanes, and a lessening of ranch activities. There is talk of a bigger military presence on the island to subsidize the economy, and maybe a high-end resort. But as of now, the land and its people are a pristine example of life without outside influence.

Outsiders question whether the people who live on Ni'ihau want this life. Know that Ni'ihau inhabitants are by no means forced to stay here. The people are allowed (and even encouraged) to leave the island for school (the Gay and Robinson folks even pay for higher education, health care, and more), shopping, and to visit friends; and most do. Some stay on Kaua'i and get married; some have been forced to leave for using (or growing) drugs. But most return after a sabbatical on Kaua'i to enjoy the solace, solitude, and simple ways.

GETTING THERE

What strikes people as strange is the isolation. Yet people can visit the island. Well, only if you're offered a formal invitation from one of the residents, or if you have a ton of cash. With no proper tourist boat or flight service connecting Kaua'i with its sister island, Ni'ihau has a culture that is closest to what Hawaii might have been if it hadn't been settled by missionaries.

If you are dying to get here, there are a couple of ways to visit, even if you don't know anyone on the island. The first is to take a dive tour through one of the dive operators listed in chapter 7. Though you won't get to visit the community (or step on the land), you will catch a glimpse of the richest marine life in all Hawai'i.

Or, if you have a wad of money to spend, the **Gay and Robinson** folks (808-335-2824; www.gandrtours-kaia.com) offer insanely expensive helicopter tours (where you land on an outer beach and don't come in contact with residents) and hunting expeditions (where you can hunt wild boar, again in an unpopulated stretch of the island). All in all it is best to remember that the beauty of this land lies in its isolation.

10

INFORMATION

Ho'ike

Below are some practical matters that might help make your stay easier. My hope is to touch on basic information that will help both locals and visitors. This chapter covers the following topics:

AMBULANCE, FIRE, AND POLICE

The general emergency number in Kaua'i is 911. Other emergency numbers are as follows:

Coast Guard: 800-424-8802

Poison Control: 800-222-1222

Police: 808-241-1711

Sexual Assault Crisis Line: 808-245-4144

You can escape the masses at Lumiha'i Beach.

AREA CODE, LOCAL GOVERNMENT, TIME ZONE, AND ZIP CODES

The area code for all Hawai'i is 808. When a hotel says "free local calls," however, that means on Kaua'i only. If you choose to bring your cell phone to the island, know that many companies only get signals in the Lihu'e and Kapa'a/Wailua areas.

All of Hawai'i is on Hawaiian Standard Time, which is 10 hours behind Greenwich Mean Time for *half of the year*, since Hawai'i does not observe daylight saving time. Also of note is that Hawaiian people live on what locals call Hawaiian Time, which does not refer to the time zone. Instead people tend to move slower (sometimes really slow). Events often start late and last longer than planned. You'll notice stark differences from the mainland: That shop owner will actually want to chat with you about your sandals, or the bank teller will want to know about customs in your hometown. This is called talking story and is the best way to soak up the true Kaua'i atmosphere.

The county of Kaua'i consists of Kaua'i and Ni'ihau, plus all other islands located within 3 nautical miles of their shores. These islands are governed by the mayor and taken care of by a seven-member city council. County government offices are all located in Lihu'e. For general information about local affairs, call **Kaua'i County Information** (808-241-6303) or visit their web site at www.kauai.gov.

Even the phone booths honor the Garden Isle.

Kauaʻi zip codes are listed below:

Anahola	96703
ʻEleʻele	96705
Hanalei	96714
Hanamaʻulu	96715
Hanapepe	96716
Princeville	96722
Kalaheo	96741
Kapaʻa	96746
Kaumakami	96747
Kealia	96751
Kekaha	96752
Kilauea	96754
Koloa	96756
Lawaʻi	96765
Lihuʻe	96766
Makaweli	96769
Waimea	96796

BANKS

Most banks in Kauaʻi are linked to ATM machines electronically. Listed here are branch locations of these banks.

EAST SHORE

American Savings Bank
Kapaʻa: 808-822-3427; 4-1177 Kuhio Hwy., Suite 110.
Lihuʻe: 808-246-8844; Kukui Grove, 3-2600 Kaumualiʻi Hwy.
808-245-3388; 4318 Rice St.

Bank of Hawaii
Kapaʻa: 808-822-3471; 1407 Kuhio Hwy.
Lihuʻe: 808-245-6761; 4455 Rice St.

First Hawaiian Bank
Lihuʻe: 808-245-6394; Kuhui Grove Shopping Center.
808-245-4024; 4423 Rice St.
Kapaʻa: 808-822-4966; 4-1366 Kuhio Hwy.

SOUTH SHORE
First Hawaiian Bank: 808-742-1642; 3506 Waikomo Rd., Koloa.

WEST SHORE
American Savings Bank: 808-335-3118; 4548 Kona Rd., Hanapepe.
Bank of Hawaii: 808-338-1636; 9801 Waimea Rd., Waimea.

First Hawaiian Bank
Hanapepe: 808-335-3161; Ele'ele Shopping Center, Building 606.
Waimea: 808-338-1611; 4525 Panako Rd.

NORTH SHORE
First Hawaiian Bank: 808-826-1560; Princeville Shopping Center, 5-4280 Kuhio Hwy.,
Princeville.

BIBLIOGRAPHY

Strangely, not many books have been written about Kaua'i. Though the island has inspired
many, the majority of creative endeavors to come out of the isle are film and visual arts.
Below are some interesting finds.

Blay, Chuck, and Robert Siemers. *Kaua'i's Geological History: A Simplified Guide*. Teok
        Investigations, 1998.
Cook, Chris. *Kaua'i Movie Book*. Mutual Publishers, 1996.
——. *A Kaua'i Reader: The Exotic Literary Heritage of the Garden Island*. Mutual, 2007.
——. *Kaua'i The Garden Island: A Pictorial History*. Donning Co., 1999.
Dawes, Gavan. *Shoal of Time: The History of the Hawaiian Islands*. Macmillan, 1968.
Denny, Jim. *The Birds of Kaua'i*. University of Hawai'i Press, 1999.
Joesting, Edward. *Kaua'i: The Separate Kingdom*. University of Hawai'i Press, 1984.
Krauss, Bob. *Grove Farm Plantation*. Pacific Books, 1983.
Michener, James. *Hawaii*. Fawcett, 1996.
Morey, Cathy. *Kaua'i Trails*. Wilderness Press, 2005.
O'Connor, Dan. *Sugar: A Hawaiian Novel*. Waterton Press, 2001.
Penhallow, David. *The Story of the Coco Palms Hotel*. Rice Street Press, 2007.
Ronck, Ron. *Kaua'i: A Many Splendored Island*. Mutual, 1985.
Stone, Robert. *Day Hikes on Kaua'i*. Day Hike Books Inc., 2001.
TenBruggencate, Jan. *Kaua'i*. Mutual, 2002.
Wichman, Frederick. *Kaua'i: Ancient Place Names and Their Stories*. University of Hawai'i
        Press, 1998.
——. *Kaua'i Tales*. Bamboo Ridge Press, 1985.
——. *More Kaua'i Tales*. Bamboo Ridge Press, 1997.
——. *Pele Ma: Legends of Pele from Kaua'i*. Bamboo Ridge Press, 2001.
——. *Polihale and Other Kaua'i Legends*. Bamboo Ridge Press, 1991.

CHAMBER OF COMMERCE

The Kaua'i Visitors Bureau and Chamber of Commerce are wonderful resources to help you
plan your trip. The visitors bureau will send you their free tourist guide (which has a great
map and pictures) and assist you with any questions you might have. Recently, they began
making advertisements geared to tourists, encouraging responsible travel. I'd recommend
contacting them in advance if you have questions about the current safety of particular
hiking trails, helicopter tours, or the like.

Chamber of Commerce of Kaua'i: 808-245-7363; 2970 Kele, Suite 112, Lihu'e; www
.kauaichamber.org.

Kaua'i Visitors Bureau: 808-245-3971; 4334 Rice St., Suite 101, Lihu'e; www.kauai discovery.com.

Kaua'i Visitors Information: 800-262-1400.

Poipu Beach Resort Association: 888-580-8555.

CHILD CARE

In addition to Kids' Clubs and child care at most resorts (listed in chapter 7), the following companies also babysit. Some will come to your condo or hotel.

Aloha Child Care: 808-652-8312. They come to the clients; this is not a drop-off site.

Babysitters of Kaua'i—Happy Kids: 808-632-2252; www.babysittersofkauai.com. This 7 1/2-year-old company sends female sitters all over the island. All sitters are CPR certified, background checked, and experienced.

Local keikis head to the beach after school.

Megan Irvine: 808-647-4263 or 808-332-0330; www.islandnanny.net. This CPR-certified nanny comes highly recommended, but at a steep price. She also gives swim and surf lessons.

PATCH: Childcare Resource and Referral Agency: 808-246-0622.
Also, if you need to rent high chairs, cribs, gates, or other baby gear, contact **Ready Rentals** at 800-599-8008.

CLIMATE, WEATHER REPORTS, AND WHAT TO WEAR

For most of us, the weather on the island is divine—warm sunny mornings give way to tropical rain that gathers just in time for an afternoon siesta, and then breezes cool the evening just enough in winter to bust out a light sweater (in warm seasons you'll get to show off that itsy-bitsy summer dress). However, it is tough to categorize the climate on Kaua'i: It has seven microclimates. The north shore (which is also the greenest) is, as you might guess, the rainiest, while the west shore has almost desert-like conditions year-round. Weather varies dramatically from one part of the island to the other, so you might be lazing in the Poipu sun and then arrive in

Hanalei to find waterfalls of rain. (If you are staying in the north shore in winter, it could shower every day of your vacation.) Since you will spend the majority of your time along the coasts, know that these areas get between 20 and 40 inches of rain annually; however, the interior is one of the rainiest places on earth, getting up to 500 inches of rain per year!

In general, daytime temperatures range from the mid-70s to mid-80s Fahrenheit; evenings from the mid-60s to mid-70s. In summer, expect warmer temperatures and lots of humidity. Ocean temperatures stay perfectly between 72 and 76 degrees Fahrenheit year-round. You can check island and ocean temperatures, surf reports, and tides at www .kauaiexplorer.com, *The Garden Island* newspaper, and on local television stations listed below. There is also a tide chart in the *Hawaiian Telecom Yellow Pages*.

The unfortunate realities of this Pacific island are that hurricanes (from June through November), earthquakes, flooding, and tsunamis can occur—though all of these events are rare. In case of an emergency, it is best to keep your gas tank full to at least halfway. If something should happen, sirens will sound. Tune in to a radio or television station for instructions. For more information, refer to the local phone book or call the **Kauaʻi Civil Defense Agency** (808-241-1800).

Of course the biggest question for any traveler is what to wear. Luckily for Kauaʻi visitors, the answer is not much. The dress here is casual—flip-flops, board shorts, and T-shirts for men and about the same for ladies. Bring light-colored clothing that breathes for the day, and a light sweater or jacket for the evenings and treks into Kokeʻe. I always have a raincoat with me, but never seem to bust it out; if you plan to stay on the north shore in winter, though, I'd definitely advise a raincoat. For even the most high-end restaurants, you can get away with resort wear, which consists of a Hawaiian shirt and nice shorts or summer dresses and sandals. Leave that suit and tie at home. It's okay.

Finally, even though you might want to come home looking like you just sunned your days away on the islands, you should always wear sunscreen of SPF 15 or higher, even when it is cloudy. You can still get a healthy tan wearing sunblock; you just won't become such a blistering lobster that the rest of your stay is uncomfortable. And make sure to reapply often. The sun is much stronger than it feels. Also, mosquitoes are a serious annoyance on Kauaʻi, so wear insect repellent or thin long-sleeved shirts and pants, especially at dawn or dusk.

GAS STATIONS

As you might have guessed, Hawaiʻi has some of the priciest gasoline in the country. Current gas prices can be found in *The Garden Island* newspaper (www.kauaiworld .com); budget accordingly. Below are places to fill up your tank.

EAST SHORE
76 Kukui Grove Self-Service: 4360 Kukui Grove St., Lihuʻe.

76 Paradise Service: 3155 Kuhio Hwy., Lihuʻe.

Chevron Lihuʻe: 3187 Kuhio Hwy., Lihuʻe.

Chevron Kapaʻa: 4-994 Kuhio Hwy., Kapaʻa.

Lihuʻe Shell Station: 3-3178 Kuhio Hwy., Lihuʻe.

A gas station pump from another era in Old Koloa Town.

Rainbow Gas and Mini-Mart: 4-350 Kuhio Hwy., Kapa'a.

Rice Street Chevron: 4411 Rice St., Lihu'e.

SOUTH SHORE
Kalaheo Shell Station: 2-2416 Kaumuali'i Hwy., Kalaheo.

Koloa Chevron: 3486 Poipu Rd., Koloa.

West Shore 76: 9935 Kaumuali'i Hwy., Waimea.

Chevron: 2-2489 Kaumuali'i Hwy., Waimea.

NORTH SHORE
The North Shore only has one service station, in Princeville. Make sure to fill up before heading out to Ke'e Beach.

Princeville Chevron: 5-4280 Kuhio Hwy., Princeville.

GUIDED TOURS

There are a number of guided tours listed in chapters 4 and 7. Most are focused on hiking, boating, snorkeling, or diving, but there are also movie, walking, and historical jaunts.

The only additional tour group to know about is **Encounter Kaua'i** (808-634-6812; P.O. Box 998, Kilauea 96754; www.encounterkauai.com). Koa Kahili and his crew offer "transformational healing retreats" that focus on a mind–body experience. Retreats last for a week or weekend. Guests can camp, or stay at a resort or B&B. All retreats offer gourmet organic food, yoga, hiking, and the ability to enjoy the natural beauty of Kaua'i. Some retreats gear more to the adventurer, others to the spa junkie, and still others to those who are searching for the spiritual center of the island. Rates include transportation (except flights), gear, food, lodging, taxes, and fees. See their web site for details. They also have group rates.

HANDICAPPED SERVICES

Officially, it is the law that all handicapped persons have access to all buildings on the island. However, the facilities at some condo complexes and restaurants have been "grandfathered" in and needn't abide by these laws. Make sure to inquire about your hotel/condo before booking. If you have any questions or complaints, contact the **Mayor's Office** (808-241-6203), the **Hawai'i Disability Rights Center** (800-882-1057), or the **Disability and Communication Access Board (DCAB)** (808-586-8121) (V/TTY).

On Kaua'i, there are no rental car companies with lift equipment. For transportation, people either use the Kaua'i Bus, or rent a van from a rental car agency along with a ramp from **Gammie Homecare** (808-632-2333) to get into the van.

For rental of wheelchairs, including Landeez chairs and portable ramps, other equipment, and helpful island advice, call Clyde Silva at **Gammie Home Care** (808-632-2333 www.gammie.com), or **Ready Rentals** (800-599-8008).

Kaua'i County provides Landeez all-terrain wheelchairs at three beach parks on the island: Poipu Beach Park, Lydgate Beach Park, and Salt Pond Beach Park. Beachgoers wanting to use the all-terrain beach chairs can go to the lifeguard stations and ask the lifeguard for help getting one. The beach chairs cannot be taken out of the park. The above-mentioned parks have accessible parking, pathways, pavilions, restrooms, and showers. For more information about all-terrain beach chairs, call **Kaua'i Recreation Agency** (808-241-4467). Lydgate Beach Park is slated to have camping areas with handicapped-accessible campsites.

Some boat harbors (Kukuiula Boat Harbor, Port Allan Boat Harbor, and the Nawiliwili Boat Harbor) have accessible ramps and services.

Tour companies and outfitters that make a special effort to provide access for the handicapped are **Water-sports Adventures** (808-821-1599), **Kaua'i Nature Tours** (888-233-8365), and **Liko Kaua'i Cruises** (808-338-0333).

For ASL interpreters, contact **Susan Warren** (808-241-1386) (V) or **Robert Revel** (808-332-0830) (V).

HELPFUL WEB SITES

www.alternative-hawaii.com
www.hawaiistateparks.org
www.hawaiiweb.com
www.islandsource.com
www.kauaidiscovery.com
www.kauaiexplorer.com
www.kauai.gov
www.kauai-hawaii.com
www.kauaiworld.com
www.wehewehe.org

HOSPITALS

Kaua'i Medical Clinic: 808-245-1500; 3-3420 Kuhio Hwy., Suite B, Lihu'e.

Mahelona Medical Center: 808-822-4961; 4800 Kawaihau Rd., Kapa'a.

St. Francis Medical Center: 808-547-6411; 4643A Waimea Canyon, Waimea.

West Kaua'i Clinic: 808-338-8311; 4643 Waimea Canyon Dr., Waimea.

West Kaua'i Medical Center: 808-338-9431; 4643 Waimea Canyon Dr., Waimea.

Wilcox Memorial Hospital: 808-245-1100; 3420 Kuhio Hwy., Lihu'e.

INTERNET AND WIRELESS LOCATIONS

Most hotels, condos, and even rental houses supply free wireless (or at least offer Internet access for a fee). If your lodging does not offer this service, don't fret: There are plenty of places to surf the web when you get tired of surfing the waves.

If you plan to be on the island for a while, for $10 you can purchase a three-month library membership. This gets you free Internet, movie and book rentals, and a quiet place to hang on rainy days.

EAST SHORE
Java Kai: 808-823-6887; 4-1384 Kuhio Hwy., Kapaʻa.

Small Town Coffee: 808-821-1604; 4-1495 Kuhio Hwy., Kapaʻa.

WEST SHORE
Aloha-n-Paradise: 808-338-1522; 9905 Waimea Rd., Waimea Town.

The Waimea Visitor and Technology Center: 808-338-1332; where Waimea Canyon Dr. meets Kaumualiʻi Hwy. in Waimea.

NORTH SHORE
Java Kai: 808-826-6717; 5-5183 Kuhio Hwy., Hanalei.

Na Pali Art Gallery and Coffee Shop: 808-826-1844; Hanalei Colony Resort, Haena.

LICENSES

There are a number of licenses required if you want to engage in some good old Kauaʻi fun. It is highly recommended to get these licenses taken care of *before* arriving on the island. In chapter 7, I have detailed which license you need for specific camping/hiking locations.

Camping Licenses
Beach Camping: Division of Parks and Recreation: 808-241-4463; www.kauai.gov; 444 Rice St., Piʻikoi Building, Suite 350, Lihuʻe.

Park Camping: Department of Land and Natural Resources Division of State Parks: 808-274-3444; www.hawaii.gov/dlnr; 3060 ʻEiwa St., Room 306, Lihuʻe.

Forest Camping: Division of Forestry and Wildlife: 808-274-3433; www.hawaii.gov/dlnr; 3060 ʻEiwa St., Room 306, Lihuʻe.

Other Licenses
Fishing License: 808-274-3344.

Hiking License: DLNR State Parks Office: 808-274-3444; www.hawaii.gov/dlnr; 3060 ʻEiwa St., Room 306, Lihuʻe.

Marriage License: 808-241-3498.

MEDIA

Magazines and Newspapers

This small island can really make you want to disconnect from the world. And the lack of media helps. There are three daily newspapers serving Kaua'i: the local *Garden Island* newspaper and the statewide *Honolulu Advertiser* and *Honolulu Star Bulletin*. All are easy to access on the island and focus mainly on island happenings. Local magazines to look for (which are free at the airport) are *101 Things to Do*, *This Week Kaua'i*, and *Essential Kaua'i*.

Radio Stations

87.7: 1980s, '90s, and current hits.

90.9/91.9/92.7/95.1: Community news, stories, and local music.

93.5: Island hits.

95.9/103.9: Surf and island music

98.9: Island music.

99.9: Oldies.

103.3: Rock and roll.

Television Stations

ABC: Channel 51.

CBS: Channel 57.

FOX: Channel 55.

NBC: Channel 8.

PBS HAWAI'I: Channels 10 and 11.

PHARMACIES

EAST SHORE
Lihu'e Pharmacy: 808-246-9100; 4484 Pahee St., Lihu'e.

Longs Drugs:
Kapa'a: 808-822-4918; 4-831 Kuhio Hwy.
Lihu'e: 808-245-7771; Kukui Grove Shopping Center.

MedCenter Pharmacy: 808-245-2471; 3-3420B Kuhio Hwy., Lihu'e.

SOUTH SHORE
Kalaheo Pharmacy: 808-332-7660; 4489 Papalina Rd., Kalaheo.

Papalina Pharmacy: 808-332-9130; 4469 Papalina Rd., Kalaheo.

Southshore Pharmacy: 808-742-7511; 5330 Koloa Rd., Suite 2, Koloa.

WEST SHORE

MedCenter Pharmacy: 808-338-0600; 4643A Waimea Canyon Dr., Waimea.

Menehune Pharmacy: 808-338-0200; 9665 Kaumualiʻi Hwy., Waimea.

Westside Pharmacy: 808-335-5342; 1-3845 Kaumualiʻi Hwy., Hanapepe.

NORTH SHORE

North Shore Pharmacy: 808-828-1844; 2460 Oka St., Kilauea.

REAL ESTATE

Chances are that at some point of your vacation, you will play out the option of moving here. Everyone does. That's why there are so many transplants. It's also why there are so many real estate agents, condominiums, and construction projects. You can find a variety of real estate listings in the yellow pages as well as in most of the free periodicals at the airport and visitor information booths.

If moving to Kauaʻi is your dream, it is wise to understand the technical aspects of moving here (zoning laws, pet quarantine information—three months!—and so on) and the social issues associated with such an endeavor. Over the past 20 years, Kauaʻi has become popular with mainlanders—many of them rich and/or famous—who buy beachfront property at inflated prices. Though this gives the island some bragging rights to the largest

While you search for your dream home, Fluffy will have to wait in quarantine.

population of celebrities and millionaires of the Hawaiian Islands, it has also made it almost impossible for native Hawaiians to purchase land—or even afford to live here at all. Many of my friends have had to move to the Big Island, where they can still afford to rent. The effect of this can be seen in the attitudes of locals, who are very happy to welcome visitors, but are also very happy when they don't stay. If that hasn't scared you off, a good book about relocating to the island is Toni Polancy's *So You Want to Move to Hawai'i*.

Another option for out-of-towners is to buy a time share. For information about time shares, contact the buildings you are interested in—most of them are in Poipu and Princeville (see the yellow pages for details). If you sign up for a tour, they often offer free diving or boat trips.

Finally, for those of us who aren't rich (or famous), another option is to buy (or rent) a condo. Since buildings shoot up faster than trees, you will see loads of listings in the local paper as well as advertised on placards in resort areas.

RECYCLING CENTERS

One of the biggest bummers of Kaua'i is that there are no at-home recycling services. An even bigger issue is that the landfills are overflowing with waste. The best way to help is to limit the amount of waste you have by bringing your own reusable water bottle, and buying fewer packaged goods. When you're on vacation of course, that is often tough. So the next best thing you can do for both the island and its people is to recycle your bottles, cans, paper, etcetera. But it takes a little work on your part. Just a little. Below are recycling drop-off locations. If you can't make it there, ask your hotel or condo to do it for you.

EAST SHORE
Kapa'a: At the end of Kahau Road past the Kapa'a Armory, where the farmer's market is held.

Lihu'e: In the back of the Kmart parking lot, on the pavilion side of the store.

SOUTH SHORE
Poipu: In the Brennecke's parking lot.

Lawa'i: At the Lawa'i Post Office.

WEST SHORE
'Ele'ele: At the 'Ele'ele Shopping Center.

Kekaha: At the Kekaha Landfill.

Waimea: At Waimea Canyon Park.

NORTH SHORE
Hanalei: At the Hanalei Transfer Station.

ROAD SERVICES

A Tow in Paradise: 808-245-8818.

DK Towing: 808-821-0200.

Kauaʻi Roadside Service and Towing: 808-245-1892.

Nalaʻs Towing: 808-632-0333.

WEDDINGS

If you dream of exchanging vows on a white sand beach with the golden sun setting over the crystal blue sea, palms gently swaying in the distance, you can be like many others before you and get married on Kauaʻi. Though most locals head over the Las Vegas to exchange vows, heaps of mainlanders have made Kauaʻi the wedding destination of choice. Since this is an already paved road, there is a big business set up to help with wedding plans—from coordinators to florists, DJs to luʻau organizers, folks who will marry you in the sky or underwater, as well as at sunrise weddings along the Coconut Coast. Basically anything you can imagine has been done. For a price. As with any other popular destination wedding locations, when people hear weddings, the dollar signs pop up in their eyes.

The romantic breeze, the salty sweet air, and the crashing waves will make you want to get married on Kauaʻi.

For a traditional wedding package, organized through any of the major resorts, expect to pay a lot, but not to do much work. Each resort has a variety of packages, including intimate affairs of candlelit dinners on the sand to blow-out parties for every person you know. The resorts that specialize in weddings are the Waimea Plantation Cottages, Grand Hyatt Resort, Princeville Hotel, Hanalei Bay Resort, Hanalei Colony Resort, Sheraton Kaua'i, Hilton Resort, and Lihu'e Marriott.

Many of my friends have chosen to stitch together an affair on their own. Unless you are local (or plan to live on the island until your wedding), most people recommend getting a wedding coordinator. The Kaua'i Visitors Bureau (808-245-3971; www.kauaidiscovery .com) has a comprehensive listing of wedding service providers both online and in their travel planner. Some coordinators popular with tourists are:

A Vow Exchange: 800-460-3434; www.vowexchange.com.
Island Weddings and Blessings: 808-828-1548; www.weddings-kauai.com.

Rainbow Weddings and Celebrations: 808-822-0944; www.rainbowweddings.com. They also perform commitment ceremonies for gay and lesbian couples.

If you choose to skip the whole coordinator thing, you might want to explore the **Kaua'i Wedding Professionals Association** (www.kauaiwedpro.com) website for information about locations, caterers, florists, photographers, carriages, tent rentals, and so on. The yellow pages offers comprehensive listings of wedding services, including the above-mentioned information, officiants, churches, rehearsal dinner locations, musicians, and more. It is important to note that if you want a friend or family member from the mainland to perform your ceremony, you must also hire a locally certified officiant to preside over the event (and make it legal).

So what happens if you arrive here and are swept away by the romance of the isle and decide at the last minute to get hitched? Plan to stay a few extra weeks, because Hawai'i has some strict licensing requirements. Though no blood tests are required, both parties need to be present (with *cash* in hand and valid ID) *before* the date of the wedding at the **Kaua'i Governor Liaison's Office** (808-274-3100; www.hawaii.gov/health). You must make an appointment (and often they only accept them two weeks prior to the event) with an agent to sign the appropriate papers. Note that licenses only last for 30 days.

IF TIME IS SHORT

I can't imagine having only a day to spend on the island the way most cruise ship passengers do. Or even only having a week to explore this abundantly beautiful locale. However, if you have but a few spins of the earth on Kaua'i, I have included some of my personal do-not-miss locations here. Hopefully you will be as smitten with this tropical paradise as everyone else and return for a longer stay soon.

Lodging

EAST SHORE
Rosewood Inn (808-822-5216; 872 Kamalu Rd., Kapa'a). This Victorian-style compound, with bunkhouses, B&B rooms, and private cottages, is the best deal on the island for such tastefully decorated lodgings.

SOUTH SHORE

Bamboo Jungle House (808-332-5515 or 888-332-5115; 3829 Waha Rd., Kalaheo). This B&B is a tropical oasis in the residential south shore town of Kalaheo.

Grand Hyatt Kaua'i (808-742-1234: 1571 Poipu Rd., Koloa). The most extensive and luxurious resort on the island is worth every cent.

WEST SHORE

Waimea Plantation Cottages (808-338-1625; 9400 Kaumuali'i Hwy., Waimea). Return to the plantation days in sunny Waimea Town to relax in a private beachfront cottage.

NORTH SHORE

Aloha Sunrise Inn & Aloha Sunset Inn (808-828-1100; 4899-A Waiakalua St., Kilauea). Tastefully decorated cottages nestled in an organic Kilauea eco-farm.

Hanalei Colony Resort (808-826-6235; 5-7130 Kuhio Hwy., Hanalei). Like a grown-up summer camp, these remote condos bring out the kid in us all.

Cultural Attractions

Hanapepe Art Night. Friday evening 6–9 PM, the whole island seems to gather in downtown Hanapepe to celebrate art and music.

A lonely beach. Photo taken by Oliver Reyes

Limahuli Garden and Preserve (808-826-1053; located on H 56 in Haena, 0.25 mile before Ke'e Beach). The lush north shore outpost of the National Tropical Botanical Garden offers stellar views of native plants and the expansive ocean below.

Sheraton Surf to Sunset Oceanfront Lu'au (808-742-8205; 2440 Ho'onani Rd., Poipu). If you've never been to a lu'au, this is the one to attend. Great food. Great views. And the cheesiest show on the island.

Recreation

Koke'e State Park and Waimea Canyon (at the end of H 550). This expansive state park offers stellar views and hikes galore.

Lydgate Beach Park (on the south side of the Wailua River, off H 56). A lava rock barrier creates a natural swimming and snorkeling area that is perfect for the *keikis*.

Na Pali Coast State Park (at the end of H 56 on the north shore). Hike the **Kalalau Trail**, a steep 11-mile trek along the Na Pali cliffs with stops at rocky beaches, to get to waterfalls and unmatchable views.

Poipu Beach Park (where Ho'owili Rd. meets Pe'e Rd.). Voted one of America's top beaches by numerous travel magazines, this is one of Kaua'i's best-developed beach parks.

Wailua Falls (from Lihu'e, take Kuhio Hwy. north, and turn left onto Ma'alo Rd.; drive 4 miles until the road ends). This gushing waterfall proves just how lush the inland of Kaua'i is.

Dining

EAST SHORE

Blossoming Lotus (808-822-7678; 4504 Kukui St., Kapa'a). This vegan oasis is sure to convert even the most committed carnivore.

Hamura's Saimin Stand (808-245-3271; 2956 Kress St., Lihu'e). Heaping bowls of steaming saimin for a steal.

Hukilau Lanai (808-822-0600; Kaua'i Coast Resort at Beach Boy, 520 Aleka Loop, Wailua). Here you'll find one of the most creative and dependable seafood restaurants on the east shore.

SOUTH SHORE

Plantation Gardens Restaurant and Bar (808-742-2121; Kiahuna Plantation, 2253 Poipu Rd., Koloa). Classic island-style dining in an open restaurant, with gourmet takes on local food.

Tidepools (808-742-1234; Grand Hyatt Hotel, 1571 Poipu Rd., Koloa). The most expensive restaurant on Kaua'i has a decadently romantic setting and menu.

WEST SHORE

Hanapepe Café (808-335-5011; 3830 Hanapepe Rd., Hanapepe). They serve healthy vegetarian and seafood lunches, plus Friday-night dinners at decent prices.

Sunsets look different from each side of the island. Photo taken by Oliver Reyes

North Shore

Bar Acuda (808-826-7081; 5-5161 Kuhio Hwy., Hanalei). You'll feel like you are in a big city at the only tapas and wine bar on the island.

Kilauea Fish Market (808-828-6244; 4270 Kilauea Lighthouse Rd., Kilauea). These folks serve up the cheapest, freshest, and biggest organic wraps on the island.

Postcards Café (808-826-1191; 5-5075A Kuhio Hwy., Hanalei). Organic and sustainable locally grown produce gives this little cottage the freshest dishes on the island.

General Index

Lodging by Price

EAST SHORE

Inexpensive
Aloha Beach Resort, 50
Anuenue Plantation, 50–51
Kaua'i Inn, 57–58
Mohala Ke Ola, 53
Tip Top Motel, 59

Inexpensive to Moderate
Garden Island Inn, 56
Hotel Coral Reef Resort, 51
Kapa'a Sands, 51
Kaua'i Country Inn, 52
Rosewood Inn, 55–56

Moderate to Expensive
Kaua'i Coast Resort at Beachboy, 51–52
Resortquest Islander on the Beach, 54

Moderate to Very Expensive
Hilton Kaua'i Beach Hotel and Resort, 56–57

Expensive to Very Expensive
Kaha Lani Resort, 57
Kaua'i Marriott Resort and Beach Club, 58–59
Lae Nani, 52–53
Lanikai, 53
Outrigger Waipouli, 53–54
Resortquest Kaua'i Beach at Maka'iwa, 54–55

SOUTH SHORE

Inexpensive
Bamboo Jungle House, 60–61
Kaua'i Banyan Inn, 71–72
Prince Kuhio Condos, 68–69
Strawberry Guava B&B, 72, 74

Inexpensive to Moderate
Hale Kua Guest Cottages, 71
Kalaheo Inn, 61
Koloa Landing Cottages, 65
Marjorie's Kaua'i Inn, 72
Poipu Crater, 66
Poipu Plantation Resort, 68
Waikomo Stream Villas, 70

Inexpensive to Expensive
Sunset Kahili Condos, 69–70

Inexpensive to Very Expensive
Hale Pohaku Beachside, 63–64

Moderate to Expensive
Makahuena, 65–66
Poipu Kai Resort, 67

Moderate to Very Expensive
Nihi Kai Villas, 66

Expensive
Alihi Lani Poipu Condos, 61–62

Expensive to Very Expensive
Kiahuna Plantation, 64–65
Poipu Kapili Condos, 67–68

Very Expensive
Grand Hyatt Kaua'i, 62–63
Sheraton Kaua'i, 69
Whalers Cove Condo Resorts, 70–71

WEST SHORE

Inexpensive
Waimea Inn, 75

Inexpensive to Moderate
Hale Puka Ana B&B, 74–75

Moderate to Very Expensive
Waimea Plantation Cottages, 75, 77

NORTH SHORE

Inexpensive
North Country Farms, 79–80
Sealodge, 84–85

Inexpensive to Moderate
Hanalei Bay Inn, 78–79
Hanalei Inn, 78–79
Kamahana Townhomes, 82

Moderate
Ali'i Kai I and II, 80–81
Aloha Sunrise Inn, 79
Aloha Sunset Inn, 79
Cliffs @ Princeville, 81
Emmanlani Court, 81

Dining by Price

Dining by Cuisine

EAST SHORE

SOUTH SHORE

WEST SHORE